THE DIARY OF A MANCHU SOLDIER IN SEVENTEENTH-CENTURY CHINA

The Manchu conquest of China inaugurated one of the most successful and long-living dynasties in Chinese history: the Qing (1644–1911). The wars fought by the Manchus to invade China and consolidate the power of the Qing imperial house spanned over many decades through most of the seventeenth century. This book provides the first Western translation of the diary of Dzengšeo, a young Manchu officer, and recounts the events of the War of the Three Feudatories (1673–1682), fought mostly in southwestern China and widely regarded as the most serious internal military challenge faced by the Manchus before the Taiping rebellion (1851–1864). The author's participation in the campaign provides the close-up, emotional perspective on what it meant to be in combat, while also providing a rare window into the overall organization of the Qing army, and new data in key areas of military history such as combat, armament, logistics, rank relations, and military culture. The diary represents a fine and rare example of Manchu personal writing, and shows how critical the development of Manchu studies can be for our knowledge of China's early modern history.

Nicola Di Cosmo joined the Institute for Advanced Study, School of Historical Studies, in 2003 as the Luce Foundation Professor in East Asian Studies. He is the author of *Ancient China and Its Enemies* (Cambridge University Press, 2002) and his research interests are in Mongol and Manchu studies and Sino-Inner Asian relations.

ROUTLEDGE STUDIES IN THE EARLY HISTORY OF ASIA

THE DIARY OF A MANCHU SOLDIER IN SEVENTEENTH-CENTURY CHINA

"My service in the army,"
by Dzengšeo

Introduction, translation, and notes by Nicola Di Cosmo

Routledge
Taylor & Francis Group

LONDON AND NEW YORK

First published 2006
by Routledge
2 Park Square, Milton Park, Abingdon, Oxon, OX14 4RN

Simultaneously published in the USA and Canada
by Routledge
270 Madison Ave, New York NY 10016

Routledge is an imprint of the Taylor & Francis Group, an informa business

Transferred to Digital Printing 2009

© 2006 Introduction, translation and notes, Nicola Di Cosmo

Typeset in Times New Roman by
Newgen Imaging Systems (P) Ltd, Chennai, India

British Library Cataloguing in Publication Data
A catalogue record for this book is available from the British Library

Library of Congress Cataloging in Publication Data
Dzengseo, fl. 1680–1681.
The diary of a Manchu soldier in seventeenth-century China: my
service in the army / by Dzengseo; introduction, translation and
notes by Nicola Di Cosmo.
p. cm.—(Routledge studies in the early history of Asia; 4)
Includes bibliographical references and index.
1. China—History—Rebellion of the Three Feudatories,
1673–1681—Sources. 2. Mongols—History—Sources.
I. Di Cosmo, Nicola, 1957– II. Title. III. Series.
DS754.66.D94 2006
951'.032092—dc22   2005036379

ISBN10: 0–700–71611–4 (hbk)
ISBN10: 0–415–54447–5 (pbk)

ISBN13: 978–0–700–71611–1 (hbk)
ISBN13: 978–0–415–54447–4 (pbk)

FOR LIA

CONTENTS

ACKNOWLEDGMENTS

This book has been in the making for a long time, mainly because it did not intend to become a book (if books can be said to have intentions of their own) until I was persuaded that the text could profit from an integral translation into English, with introduction and notes, and that the resulting work could not be possibly published as an article. Over the many years in which I kept this text in the "Manchu materials" drawer, I received valuable suggestions, comments, and corrections from teachers, students, and colleagues with whom I shared it.

I must start by expressing my sincere admiration for Professor Ji Yonghai, who first found, studied, and published the text of Dzengšeo's diary, as mentioned in the Introduction. Without his discovery, this important source would still lie unrecognized and unknown in some dusty archive.

My deepest gratitude goes to Lynn Struve, Geoffrey Parker, and Mark Elvin, who have at various stages offered generous comments, corrections, and suggestions on the draft text of the translation either in writing or in conversations. Among those colleagues who have commented on talks I have given about Dzengšeo's war experience, I would like to thank in particular Alexander Woodside for the insightful remarks made at a conference in Lund some years ago. They have helped me delve more deeply into substantial issues of content as well as problematic points in the translation. Comments by Robert Hegel and again Lynn Struve at a conference at McGill were also very helpful as I revised the Introduction. I also extend my collective, but no less heartfelt, thanks to all friends and colleagues who asked questions and made observations as conferences and in private, and are too numerous to name.

This text was used first as teaching material in Manchu classes I taught at Indiana University and Harvard University. As such, a portion of it (especially the first 4 or 5 pages) have benefited greatly from the advice and suggestions that came from students. I would like to thank especially the following former students of my Manchu class: Annika Culver, Vernon Eagle, Dorothea Heuschert, Lan Mei-hua, Li Ruohong, Ellen McGill, Pat Giersch, Gray Tuttle, and Kenji Schwarz. I am delighted to recognize everyone's contributions, and if I am forgetting anyone, please forgive me as my notes are probably not as comprehensive as they ought to be.

ACKNOWLEDGMENTS

A special word of gratitude must be extended to several institutions. First, those that allowed me to teach Manchu, namely Indiana University and Harvard University. The need to train students in this important research language is still felt deeply in the field of Qing studies, and it is extremely gratifying to see that both institutions offer instruction in Manchu at the highest scholarly levels. Second, I would like to thank those institutions that made it possible for me to make progress on this book. I finished the translation while at the Institute for Advanced Study, where I was a Member in the Spring of 1999. I also benefited greatly from a grant of the Marsden Fund of the New Zealand Royal Society, which paid for time release, research support, and contributed funds for the maps included in this book. The good-humored and unflinching assistance from the Chair of the History Department at the University of Canterbury, Professor Peter Hempenstall, has been warmly appreciated.

Finally, my assistants Dr Naimah Talib at the University of Canterbury and Maria Tuya at the Institute for Advanced Study have dedicated time and effort toward the completion of this book, for which I am extremely grateful. Mrs Tuya was particularly supportive, as she adroitly responded on my behalf to the constant demands posed by technological progress. Dr Tim Nolan, the cartographer, was simply a pleasure to work with, and the Publisher's Editors, Ms Dorothea Schaefter and Mr Tom Bates, have been helpful, patient, and professional. Ms Maria Tuya and Ms Julia Bernheim have provided invaluable assistance with indexing and proofreading.

Needless to say, I alone remain responsible for all the mistakes and shortcomings in this book.

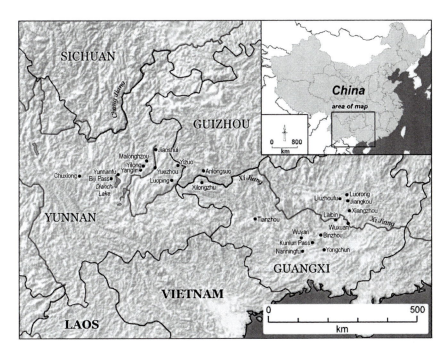

Map 1 Dzengšeo's campaign in southwestern China.

Map 2 Dzengšeo's itinerary from Yunnanfu to Beijing.

INTRODUCTION

In the Spring of 1644 victorious Manchu armies entered Beijing, the hitherto Ming capital, thus marking, at least by convention, the transition between the Ming (1368–1644) and the Qing (1644–1912) dynasties. We say "by convention" because the Qing dynasty had already been proclaimed in Manchuria eight years earlier, in 1636. On the other hand, the last claimant to the Ming throne, emperor Yongli, was only captured and executed in 1662, thus putting an end to the period known as the "Southern Ming" (1644–1662).[1] Not a small role in the Manchu conquest had been played by General Wu Sangui (1612–1678). This complex and tragic historical figure had been central to the Manchus' ability to conquer China in several respects. As Commander of the Ming army on the Manchurian border, his defection to the Manchus allowed the latter's nearly unopposed invasion of China. Moreover, his troops were used effectively against the peasant rebel troops that had seized the Ming capital and would have offered resistance to the Manchus. Finally, he played a critical role in the pursuit and destruction of "Southern Ming" armies, finally capturing the fleeing would-be Ming emperor in Burma and executing him in Yunnan.

Would the Manchus have been able to carry out their "great enterprise" and conquer China had the Ming general not defected? Surely the Manchu leaders recognized his contribution to their victory by piling on him honors and rewards that had few if any equals among the Ming military leaders that switched allegiance to the Manchus.

For reasons that will be described in some detail below, at the end of 1673 an aging Wu Sangui started a rebellion that shook the very foundations of the dynasty. Coping with the rebellion was a major test for the Qing leadership in general, but in particular for the young emperor Kangxi, installed as a child in 1661, and by then only 19 years old. Contemporary European observers expressed concern that the Manchus (the "Tartars") may not be able to withstand the rebellion, and to some the flight of the Manchu court to their homeland in the northeast appeared imminent after the early successes of the rebellious general were reported.[2] The war lasted, in all, about eight years, from the end of 1673 to 1681, although troops were not completely demobilized until 1682. This was certainly the greatest military threat confronted by the Kangxi emperor, and

1

possibly one of the bloodiest wars in the history of the Qing dynasty, at least before the Taiping rebellion.

* * *

The diary introduced here to a Western audience is authored by a mid-ranking Manchu soldier called Dzengšeo, who fought in that war and put his memoirs in writing in the form of a journal. The diary originally comprised four fascicles, but of these only the last could be found. This was published by Ji Yonghai in China in 1987 in a short book that included a Chinese translation, transcription of the Manchu text with interlinear word-by-word rendition in Chinese, and facsimile reproduction of the Manchu text itself (see the description of the text below).[3] Of course without Professor Ji Yonghai's discovery and publication we would not know anything about the extraordinary adventures of Dzengšeo. The extant portion of the diary covers the last period of the war, beginning on New Year's Day of 1680 and ending with the return home of the soldier, almost two years later.

Although this diary has been known for a while, only a small number of scholars have referred to it in their research.[4] A full translation of the diary, however, has not been produced, to my knowledge, in any Western language. The work I am presenting here began as a simple translation I made many years ago, when I began to use it as a reading text for Manchu language classes. After translating the diary, excerpts have been presented at two workshops. This translation is now presented here integrally with notes, an introduction, and the transliterated Manchu text. The latter is present also in the book published by Ji Yonghai, but because these are rare and difficult to acquire, I have chosen to add the transliterated text as an appendix in order to allow colleagues to correct and improve upon my translation.

The notes are possibly not as extensive as they could be. I have concentrated on explaining technical terms, information about people that I could identify, and clarifying some geographical issues whenever this was useful and conducive to a better understanding of the text. This introduction includes two sections. The first is a brief analysis of the Manchu conquest of China, of Wu Sangui as a historical character, and of the rebellion of the "Three Feudatories" in order to provide a modicum of historical background. In the second section I discuss a few aspects of the text, namely its authorship, style, and some aspects of the narrative that I regard as especially significant in terms of our knowledge of the nature of war in seventeenth-century China.[5]

Historical background

The Manchu conquest of China

The actual conquest of China by the Manchus was preceded by over five decades during which the tribes of southern Manchuria and eastern and southern

Mongolia were gradually united into a powerful regime by two farsighted leaders, Nurhaci (1554–1626) and his son Hong Taiji (1592–1643). Politically, the progress of this process was marked by two milestone events, the proclamation of the Latter Jin dynasty in 1616 and the proclamation of the Qing dynasty in 1636.[6]

The name "Manchu" itself was an innovation—whose etymology is still disputed—since it was adopted officially only in 1634 to designate the inhabitants of the region to the northeast of China, known as Jurchen. Divided into three major groupings, the Jianzhou, the Hada, and the Haixi, during the Ming dynasty the Jurchen nations had been gradually reduced to a condition of vassalage with respect to the Chinese emperor, to whom they continued to pay tribute in exchange for commercial and political advantages. Increasing commercial activity along the northeastern Chinese frontier and the development of agriculture in southern Manchuria brought economic prosperity to several Jurchen tribes, while political instability began to brew as a consequence of regional competition over the titles of nobility accorded by the Chinese emperor that guaranteed privileged access to border markets. Low-grade conflicts escalated into minor regional wars, bringing about a substantial increase in the military activity in the region, and favoring the rise of gifted military commanders, of whom Nurhaci was certainly one. Emerging as the leader of the Jianzhou Jurchen, he gained the support of the Ming court as a person who could be trusted to maintain order in the region. In 1595 he was given the title of Dragon and Tiger General, which was the highest honor a Jurchen tribal leader could receive from the Ming emperor. Nurhaci skillfully used his political influence and military ability to organize a series of campaigns against his Jurchen rivals. Fearful of his ambitions, these tried to stem his rise, formed a coalition against him, and attacked him in force, but were defeated. By the beginning of the seventeenth century the strength of Nurhaci was already taking shape. Key innovations, such as the adoption of the Manchu script (1599), the reorganization of the military in 1601—which would lead eventually to one of the hallmarks of the Manchu state, the Banner system—and the establishment of commercial monopolies, show that a process much larger than the mere establishment of a tribal kingdom was under way.

A group of Mongol aristocrats recognized Nurhaci's ascent to power in 1607 by offering him the title of "Honored Ruler" (Kündülen Khan). In 1616, having almost completed the conquest and unification of the Manchurian people, Nurhaci proclaimed himself the founder of a new dynasty, the Jin, thereby making himself fully independent of the Ming, while also challenging openly the Chinese authority in the region. His rise to regional hegemony had taken thirty-four years of nearly uninterrupted wars and sustained "state-building" efforts (1582–1616), partially aided and abetted by the Ming dynasty itself, which had often supported Nurhaci in his political claims.

After 1616 differences with China became irreconcilable, and hostilities open. The Ming, feeling self-confident about their power, mounted a large military offensive in 1619 aimed at annihilating Nurhaci's power base in Manchuria. At the battle of Sarhū their large expeditionary army of about 110,000 soldiers, supported by Korean and allied Jurchen troops, was shamefully defeated and routed by a much smaller Jin force.[7] Capitalizing on this major victory, in the early 1620s Nurhaci continued his expansion into the forest and steppe regions of Manchuria and Mongolia, and, far more significantly, into areas to the south of his base in Manchuria that were inhabited by Chinese peasantry and protected by the Chinese army, finally establishing his rule over the entire Liaodong peninsula. Nurhaci had become a serious problem for China, but many weaknesses hampered the progress of his political project: divisions within his regime, resistance to his rule in the occupied areas, the rise of a rival Mongol power in the west, the strengthening of the Chinese military defenses in the south, and potential conflicts with Korea in the east. In addition to these external and internal threats, the Manchus had not yet developed the administrative structure, economic power, and military force to invade China proper.

Nurhaci continued his campaign of pressure against the Ming border defenses, and in 1626 he was wounded in battle while attempting to storm the fortress of Ningyuan, protected with powerful European-style cannons. Apparently the battle injuries led eventually to his death a few months later, at the age of 62. Most worrying for Nurhaci had been, in the latter part of his life, the question of succession, the true Achilles' heel of all dynasties of Mongolian or Manchurian origin that started out as the personal creation of a charismatic leader. His political testament was to leave the leadership of the state to a "committee" of eight high-ranking members of the imperial clan in the belief that one of the senior aristocrats would emerge as the next emperor. There was, of course, the possibility that internal rivalries might have torn the state apart, but instead a certain wisdom prevailed, and while the process was by no means entirely smooth or bloodless, the rise of Hong Taiji, eighth son of Nurhaci, as successor to the Jin throne was successful in that it undoubtedly strengthened the still unstable dynastic political edifice of the dynasty. The personal qualities of Hong Taiji as a farsighted, courageous, decisive, and politically acute leader emerged immediately as he continued the process initiated by his father but gave it greater solidity by quickly developing the structures and institutions that were going to be the foundations of Manchu rule in China, in particular the expansion of the Banner system to Chinese (Han) and Mongol subjects, and the resolution of a number of military issues. In 1627 he invaded Korea to force a payment from it and forestall a possible military attack from the east, then turned his attention to the southern Mongols, who were "pacified" by both peaceful and military means, and largely incorporated in the Manchu military apparatus. All along he continued to put military pressure on the Chinese northeastern defenses. This resulted in a number of victories and in the defection of Chinese advisors and military commanders. These were brought into the state apparati and lavishly treated for their services. Thus a multinational political and military force began to take shape.

The state founded by Nurhaci changed dramatically under Hong Taiji's rule, whereby both government and army were greatly expanded, the first with the establishment of various offices such as the Six Ministries in 1631, the

Grand Secretariat, and later the Court of Colonial Affairs (Li Fan Yuan), the latter with the creation of the Mongol and Chinese Eight Banners.[8] In 1636 he proclaimed himself emperor of a new dynasty, the Great Qing or "pure" dynasty. This was followed by a period of further consolidation, with a new war against Korea, fresh raids into China, and general military build-up, waiting for an opportunity to launch a military offensive that would take the Manchus into China proper. This opportunity was going to elude Hong Taiji who died on September 21, 1643. He was succeeded by his young son Fulin (Shunzhi emperor, r. 1644–1661), aged 5, while two leading members of the royal clan, Dorgon (1612–1650)[9] and Jirgalang (1599–1655),[10] respectively Hong Taiji's brother and cousin, were appointed as co-regents.

Long poised to invade China, the Qing armies took their chance in 1644. Ravaged by over a decade of rebellions led by two competing leaders, Li Zicheng in Shaanxi and Zhang Xianzhong in Sichuan, the capital of the Ming had fallen to Li Zicheng's peasant army in April 23, 1644. The reigning Ming emperor committed suicide, days of carnage ensued, and Ming loyalists were left to cope with the agonizing dilemma of what to do: join the rebels, fight them to restore the Ming, or join the Manchus. A key figure at this extremely critical time was General Wu Sangui (1612–1678), whose contribution to the Manchu success is described in greater detail below. In the end Li Zicheng's army, 200,000 strong, was defeated by the combined forces of Wu Sangui and Dorgon, when the Manchu troops victoriously entered Beijing on June 6, 1644.

Thus began the Manchu rule of China, but the outcome of the invasion could not, at the time, have been predicted. Although the Manchus had prepared for years for the conquest of China, and had presented themselves in as positive a light as a foreign conqueror could hope to be perceived, they faced a most uncertain future, as a small minority of "barbarians" who were about to establish their rule and restore order in an immense country ravaged by famine, rebellions, and political chaos.

Members of the former Ming court that had meanwhile fled to the southern capital, Nanjing, continued to regard themselves as the rightful rulers of China, and called upon local troops and governors to join them in the resistance to the invasion. Organizing the resistance was, to put it mildly, a messy business, and conditions varied greatly from one province to the next. Dissent among the Ming loyalists, lack of leadership, the presence of a large number of outlaw elements and bandit armies, and the persistence of famine and disease in many regions made the two years that followed particularly critical. The Manchus, for their part, advertised themselves as saviors of the country for having snatched it from the clutches of the bandit rabble, and to attract support on the promise to restore law and order. At the same time, they undermined their considerable attractiveness (after all, many of the former Ming generals had already defected to the Qing), by enforcing the much hated "hair and dress" regulations. They decreed that adult males should shave their foreheads and braid their hair in a queue in the "tartar fashion." Chinese male subjects were also forced to adopt a Manchu-style dress with rigid upright collar and tapered sleeves. It was in particular the shaving decree that inflamed the Chinese population, and resisting it became the rallying cry of Ming loyalists throughout China.

In itself, the stiffness of the resistance was not the major obstacle to the Manchus' completion of the conquest. Restoring social order, returning to a condition of administrative viability, and, at the most basic level, ensuring that the areas most badly affected by war and famine obtained economic relief were more difficult objectives to achieve. An important advantage for the Manchus was the disaffection of the military class from Ming politics on account of the isolation and humiliating subordination to which they had been relegated for centuries by the civil administrators and court literati. This made Ming generals and their troops particularly vulnerable to Manchu propaganda, which emphasized martial vigor and rewarded military merits. The Manchus' success also depended on making the social and political elites switch sides rather quickly since they were needed as the backbone of any plan of social and economic recovery at the local level.

The conquest was unquestionably a bloody affair, and episodes such as the "massacre of Yangzhou," where a city that had not surrendered to the Manchus was allowed to suffer ten days of unrestrained pillage and killing by the Manchu troops, will remain forever as a somber testimony to the savage and merciless violence that the Manchu military could and did inflict on the local population.[11] While this was not an isolated occurrence, one must also say that the Manchu army, in comparison with the bands of renegades, bandits, and the same Chinese armies fighting on the Qing side, was fairly disciplined, and surely did less damage overall than their "competition." Still, many Chinese preferred to resist to the death or commit suicide and sacrifice their and their families' lives rather than surrender to the "slave barbarians." Others chose to struggle through the Ming debacle and, seeking a realistic accommodation, accepted positions and honors under the new regime.

By 1645 the southern Ming capital Nanjing had been taken and the Manchus called the Chinese advisor and strategist Hong Chengchou from Beijing to take charge of restoring taxation and collection of resources from the rich area of Jiangnan to keep the Qing army supplied for the rest of the campaign. The Manchus' march continued first east of Nanjing, and then to the south toward Zhejiang and then Fujian, where another Ming prince chosen to be the next emperor (Longwu, r. 1645–1646) became the rallying point of the Ming resistance. Manchu forces under the command of Bolo defeated, captured, and executed the short-lived emperor. At this point a new prince was installed with the reign title of Yongli, who was going to be the last emperor of the "Southern Ming" dynasty.

By then, the fate of the Ming had been sealed, since the residual loyalist forces were caught in a stranglehold that was going to grow ever tighter. This is not to say that the progress of the Qing to establish their rule over southern China was quick or unimpeded; indeed, fighting continued until 1662, and the confrontation with the military warlord Zheng Chenggong (Koxinga) in Taiwan, proved particularly long and hard. But the dramatic shift in the balance of military forces, the lack of resources at the disposal of the Ming camp, and its disorganization and fractiousness made the final Manchu victory just a matter of time.

For our purpose, we should focus on the roles played during this phase by some of the chief protagonists of the later events that constitute the historical backdrop of the Diary. These are Kong Youde (d. 1652), Geng Zhongming (d. 1649), and Shang Kexi (1604–1673).[12] These three were military commanders originally from Liaodong who had defected to Hong Taiji in the early 1630s and, together with their troops, had formed the initial nucleus of the Chinese Banners. They remained loyal to the Qing through the conquest and fought hard against the Ming in the south of China, in particular Guangdong and Guangxi. In 1648 they were given titles equivalent to viceroys and put in charge of the government of the southern provinces, which became virtually semi-independent hereditary satrapies. Kong Youde, with the title of "Prince Who Stabilizes the South" (Dingnan Wang) was put in charge of the Guangxi Province. Geng Zhongming was appointed "Prince Who Pacifies the South" (Jingnan Wang) with control over Fujian Province. Shang Kexi was given the title of "Prince who Appeases the South" (Pingnan Wang) and, after some heavy fighting in the early 1650s against the loyalist Ming armies led by Li Dingguo, became the virtual ruler of the Guangdong Province, and held it securely through the end of the conquest and until his fateful request for retirement, in 1673, which precipitated the rebellion of the Three Feudatories.[13]

The three generals distinguished themselves before and during the course of the conquest fighting side by side with Manchu and Mongol troops. In 1644 and 1645 Shang Kexi joined the Manchu Prince Ajige and Kong Youde and Geng Zhongming joined the Manchu Prince Dodo, one of the most effective commanders on the Qing side, in the operations to wipe out the Shun army, that is, the rebel forces of the extremely short-lived dynasty founded by Li Zicheng upon his capture of Beijing.[14] The three of them participated in the two-pronged campaign against the southern Ming forces in the late 1640s in central and south China. Then again in 1649 they were summoned by the court to take the command of the renewed campaign into Guangdong and Guangxi against the Ming forces of the Yongli emperor. In 1652 Kong Youde's troops, stationed in Guilin, were overrun as the city was stormed by the Ming troops of Li Dingguo during the loyalist counteroffensive in the southeast that lasted from 1651 to 1655. Kong Youde, to avoid capture, killed most of his family and then committed suicide.[15] The only surviving family member was his daughter Kong Sizhen, about 11 years of age at the time of the death of her father. Thereafter, due to the unflinching loyalty of her father, she received many honors from the Manchu court, and her husband Sun Yanling was given the post of military governor in Guangxi.[16] He was criticized by the court several times on account of poor judgment and excessive freedom in the exercise of his power, and eventually he joined half-heartedly the rebellion of Wu Sangui. But he was not trusted by Wu Sangui, who had him killed, while his wife, Kong Sizhen, remained staunchly loyal to the Qing court.

Geng Zhongming was the grandfather of Geng Jingzhong, who would later join the anti-Qing rebellion started by Wu Sangui, and father of Geng Jimao, who fought successfully throughout the conquest, and was on a campaign together with his father when Geng Zhongming committed suicide. Apparently the reason for this was his responsibility in a crime committed by his subordinate officers, accused of concealing runaway slaves.[17] Nonetheless, on account of his father and grandfather's merits and long service for the Qing, Geng Jingzhong married into the Manchu nobility and inherited the title of "Prince who Pacifies the South" and the post of governor of Fujian. But the most important of the Chinese generals who sided with the Manchus was Wu Sangui, whose career path had been very different from that of the other three generals, and whose contribution to the completion of the conquest had been even more critical.

Wu Sangui

Born in 1612 in a military family from Liaodong, Wu Sangui was of exactly the same age as the Manchu leader Dorgon when the two confronted each other in 1644 across the Shanhai Pass, the frontier gateway between China and Manchuria. Foremost among his peer military commanders for reputation, ambition, and the quality of his troops, under the Ming Wu Sangui rose through the ranks to become Brigadier-general stationed at the strategically crucial Ningyuan garrison in Liaodong. With peasant rebellions ravaging China, and several Chinese military men already gone over to the Manchus, he was in charge of the sole sizeable Chinese force between the Manchu capital, Mukden, and Peking.[18]

The facts surrounding the position taken by Wu Sangui in the fateful days of the fall of the Ming have been debated by generations of historians. The personal accounts written by people who lived through those events appear to be in conflict with later historical accounts, especially those that go back to after the rebellion of Wu Sangui, which tended to portray the former Ming general's moral character as less than palatable: fickle, ambitious, and somewhat debauched. A popular version of his behavior claimed that he responded slowly and half-heartedly to the Ming emperor's request for help, therefore not arriving in time to save the capital from the rebel forces. Then, after Li Zicheng entered the capital, Wu Sangui was asked to join him but he hesitated, thus angering the "Dashing Prince"—as Li styled himself—who proceeded to torture Wu Sangui's father and grab his favorite concubine. At this point Wu was attacked by Li's forces, and in order to exact his revenge he invited the Manchus into the Shanhai pass and joining forces with them beat the rebel army back and recovered the capital.

Based on sources not tainted by later historical judgments of Wu's role, a different and more accurate account of the events has been produced.[19] According to Angela Hsi's study, there was no real awareness in the capital that Li's forces were so close to capturing the city, and therefore Wu was not called to rescue it. His advance toward the capital was due to the mutiny of a Chinese garrison, which he was asked to suppress, as indeed he did, thereafter returning dutifully to his post on the frontier. When he got word of the fact that his father, like many other Ming officers, had been tortured by Li Zicheng to extract money from him he turned definitely against Li, and began recruiting efforts to add new troops to his army in order to march against the rebels. At this point, Li's troops advanced against him, but were met and defeated by Wu Sangui. Since the only army that could have stopped the Manchus was engaged in combat with Li's troops, Dorgon and his Manchu Bannermen crossed the border into China unopposed. Dorgon then forced Wu Sangui to join the Qing, as he had very little choice but hope to use the Manchu troops to avenge the Ming and clear Beijing and the rest of the country of the rebel armies. It is also possible that Wu intended to "buy time" in order to try to oppose the Manchus later, but this notion is only a speculation based on events that took place thirty years later, when Wu rebelled against the Qing. It is certainly likely that, from a strategic point of view, Wu Sangui's choice to side with the Manchus, and thus ensure his own and his troops' survival in order to free the capital from the scourge of Li Zicheng's army is correct, but no further intention should probably be attributed to him at this stage.[20]

It is also true that the Manchus had been conducting raids into China and exploring opportunities to exploit China's weaknesses for a long time. In 1644 the Manchu court was going through a period of instability due to the questions inherent to the succession to the throne that emerged at the death of Hong Taiji in 1643, but the aforementioned regents, that is, Dorgon, then 32 years of age, and the 44-year-old Jirgalang, uncle of Dorgon, were both strong and experienced military commanders. Dorgon distinguished himself already at 16 years of age in the wars against the Chakhar Mongols (1628), and Jirgalang was a veteran commander who had served in countless campaigns against Korean, Chinese, and Mongol enemies. They would not have shrunk at a chance to invade China when it presented itself. Given that the army of Wu Sangui was well trained and armed and about 40,000 strong, without counting the reserves that could be raised in the frontier region, a direct clash with it would have been potentially extremely damaging to the Manchu army. Estimating about 100 fighting men per company and multiplying this by the number of companies available in 1643 (554) we obtain a number of 55,400, which was small compared to even regional Ming forces or rebel armies.[21] Suffering heavy losses would have therefore prejudiced from the start the whole conquest of China. In fact, the Manchus regularly placed the surrendered Chinese military units in the very front line, while keeping Banner forces in reserve or in the rear, to be used predominantly to strike quickly and with maximum impact the enemy, so that Manchu and Mongol losses would be minimized. The terrible punishment inflicted on cities that resisted the Manchus, thus prolonging the fight and causing greater losses than expected, has been also attributed to the desire to preserve one's forces by inducing the enemy to surrender by means of "psychological warfare." Manchu military strategy did not rely on scorched earth approaches, but on a carefully calibrated balance of proportionally applied violence, so that those who resisted more vigorously received the heaviest punishment, while those who did not were rewarded. The incorporation of the former Ming forces into the Green Standard army stems from the dual need, on the one hand, to allow surrendered Ming troops to remain occupied as a military force in the government's service (rather than joining the ranks of the rebels), and, on the other, to reduce the use of Bannermen in combat.

Thus we can explain why, as the battle-hardened Shun soldiers of Li Zicheng marched to crush Wu Sangui's valiant but numerically inferior force, and Wu Sangui struck a deal with Dorgon, switching sides in exchange for military assistance, the brunt of the Shun troops' assault was still borne by Wu's troops. It seems (but the evidence is murky) that only after both sides had suffered heavy losses the Manchu cavalry joined battle, wreaking havoc among the rebel soldiers, who fled. They were pursued relentlessly to the capital, where news that the Manchus were about to arrive favored the recapture of the capital as the occupants panicked.

Following that, Wu and his troops were dispatched to pursue and destroy the remaining Shun forces outside Beijing, and fought together with the Manchu prince Ajige in the provinces of Shaanxi, Hunan, and Hubei. Coming back from this campaign he was raised to the exalted rank of Qin Wang, or Prince of the Blood, a title that he first accepted but then renounced shortly afterwards. He was then ordered to move his troops to Jinzhou and garrison it. With the continuation of the hostilities in south China he asked and was allowed to join the other Chinese generals dispatched to fight against the southern Ming in central and southern China.

In 1648 he was transferred by imperial order and appointed General at Hanzhong, in Shaanxi. The following year together with the banner general Li Guohan he struck other rebel forces at Jiezhou, in Gansu. After various locations in Shaanxi had been cleaned up, the rebels were gradually subdued. He was then commanded to undertake a military expedition to Sichuan. After the annihilation of the remaining rebels of Zhang Xianzhong he was forced to go back to southern Sichuan by the remaining forces of the Southern Ming generals Sun Kewang, Li Dingguo, and Bo Wenxuan.[22] As reward for his efforts, at a court audience in 1651 the emperor gave him a golden suit of armor and a golden diploma. His son Wu Yinxiong was also given a nobility title.

In 1657 the Ming loyalist Sun Kewang surrendered to the Manchus, and at this point a new Qing offensive began, in which Wu Sangui played a major role. In January 1658 Wu Sangui was ordered to proceed, in coordination with two other route armies, from southern Sichuan to Guizhou. Having amassed a considerable force in Guizhou, at the end of 1658 and beginning of 1659 the Qing forces moved against the defenses organized by Li Dingguo, the most successful of the Southern Ming generals. At the head of one of three expeditionary armies—the other two being under the Manchu generals Doni and Jobtei—Wu proceeded to march into Yunnan, and his forces pressed against the remnant Ming forces aiming to capture the southern Ming Yongli emperor (Zhu Youlang).[23]

An increasingly desperate Ming court, reduced to a party of destitute followers on the run, crossed into Burma. For the following two years the Yongli court, initially welcomed by the Burmese monarch, had to struggle with a Burmese court that had grown hostile because of the marauding activities of the Ming troops led by Li Dingguo. Eventually, in August 1661, the Ming court officials and every male older than fifteen were slaughtered by the Burmese, who left only children and women alive, in addition to the emperor. Meanwhile, Wu Sangui had been put in charge of the final conquest and pacification of Yunnan. Already in 1657, at the recommendation of Hong Chenzhou, he had received the title of "Generalissimo Who Pacifies the West" (Ping Xi Dajiangjun), and that of "Prince Who Pacifies the West" (Ping Xi Wang).

During this time the foundations of his monarch-like power in Yunnan were laid, as Wu Sangui insisted to retain a large force at the cost of the central government, increased taxes for his own local government, established monopolies on gold and copper, salt, and on the trade of ginseng and rhubarb. At the same time, he fought native leaders and residual Ming troops that, according to a memorial he had sent to the throne, were being supplied and instigated by the Ming generals in Burma.[24] Notwithstanding the prohibitive costs of pacifying the southwest, the court agreed to fund a campaign into Burma, which got under way in 1661.[25] After entering Burma Wu Sangui and the Manchu general Aisinga, in compliance with their requests, received from the Burmese king the Yongli emperor and the remainder of his party. Taken into custody, the party was transported to Yunnan. Here the emperor (no doubt close to death because of an increasingly serious asthma condition) and his teenage son were executed on June 11, 1662, probably by strangulation.[26]

Having achieved full control of Yunnan, and having added to that also the province of Guizhou, during the eleven years from the regicide of the Yongli emperor in 1662 to the revolt he initiated in 1673 Wu Sangui consolidated his hold on the southwest. His army was well equipped and well trained. Weapons and money were stockpiled, and the military and civilian ranks staffed with people he had personally selected and appointed, overriding any central authority. It seems peculiar that he could do so without powerful support at court, and one wonders whether the rise of an autonomous native Chinese power in the south may not have been seen with some sympathy by those Chinese advisors of the Manchus that had been the staunchest supporters of Wu Sangui and other Chinese generals serving under the Qing. In another sense, the growth of his independent power in the southwest resembles the early phase of the Manchu rise in the northeast. Wu, like Nurhaci, established trade monopolies and began building a centralized military and civil administration.

The Three Feudatories' rebellion

After the completion of the conquest of China, and with the greater part of the Banner forces concentrated in the north, the military security and political loyalty of the south had been entrusted to three prominent military leaders, Wu Sangui in

Yunnan, Shang Zhixin in Guangdong, and Geng Jingzhong in Fujian. They wielded virtually absolute power over their jurisdictions, and the central government's role and presence were minimal. They retained command of their own armies, and Wu Sangui had the best-trained soldiers, amounting in 1665 to 64,000 men, of which 48,000 were Green Standard troops. Administrative and financial powers were also firmly in their hands. Geng Jimao had under his command about 20,000 troops, and Shang Kexi 10,500.[27]

At the root of the rebellion, for what is possible to gather from the oblique political positions that emerged at this time, were a combination of autonomist tendencies that had been allowed by the court to become entrenched and the court's own indecision and internal dissensions about how to confront Wu Sangui.[28] As it was later recognized by the Kangxi emperor, the Qing court had failed to check the growth of the powerful Chinese "warlords" and allowed the remote provinces of the south to become the cradle of anti-government military factions. The facts are well known. In April 1673 Shang Kexi, the old general who was to remain loyal to the Qing, submitted to the emperor a petition requesting that, because of old age, he be allowed to retire to his birthplace in Liaodong with a suitable retinue. The request was granted and Shang was ordered to transfer to the north with his army and family.[29] However, the emperor did not agree to the further request that his "fiefdom" be inherited by Shang's son, Zhixin, and used this opportunity as a wedge to abolish his "fiefdom" in Guangdong and re-establish full central control over the province. It is likely that this decision was regarded, in the emperor and his advisors' intention, as the first move toward the abolition of all the independent powers in south China, and the other two "feudatories" were to follow suit.

In August of the same year Wu and Geng submitted similar petitions, which could be interpreted as a covert challenge to the central power. Would the Manchu emperor dare abolish their principalities, too? Geng's petition for retirement was accepted without much discussion, but Wu Sangui's presented a greater challenge, and the emperor's advisors could not agree on how to proceed. The majority of the members of the Deliberative Council, including the extremely influential Songgotu, were against granting Wu's petition. The formal reason for it was the claim that the transfer of all the people in Wu Sangui's service to Liaodong would have caused a major disruption in Yunnan, but the real reason was, most likely, that they feared Wu's reaction, and that they felt uneasy about the possibility of precipitating a major revolt. The decision was difficult, since the newly created unity of China was still weak and vulnerable. On the other hand, the dynasty had to assert itself, and allowing the existence of personal "fiefdoms" would have been tantamount to conceding the existence of a *de facto* separate political authority over the country.

The outcome of a major war would have been impossible to predict, yet the 19-year-old emperor decided to respond to Wu's challenge by accepting his retirement, and implicitly abolishing his principality. He was supported in this decision only by a small group of four advisors, against the exhortations of the majority to temporize and seek a compromise. An edict was therefore issued in October 1673 accepting Wu's retirement and inviting him to move to his birthplace in the northeast. Wu rejected the edict and on December 28 rebelled openly and irrevocably by proclaiming a new dynasty, which he called Zhou in deference to the long-lived native Chinese dynasty of ancient times.[30]

Wu felt fully in control of the military situation and of the support he would enjoy from the military commanders of other provinces. The rhetoric of the revolt emphasized Ming loyalism and anti-Manchu patriotism, and the slogan "fight the Qing and restore the Ming" aimed to mobilize patriotic forces eager to see the foreign conquerors driven out of the country. But of course, coming from one of the most effective supporters of the Manchus, who were also responsible for killing the last Ming scion, such arguments sounded hollow to anybody who had cared about the Ming, and therefore those who joined the rebellion did so purely on the basis of political calculus. At the same time, Wu Sangui was so emboldened by his early success that he sent a letter to Kangxi suggesting that he should take his Manchus back to Manchuria, and that, if he did so, he would be able to keep Korea as well.[31] The emperor's response was unambiguous: Wu's son Wu Yingxiong, who was in residence at the capital, was seized and summarily executed.

There are indications that the extent of the threat and magnitude of the rebellion may have been at first underestimated by the Qing emperor. An estimate of the first contingent sent to quell the rebellion seems to number only a little over 10,000 troops, inclusive of soldiers from the Mongolian and Manchu Vanguard Regiment, Guards Regiment, Cavalry Regiment, and from the Chinese Firearms Battalion.[32] This appears extremely small if compared to the total number of Banner and Green Standard soldiers that would be mobilized by the end of the rebellion, numbering over half a million troops.

The initial strategy of the Kangxi emperor was to deploy these troops so as to contain the rebellion, and prevent its spreading north of the Yangzi River. In order to protect Hubei and the main routes between southern and northern China, Lergiyen, son of the famed general Lekdehun, was appointed commander-in-chief of the Qing forces, and sent with a contingent of Banner troops to defend the strategic city of Jingzhou. It was also essential to prevent the advance of the rebels in Sichuan in the west, and in the Jiangnan region, that is, the richest and most populous area of China, in the east. For that reason troops were also deployed along the Yangzi River. This general strategy paid off because, although the government troops suffered a series of defeats in the early stage of the rebellion, the rebels' inability to tap into the resources of the richest areas made it impossible for them to advance beyond their initial thrust into central China. Thus, the rebellion began to lose impetus, divisions started to emerge within the rebels' ranks, and gradually the central government managed to recover territory and gain its own military momentum. Geng surrendered in 1676, Shang in 1677, Wu passed away in 1678, and the Qing would achieve final victory at the end of 1681.[33]

The early phase of the war was hugely favorable to the secessionist forces, as they proceeded from victory to victory, and more local military commanders and governors appeared to support the rebellion. Wang Fuchen, the provincial governor of Shaanxi, revolted, and killed the Manchu commander Molo in the process. Another blow to the government forces in the south was the defection of Sun Yanling, military governor of Guangxi, to the rebels' camp, which led to Wu Sangui's control of Guangxi. In 1674 the "rebels" invaded the once prosperous province of Hunan. The capital Changsha was quickly occupied and by April Wu Sangui's control of the province was complete. Local officials who remained loyal to the Qing did not take action or were exceedingly slow to respond. At the same time the rebel general Wang Pingfan was sent to invade Sichuan, which he controlled by March 1.

Aside from a general deterioration of the fighting quality of the Banner troops, which for some years had grown complacent about training and discipline, the major problems that the Qing forces had to face were of a logistic nature, that is, they had long supply lines and severe shortages of food and horses for the expeditionary armies.[34] These shortages became ever more serious as they advanced into southern China, which had of course been stripped to the bone by the rebel forces. Coordination of the troops at the front was not easy to achieve either, as the command structure was not clearly demarcated and various Banner and Green Standard armies in the field responded to central orders but were at times unable to agree at the operational level.

In April, Geng Jingzhong joined the rebellion, probably betting on Wu's strength and impressed by his early success. His forces obtained victories in Fujian and entered Zhejiang and then Jiangxi. Kangxi mobilized both Banner and Green Standard troops under the command of the Manchu Prince Giyešu against him, but throughout the remainder of the year Geng was on the whole quite successful.[35] At the beginning of the following year Giyešu managed to keep the city of Jinhua, which had been fiercely fought over. But at this point armed operations came to a halt, and Giyešu stayed at Jinhua for over a year, until the Kangxi emperor, in April 1676, became angry at his inactivity and forced him to advance further into Zhejiang and enter Fujian. The offensive was successful, Geng surrendered on the promise that his life would be spared. This promise was one that the Kangxi emperor did not keep.

Giyešu's lackluster conduct was not an isolated occurrence. One of the defining aspects of the first phase of the hostilities is the poor conduct of the Manchu military commanders and troops, which must have struck many as utterly unexpected and extremely worrying for the government. Kangxi openly vented his frustration with several of them. For instance, the Manchu general Labu, appointed as commander of the forces in Jiangxi, suffered several defeats at the hands of the rebel armies under Han Daren. He later recovered from these defeats with the help of reinforcements, but his conduct in war was severely censored by the emperor and his titles posthumously revoked after his death in 1681.[36] The hiccup progress of the war in several theaters, particularly in 1675 and 1678, proved to be particularly frustrating for Kangxi, who had to intervene personally and forcefully to spur the government forces into action. The direct involvement of the emperor in strategic and tactical decisions also provided a centralized leadership that the rebels lacked: whereas the emperor could just intervene to reprimand or replace high officers and resolve tensions among field commanders, the rebels would simply continue to argue with one another.

Meanwhile, Wang Fuchen's defection had widened the rebellion in the northwest, and had occupied parts of Shaanxi and Gansu. Several Chinese generals were appointed to fight in this region, such as Zhang Yong (1616–1684), Wang Jinbao (1626–1685), and Zhao Liangdong (1621–1697), who were to serve successfully through the rest of the campaign and make a tremendous contribution to the government's victory.[37] Also, the force assembled in Xi'an for the counteroffensive in the northwestern theater included a large number of Green Standard troops, which appear to have been preferred because of the rocky nature of the terrain, for which an infantry force would be better suited, and because of the desire to keep the Banner troops in reserve. Also, the Manchus seem to have believed that Chinese troops were particularly effective when fighting other Chinese, a somewhat ironic twist on the time-honored Chinese practice of "using 'barbarians' to fight 'barbarians'."[38]

In the meantime, the irredentist Chakhar Mongol leader Burni started a campaign in the north that could have been devastating for the government, since there were not many troops that could be diverted from fighting the rebellion in the south. Two Manchu generals, Oja and Tuhai, were appointed to quell the Mongols, a task that they accomplished quickly and efficiently with the assistance of Mongol allies even though the troops at their disposal were substandard Banner forces. The leadership qualities demonstrated by Tuhai in this circumstance gained him imperial favor, and as soon as Burni's revolt was repressed he was appointed, in 1676, commander-in-chief of all forces fighting in the northwest (Gansu and Shaanxi) against Wang Fuchen.

During the first eighteen months of military operations, through 1674 and most of 1675, the success of the rebels had been so impressive that the Dalai Lama, in an attempt to act as political intermediary, suggested that peace might be achieved by dividing the empire and allowing Wu to keep part of China. Needless to say, the Kangxi emperor did not appreciate the suggestion, and in his reply he pointed out that Wu Sangui was a petty officer under the Ming, he begged to submit to the Qing, was elevated to the highest ranks, and his son married a royal Princess, receiving the highest possible favors, and repaid them with ingratitude, stirring up dissension and oppressing people: "As the Sovereign of the people of the empire, how can we bear to allot him land and cease military operations? If he really repents of his sins and returns to the allegiance, we shall punish him with less than the death sentence."[39]

In 1676 the tide of the war was turning in the government's favor, as both the military operations and the propaganda war to persuade former rebels to surrender began to pay off. Wang Fuchen surrendered to Tuhai in July 1676, and Giyešu successfully resumed operations in Fujian, forcing Geng Jingzhong to surrender at the end of the year. The third feudatory Shang Zhixin switched sides again in January 1677 and helped the government recover Guangdong by the end of that year. His participation in the rebellion, turnabout, and final fate was played out largely against the backdrop of the deadly feud that opposed him to his brother Shang Jixiao. The denunciations and counter-denunciations of the two finally ended in a crime drama atmosphere, as Shang Zhixin hatched a plot to assassinate one of the people involved in the accusations, and was in turn discovered and sentenced to death by suicide.[40] This was not the only occurrence of deadly in-fighting. In Guangxi Wu Sangui began to suspect that Sun Yanling might betray him, and had him assassinated.

The government troops made several advances in 1677 and 1678. Yolo, after having suffered earlier defeats advanced in Jiangxi, took Changsha in March 1679, and opened a strategic route to Guizhou. Wu Sangui's generals were suffering defeats in the field, and Wu himself was losing appeal with his demoralized allies, while fearing they might betray and turn against him; in addition, his supplies were dwindling. He concentrated on defending his bases in Hunan but this was an increasingly difficult, and eventually desperate task. Showing perhaps more than a hint of delusion, in March 1678 he promoted himself from the rank of Generalissimo Commander of all the Forces of the Empire to emperor of his "Zhou dynasty." At the end of the year he fell ill and died at the age of 66 on October 2, 1678.

With all three initial leaders now out of the fray, the rebellion, remarkably, kept going on its own steam under the leadership of Wu's grandson Wu Shifan, the son of Wu Yinxiong, whom the Kangxi emperor had executed four years earlier. He was then based at Guiyang, and the territory under his control, albeit considerably reduced with respect to the heyday of the revolt, still included Yunnan, Guizhou, and parts of Hunan, Sichuan, and Guangxi.[41] Moreover, while the rebellion had lost its most important leader, and was plagued by extensive defections and internal bickering, there were still numerous capable generals and battle-hardened troops that had decided to fight to the death. On the government side, the long years of war and hardships had taken a major toll, and the troops were exhausted. The last three years of the war, from the end of 1678 to the capture of Yunnanfu (modern Kunming) in December 1681, were anything but a leisurely walk.

In 1679 Yolo, having achieved great merit in the field, stepped down from the post of commander-in-chief of the Qing forces, to which his nephew Jangtai was promoted. This was a Manchu general who had lacked distinction in the initial phase of the war but later redeemed himself. He advanced to Guizhou in 1680 and in 1681 entered Yunnan, joined forces with Laita, who commanded the forces in Guangxi, and Zhao Liangdong, coming with his army from Sichuan. It is this last phase of the war that is the subject of the diary's surviving portion.

16

The war during the period covered by Dzengšeo's diary

At the end of 1679 the emperor had issued an edict ordering Qing generals Zhao Liangdong and Wang Jinbao to proceed to invade and recover southern Shaanxi and Sichuan. This task was going to be entrusted mainly to the soldiers of the Green Standard Army, although Manchu forces continued to be in charge of carrying supplies and other logistical tasks. Ostensibly, the Chinese Green Standard troops were going to be used for simple mopping-up operations, given that the main rebel forces had already been smashed. In reality, the Chinese infantry was better equipped to fight in the mountainous terrain of southwestern China, where substantial resistance could still be expected, than the Manchu-Mongol cavalry.

In February 1680 Zhao Liangdong captured Chengdu, while Wang Jinbao captured Baoning, in western Sichuan. In March the city of Chongqing surrendered, thus completing the recovery of Sichuan, but scattered resistance continued in the region, and as late as the fall of 1680 the rebels were still able to defeat government troops in western Sichuan. Food shortages and tensions among the leading Qing generals made matters unstable, and caused delays that allowed rebel generals Hu Guozhu, Xia Guoxiang, and Ma Bao to attempt to recapture Sichuan, coming to the rescue of the local rebels from Guizhou and Yunnan.[42]

In October 1680 the emperor then appointed a Manchu general, Laita, as commander-in-chief of all Manchu and Chinese troops in Guangxi, and gave him orders to attack Yunnan from there. At the same time, Jangtai was ordered to attack and capture Guiyang, while general Tuhai transferred more troops to southwestern Sichuan from Chengdu, so as to stifle local resistance and repel the rebel armies and then march into Yunnan. The classic three-pronged maneuver was successful, and Laita was the first of the three generals to enter Yunnan. He defeated the enemy on the Guizhou–Yunnan border, and reached Qujing in March 1681. The rebel general Li Benshen surrendered to Tuhai, and he could then march against Kunming. Meanwhile, the rebel forces that were fighting in Sichuan were recalled into Yunann to help defend the capital. Pursued by Zhao Liangdong, the rebel generals either surrendered with their troops or committed suicide. The siege of Kunming continued for months, but in December the city fell, and the suicide of Wu Shifan, on December 7, 1681, brought the rebellion to an end.

The demobilization of the Qing troops, however, was no easy matter. All together there were approximately 150,000 Banner troops and 400,000 Green Standard Army troops that had been mobilized. Already in the summer of 1679 the Mongolian troops from Hunan and Hubei had been recalled to Beijing. Also, in September 1681, before the fall of Kunming, the Manchu troops still remaining in Sichuan were almost completely called back to Beijing. Most troops from Guangxi, Guizhou, and Hunan were also recalled, with the exception of a small number left behind on garrison duty. Other troops were left behind in Hangzhou, Fuzhou, Canton, and other places.

The Green Standard Army was also demobilized and moved for the most part to Shaanxi from Yunnan. This was possibly a precautionary measure to prevent a concentration of troops that might create yet another military threat, but in light of the extremely severe shortages of food, one can also see this as a relief measure to allow the region to recover economically. Green Standard troops were placed under the direct control of the provincial governors; at the same time the military officers commanding individual units were subject to periodic controls from the capital, and replaced often in order to prevent that the troops' personal loyalty to them might lead to new instances of local focuses of rebellion.[43] These provincial commanders were either called to the capital periodically or transferred after a tour of duty from one province to another. This and other changes both in the army and in the local administration led to bringing the southern provinces once again, and far more securely, into the fold of the empire.

There are several theories as to why the rebellion failed. Wu Sangui and the other rebel leaders never received the widespread popular support they had hoped for and eventually grew isolated politically. This was allegedly the result of the imposition of extra taxes in the regions under the "feudatories'" control; moreover, lands were confiscated, and local governance became predatory and callous. Second, Wu Sangui's strategy was conservative. After the occupation of Hunan Wu Sangui enjoyed tactical advantage since the rebels' camp was united and he had under his command a large number of seasoned troops. But, instead of crossing the Yangtze and advancing right away he allowed the Qing forces to take the initiative, deploy at strategic locations, and strengthen their positions until they could start a counteroffensive. Third, the rebellion had too many leaders, all of whom tried to pursue their own individual and localistic objectives. Tensions developed among them that made coordination and cooperation effectively impossible. Finally, from the beginning Kangxi formulated a strategy that concentrated on dividing the enemy camp and isolating Wu Sangui, correctly seen as the central pillar of the revolt. Reconciliation was actively sought out and pardons were offered to those who surrendered. Some of the most crucial allies of Wu Sangui, including Wang Fuchen and the other "feudatory" Geng Jingzhong, were eventually persuaded to renounce their anti-government struggle and to seek pardon. Shang Zhixin also surrendered after having joined the rebellion only in 1676.[44]

The Kangxi emperor

It is beyond question that Xuanye, the Kangxi emperor, played a most critical role in the political decisions and strategic thinking throughout the war even though in 1673 he was a young man of barely 19 years of age. Born in 1654 as the third son of the Shunzhi emperor, he acceded the throne as a boy of 7 in 1661, while his father the Shunzhi emperor, only 23 years old, lay on his deathbed, having suffered from poor health and possibly tuberculosis for some time. A day after Xuanye's accession to the throne his father died among rumors of court intrigues, and the leadership of the country officially passed to four regents while the new emperor was a minor.

The four regents were Soni, Suksaha, Ebilun, and Oboi. All of them came from the top echelon of Manchu nobility, and displayed a distinctly different attitude in governance with respect to the Shunzhi emperor. The Shunzhi emperor had been conciliatory toward the Chinese who served under him, drawn to Buddhist mystical practices, and reliant on the palace eunuchs, but it is very likely that the Manchu aristocracy saw these tendencies as pernicious to the state and deviant from the more authentic Manchu "values." The regency concentrated on strengthening Manchu institutions, such as the Court of Colonial Affairs (Li Fan Yuan), and placed greater emphasis, at least in theory, on the need for military preparedness, fiscal efficiency, and judicial rigor. At the same time, however, the regents were jousting for power. Oboi, the most ambitious of the four, was able to achieve a high degree of influence and control over all matters of state, both within and outside the palace.

Given the intensity of the competition among the regents, the early years of the Kangxi emperor's rule were probably not devoid of danger, but he seems to have been protected and advised by his grandmother, the Empress Dowager. With her guidance, Kangxi began in 1667 and 1668, at the age of 14, his struggle to recover his rightful political role. The emperor rose to the occasion, but the fight was bloody, and involved the heavy punishment of Suksaha and his family, and various other supporters of the regents. What is particularly impressive is the swiftness and sure-footedness of the emperor's political moves, which revealed, quite apart from the political advice he received from his grandmother, acute intelligence and steadfast courage, two characteristics that continued to define his person and his period of reign.

Once firmly in power, the Kangxi emperor did not revert to the policies, or style of governance, of his father. He was a healthy man who delighted in a military life and hunts, but was also a man of intense intellectual curiosity and considerable learning. His long period of rule is generally seen as one of consolidation of Qing rule on the frontiers, reconciliation, and accommodation within the country, and economic growth. But the challenges that Kangxi faced in order to retain a firm grip on the state's rudder wheel were many, and none more testing of his abilities as a ruler and as a military strategist than the war of the Three Feudatories. This remained a critical moment of his success as a ruler, but also of his reflection about errors committed and of the disasters incurred by incorrect judgment.[45]

The Manchu army

Banner forces

An understanding of the diary's narrative requires an illustration, as cursory and incomplete as it may be, of the Qing army. The rise of Manchu power has its foundations in the Eight Banners, a system of dual administrative and military organization in which each "Banner" included a portion of the Manchu population whose male individuals were bound to provide military service. Created in 1601, this system remained a dynamic feature of the early Manchu state throughout the reigns of Nurhaci and Hong Taiji. In its finite form, achieved in the early 1640s, it included three sets of eight "Banners" each, divided along ethnic lines: Manchu, Mongol, and Chinese (Han). The "Banners" were distinguished according by four colors: yellow, white, blue, and red; each color was used for two Banners in a "plain" (i.e. without border) and "bordered" pattern. The "bordered" flags were framed with a red rim, with the exception of the red flag, hemmed in white.

The building blocks of the Banners were the companies, called in Manchu *niru* (Chinese *zuoling*). Five companies would make up a division (Manchu *jalan*) and in turn five divisions constituted a Banner. Because the number of companies tended to grow throughout the seventeenth century, the complement of companies in each Banner came to vary accordingly, although as a general principle, and as a matter of military balance among the princes that were in charge of these Banners, the number of soldiers assigned to each tended to remain roughly equivalent.

The first actual *niru* as proper military units were established by Nurhaci in 1601. They were four and distinguished by flags of many different colors: white, yellow, red, and blue. These were the seed of the future Eight Banner system. The name *niru* means "large arrow" and comes from the custom according to which each man would present an arrow to the leader when hunting or war parties were formed. Apparently the "arrow" used to designate the group's leader became the word to designate the group itself. According to the report of Sin Ch'ung-il, a Korean envoy that visited Nurhaci's capital in 1596, Nurhaci mobilized his troops by sending arrows to the tribal chiefs in the localities within his domain. These proceeded to supply themselves with weapons and provisions and then congregated in the cities.[46] The etymology of "Banner" (Manchu *gūsa*) responds to a similar process of metonymy as it indicates the military unit distinguished by a distinctive flag. Incidentally, in the Western military tradition an identical occurrence can be found in the word "bandon" (meaning also banner or standard), which in Maurice's Byzantine army was a unit of 300–400 soldiers.

The second step in the evolution of the Banner system occurred in 1615, as a direct result of the growth of the population and military forces under Nurhaci's control, as well as a step towards the greater centralization of his rule, to be formalized with the proclamation of the Jin dynasty in 1616. With the establishment of the Eight Banners the *niru* became a subunit, which is usually translated as "company" and constituted by a nominal body of three hundred men under a commander or "captain" (*nirui ejen*), a rank usually compared with that of a captain. These companies were created according to multiple criteria, and were structured according to different principles. There were two basic classes of companies: hereditary and public. The hereditary type was normally a *niru* formed at an early stage by clans and groups of people who submitted to Nurhaci, whose chiefs were appointed as commandants with the right to retain the position within their family after their death. In some cases more than one family could alternate as holder of the position of captain. The candidates for the inheritance were appointed after being interviewed by the throne. The public *niru* were created as a consequence of the increase in the Banner population, and as they did not reflect a pre-existing aristocratic hierarchy, their commanding post was not hereditary. Companies without a full complement of able-bodied men were organized initially as "half companies" before being turned into full-size ones.

If we look at the composition of the Manchu Banners before the conquest we find the following distribution between hereditary and non-hereditary companies. The total number of these companies were 265, and each of them were originally constituted, according to one estimate, according to one of the following criteria. In ninety-seven companies the members and the commanders had blood ties, which means that they were formed out of one kin group from the same area, as a chieftain submitted to Nurhaci and Hong Taiji. In thirty-six companies the members and the commander came from the same area but their blood or clan ties are not specified, although they appear to be related. In thirty-seven cases the members of the *niru* came from the same area but the commanders come from outside or are not identified as coming from the same area of the members. In eighty-one cases the regional and clan affiliations of the commanders are known but not those of the members, who probably came from a variety of areas. In eleven cases it is known that there were no relations between commanders and members, and in four cases a *niru* was made out of the members of a few clans controlled by a larger clan. The general principle seems to have been one of keeping people from the same region or clan who surrendered as a large group together in one or more *niru*, or to combine two or more smaller groups in a single *niru*. An important principle was that the *niru* in each Banner not be allowed to grow much more than the others, and that a general balance of forces should be maintained to prevent the accumulation of excessive military power in the hands of one or the other Banner commanders.[47]

The Mongol and Hanjun (Chinese) Banners were established in the 1630s as a result of the gradual expansion of the Manchu state.[48] The Mongol Banners were the end result of a long process that brought a large portion of the southern Mongol aristocracy into the fold of the Manchu state. Nurhaci adopted early on a policy of diplomatic rapprochement realized through treaties, marriages, and military alliances. The chaos that shook the Mongol political order in the 1620s due to the violent but unsuccessful bid by the khan of the Chakhar nation to restore a Mongol empire allowed the Manchus to redirect their Mongolian policy in a manner that was organic to the enlargement of the Manchu state, rather than simply based on alliances. The end result was that the Mongol aristocracy traded its independence for protection and a share of the future gains that the Manchus were promising. The Manchus were of course especially interested in the possibility to utilize Mongol warriors for the conquest of China. A portion of the Mongols (though not all of them) came to form forty Mongol companies that in 1635 were organized in a single stroke in a separate set of Eight Banners, known as the Mongol Eight Banners.

The Hanjun Bannermen were all natives of Liaodong who had previously served the Ming dynasty, and their ranks included those who had surrendered or defected to the Manchus as well as those who had been captured in war. The process of formation of these banners began in 1633 with the creation of the first body of Hanjun. The Chinese Banners became 2 in 1637, and doubled again to 4 in 1639. The process was completed in 1642 with the establishment of the Eight Hanjun Banners.[49] The Bannermen from Liaodong continued to dominate the Chinese Banners' aristocracy long after the conquest of China.

After entering Peking, the Qing government concentrated over half of the banner troops in the capital. The Plain Yellow Banner and the Bordered Yellow Banner were located in the northern part of the city, respectively to the west and east of the central axis. On the eastern side, from north to south, were located the Plain White, Bordered White, and Plain Blue Banners. Continuing clockwise from south to north on the western side were the Bordered Blue, Bordered Red, and Plain Red Banners. Moreover, the Banners were further divided into the 3 Upper Banners (the 2 yellow and the plain white banners) and the 5 Lower Banners, of which the former were controlled directly by the emperor.[50]

These were the standing forces of the Eight Banners, and in time of peace they were simply charged with the protection of the capital. At time of internal disturbances they could be dispatched to any corner of the empire. They also preserved the unity of the country, and protected the frontiers against foreign invasions. In addition, Banner garrisons were established throughout the country with the task of guarding a certain area and maintaining a non-local military presence, insulated from the local residents, that could intervene rapidly in case of trouble. As the conquest of China proceeded, contingents of Banner troops were stationed in key locations, such as Xi'an, Nanjing, and Hangzhou. These were not meant to be permanent garrisons, but rather temporary arrangements to cope with the stabilization of the military and political situation in a given area. During and immediately after the Sanfan rebellion more garrisons were added, such as the important ones at Jingzhou and Guangzhou, to keep military watch over the rebellious provinces after they had been pacified. After the rebellion was suppressed more garrisons were created in the rest of the country, with a preference for populous and rich provinces, which could afford the burden of sustaining this extra military force. Strategic importance was also, naturally, a key criterion. Garrison troops could number from 100 or 200 to several thousands, and lived in walled compounds separate from the rest of the local population. There seem to have been at least two reasons for this. One was the desire to keep the Banner forces insulated from excessive contacts with the overwhelming mass of the Chinese population, in the hope that they would be better able to preserve a distinctive identity as a conquering class. The second was, essentially, one of public order: since there had been already in 1650 considerable attrition between the

Bannermen stationed in Hangzhou and the local people from whom land for the troops had to be expropriated, the government decided to set up the soldiers' quarters in compounds kept separate from the main urban areas. The walls were therefore meant both to minimize contact and to protect the soldiers. The garrison system only became permanent in the mid-eighteenth century, and resulted in a gradual re-distribution of Banner forces, to the point that 7 percent of them were stationed in the north, largely Beijing and its environs, 35 percent in Manchuria, 12 percent were moved to the northwest after its conquest in 1760, and about 45 percent were scattered in garrisons around China which were made permanent during the period of reign of the Qianlong emperor (1736–1795). What is important to note in relation to the diary is that only after the suppression of the Three Feudatories (Sanfan) were Bannermen assigned to newly created garrisons, and the massive return to Beijing of the demobilized troops described in the diary is fully consistent with the fact that, in 1681, most Bannermen had their residence in the capital.[51]

Bannermen also had a specialization in terms of their specific military function and role, which was defined by the regiments to which they belonged. The composition of these regiments changed in the course of the dynasty, but generally speaking there were four basic unit, which we have called regiments, that combined together soldiers from all Manchu, Mongol, and Chinese Banners.[52] The most important regiments of the standing forces where the Imperial Bodyguards (Ch. *qinjunying*, Ma. *hiya*), the Guards (Ch. *hujunying*, Ma. *bayara*), the Cavalry (Ch. *xiaoqiying*, Ma. *aliha cooha*), and the Vanguard (Ch. *qianfengying*, Ma. *gabsihiyan*).[53] In addition, the Hanjun Banners provided most of the firepower, being specialized in artillery and musketry. They also had infantry soldiers armed with shields and close-range weapons, and engineers. Although the theoretical manpower of each company was between 200 and 300 soldiers, only a percentage of them were actually called to serve in the various regiments, in the proportion of 89 men from each Manchu and Mongol company and 47 from each Hanjun company. The distribution of forces drawn from each Manchu and Mongol companies according to regiment was as follows: 2 for the Vanguard, 2 for the Bodyguards, 17 for the Guards regiment (inclusive of 8 battalions), 45 for the Cavalry regiment (inclusive of 16 battalions), 20 for the Infantry corps, and 3 artisans (bowyers and ironsmiths). The Hanjun Banners had 34 men to staff the firearms battalions and 13 for the infantry corps. The total number of these forces varied according to the number of companies. The infantry corps, Manchu, Mongol, and Hanjun, were established by the Kangxi emperor in 1673 to garrison the capital.[54] Moreover, a dedicated Firearm Regiment (Ch. *huoqiying*) was created in 1691, which included musketeers and artillery specialists.[55]

Looking now to the Banner forces that were initially mobilized for the war of the Three Feudatories, we find that there were in 1673 altogether 527 Manchu and Mongol companies and 213 companies of the Hanjun Banners. Half of the men in the Manchu and Mongol companies were mobilized from the Vanguard regiment, which means that one man out of each banner was taken, totaling 527 men, and officers (not counted). From the Guards regiment they took 152 officers and

7 men out of the Manchu and Mongol companies, totaling, excluding the officers, 3,689 soldiers. The forces mobilized from the Cavalry regiment comprised 120 officers and 10 men per company, that is, 5,270 soldiers. From the Chinese Firearms regiment they took 32 officers and 5 men out of each Chinese company, which amounts to 1,065 soldiers. Hence, the number of soldiers mobilized, excluding officers and retainers, was 10,551. The total number sent from Peking from 1674 to 1681 was 50,000, in addition to 26,000 auxiliaries from Inner Mongolia and 4,000 from Manchuria, making up a total of 80,000. Counting the officers and the retainers the total number of Banner troops is a figure between 160,000 and 200,000.[56]

Green Standard forces

In addition to the pre-conquest Eight Banner forces the Qing army included an all-Chinese force called the Army of the Green Standard. This incorporated the Ming soldiers who surrendered to the Qing in the course of the conquest and were thereafter re-organized mainly as provincial forces within China proper. They were originally meant to be used for the suppression of rebellions and pacification of areas that had not been brought fully under Qing control. Later they were however used also in far-ranging wars as part of an expeditionary force. Again, we can see in the evolution of this military corps the impact of the Sanfan rebellion. Because many Green Standard soldiers had joined the rebels, after the rebellion the army was reduced by as much as one-third, going from approximately 800,000 or 900,000 (the exact number cannot be calculated) to 578,204 soldiers in 1686.[57] Before the rebellion the Green Standard troops were assigned to various Chinese commanders who had chosen to surrender to the Manchus and serve the Qing dynasty. But their concentration in the hands of powerful generals such as Wu Sangui had also provided the chief source of military manpower for the rebellion. Given that their total number was 3–4 times greater than the Banner Forces, the general tendency after the rebellion was to reduce the size of the units to an average of 5,000 soldiers, with several units having even few soldiers and scatter these troops throughout the empire.

During the Sanfan rebellion, however, both officers and troops of the Green Standard that remained loyal to the Qing, of whom as many as half a million may have been mobilized, are known to have performed well, and at least in the beginning to have outperformed Banner forces. It is well known that the Kangxi emperor became exceedingly frustrated with the initial inability of the Manchu generals and their supposedly much better troops to make progress. Then, greater weight was given to Green Standard troops under generals of considerable value such as Zhao Liangdong, Wang Jingbao, and Sun Sike. They fought against the rebellious Wang Fuchen in Gansu from 1674 to 1676, and then from 1679 to 1681 distinguished themselves in the major operations through Shaanxi, Sichuan, until they finally entered Yunnan.[58] We have mentioned above that the reason why they were employed in large numbers and as the main military force in the suppression

24

of the rebellion was the belief that Chinese troops were better at fighting other Chinese. But we should also recall that the Banner troops were fewer, and that they were forced to fight in a terrain that was extremely difficult to negotiate on horseback. Dzengšeo's testimony may in fact provide the most vivid and reliable account of the appalling difficulties met by cavalry forces in the mountains and forests of southwest China. We should also mention that not all the people who served in the Green Standard were Chinese. Manchu officers could also be appointed to serve in the Green Standard, albeit their rank and prestige would be lower than their counterparts in the Banner forces.[59]

After the Sanfan rebellion and through the eighteenth century the Green Standard Army became chiefly a local force with the function of policing the territory and intervening in case of disturbance or minor rebellion. However, its troops continued to be employed extensively in major expeditions, and were even sent to the remote northwest after the conquest of Xinjiang in a role of support of the Banner troops.[60]

The author, text, and main content of the work

The author

There is no internal evidence in the diary that allows us to identify with certainty its author, and the name Dzengšeo itself, being not uncommon, does not provide a useful clue. However, a few details permit a tentative identification. The biographical records of Manchu Bannermen are not particularly helpful. In the *Baqi Tongzhi* we find a Dzenšeo of the Mongol Bordered White Banner who became a Lieutenant of the Imperial Guards (*hujunxiao*) but since he is listed after the Bannerman Qi-shi-san, who is reported to have fought during the ninth year Yongzheng period (1723–1735) against the Zunghars, chronological reasons exclude the possibility that he could have been active during the early Kangxi period.[61]

In the *Baqi Manzhou shizu tongpu* we find as many as nine Dzengšeo belonging to various Manchu clans.[62] However, the entries are minimal and do not provide sufficient information to identify a Dzengšeo who might have been the author of the work.[63]

In the records of Manchu officials known as the *Man ming chen zhuan* ("Biographies of Famous Manchu Officials") we find an extremely concise biography of a Dzengšeo whose father, Pengcun, was a famous general of the Plain Red Banner.[64] At the death of his father in 1701 Dzengšeo inherited the family title of "duke" (*gong*), reduced in rank to duke of the third class. In 1702 he was promoted to Lieutenant-General of the Chinese Plain Yellow Banner, and two years later he was promoted to Lieutenant General of the Bordered Blue Banner, although he does not seem to have engaged in active service. In 1712 he retired from office and died in 1721. From this short biography we can probably determine the rough age of Dzengšeo. Assuming that he was around 60 at the time of his retirement, in 1712, this would place him at an age of 22 when the rebellion began in 1674, and 28–30 when the narration of the diary takes place, in 1680–1682, thus giving a possible date of birth of 1652.

From the diary we know that by the time the Dzengšeo author of the diary returned home he had served on military campaigns for ten years. We do not know whether this included the entire duration of his military service, or the time actually spent fighting, but since he returned home in 1682, he must have begun his service in the army not later than 1672.

If the two Dzengšeo were the same person, the author of the diary should therefore have been 20 years old in 1672. This may seem somewhat old for a Manchu Bannerman, since military service typically began at a younger age. According to regulations that precede the conquest of China, the drafting age for active military service could have been as low as 13.[65] As late as the nineteenth century we find that the age of recruits could be also 13.[66] However, an important clue at the end of the diary tells us that he had children whom, upon his return, he could no longer recognize, thus pointing to the fact that before he left for the military campaign he had married and had some young children. This tallies with the notion that he was an adult of about 20 when he joined the military expedition, and about 30 when he came back, thus making a birth date of 1652 plausible, and strengthening the hypothesis that the son of Pengcun and the author of the diary are the same person.

As discussed below, his rank in the army in 1680, after having served for at least eight years, was comparable to that of a lieutenant colonel in a Western army, which would not be incompatible with his age, experience, and family background. It is also possible that he joined active military service later than other youths, which would explain his higher level of education. At any rate, the dates from the evidence gathered from the diary and those from the short biography in the *Man ming chen zhuan* are sufficiently consistent to allow us to identify tentatively the author of the diary with Pengcun's son.

Unlike his father, who had a distinguished military career defending the frontiers of the empire against the Russians and the Mongols, Dzengšeo does not seem to have achieved prominence as a military man. If he is indeed the author of the diary, it is likely that he retired from active military service after this campaign, a possibility consistent with the transparent dislike of military life that surfaces at times very clearly through the pages of his journal. A minor discrepancy might be found in the fact that the Dzengšeo author of the diary appears to be in charge of a Bordered Blue Banner unit, while the Dzengšeo son of Pengcun belonged, like his father, to the Plain Red Banner, but as we have mentioned above, Dzengšeo later in life also served in other Banners, and mobility from one Banner to another was normal in the career pattern of a Manchu officer.

Dzengšeo's rank has been understood as a relatively low one, possibly one of adjutant, which would have been a grade 5a rank.[67] While there is uncertainty about his rank, there are explicit mentions of his being once demoted from and once promoted to a fairly high rank of *jalan-i janggin*, that is Colonel (or Lieutenant-colonel), a grade 3a rank. On October 20, 1680 he was dismissed from this rank because there were too many officers at that level, and was presumably demoted. Exactly a year later, on October 21, 1981, he was reinstated to this rank as a position became vacant when a *jalan-i janggin* called Fafuri was moved to another post. In battle he is often seen carrying a flag, and occupying positions of leadership. Moreover, he is well-informed about the general strategy and tactical maneuvers decided by the top military officers.

Another indication of his holding a medium-high rank is provided by the number of servants and horses he had with him. In the entry for August–September 1680 he says that only 5 of his retainers survived, having just mentioned 3 who had died. Even admitting that the 3 who died did not necessarily have to be his retainers, it is likely that at least 1 or 2 were. Since a number of 6 or 7 retainers were allowed to officers respectively in the rank of lieutenant-colonel and vice-banner commander this would again be consistent with a formal rank level of *jalan-i janggin*.[68] The loss of twenty horses he mentions at some point that belonged to him and presumably to his retainers also indicates a high rank.

Finally, a high-ranking officer named Ganduhai appears in several passages to have been his direct superior. This may have been a Banner Commander or vice-Banner Commander, although his specific rank is not mentioned, probably because given in the missing parts of the diary. On this basis, we can say that Dzengšeo had a variable military rank that, however, was often as high as a 3a level. This rank paid a yearly salary of 130 silver taels and as many bushels of rice.[69]

The text

The extant portion of Dzengšeo's diary was discovered by a Chinese scholar of Manchu language and literature, Professor Ji Yonghai, in the late 1970s in the library of what was then the Zhongyang Minzu Xueyuan (Central Institute of Nationalities, now Minzu Daxue, University of Nationalities). The diary originally comprised four fascicles, or *debtelin*, but of these only the last could be found. This was published in China by the same scholar in 1987 under the title *Annotated Translation of the "Diary of My Service in the Army"*[70] as a small book that included a Chinese translation, transcription of the Manchu text with interlinear word-by-word rendition in Chinese, and a perfectly legible facsimile reproduction of the Manchu text. This is an excellent feature of the book, since the availability of the original (albeit in reproduction) has made it possible to consult the text without having to retrieve a copy or consult the original.

The diary, written in neat and almost flawless Manchu, covers the last period of the war, beginning on New Year's Day of the nineteenth year of Kangxi (January 31, 1680) and ending with the return home of the soldier, nearly two years later. It displays a high degree of proficiency in terms of grammar and vocabulary, with the occasional inclusion of Chinese loanwords (also rendered in Manchu script), a phenomenon that should not surprise as the author was in all likelihood born in China in a family of Manchu Bannermen and educated in both languages. The style of the narrative is terse and simple, but also rich in pathos and color; in general, it conveys a distinct impression of freshness and sincerity, and is particularly felicitous in the descriptive passages, and when the author expresses sorrow for the distress caused by the war to the common people, or pity for the misery of his own condition. Above all, this work is the best available source to gain an insight of the life (and tribulations) of a Manchu soldier on active duty.

Although personal memoirs have been commonly written by literate Chinese in pre-modern times, and many of them constitute precious repositories of historical knowledge, military diaries, journals, or even memoirs written by soldiers in the field do not appear to be among them.[71] This is in sharp contrast with the tradition of writing personal memoirs of war, either as recollections or in the form of journals, in the West, especially from early modernity to our days. From the American Revolution to the Napoleonic wars and to the American Civil War, history has often been enriched by the personal views and feelings of otherwise anonymous protagonists. Without such accounts path-breaking books like John Keegan's *The Face of Battle* could not be written, or would have to rely on far less satisfactory material. Even periods of peace have produced military memoirs that remain documents of literary and historical value. In post-Napoleonic France the words by Alfred de Vigny described the feelings of a whole generation of young students imbued with a notion of martial valor that became a central element of their ethos even in the absence of an actual war:

> War seemed to us so very natural a state for our country, that when, freed from the classroom, we poured ourselves into the army along the familiar course of the torrent of those days, we found ourselves unable to believe in a lasting calm of peace ... So we trained and thus lost precious years, conjuring up the fields of battle on the Champ-de-Mars, and exhausting our formidable and futile energies with parade exercises and in personal feuds.[72]

As members of a military society, Bannermen probably shared a similar ethos, and one wonders whether, in the long periods of peace and idleness that punctuated the history of the Qing dynasty, they too felt a similar sense of personal loss and futility.

Those voices have enabled historians to instill real life into their narratives, and to reach far beyond the dry records of dates and places, the discussion of operational and tactical movements, and the count of casualties. In seventeenth-century China, and indeed for much of China's written tradition, writing about actual field operations, campaigns, and battles, was a highly bureaucratized process. The official accounts of military campaigns were the result of government-sanctioned compilations authored by committees of historiographers appointed by the emperor. Several offices were involved in the collation of documents and in the redaction of the narrative of a given war, which was eventually released "under imperial auspices."[73] Hence, the diary, as a personal memoir, offers a unique, or at least extremely rare opportunity to obtain a glimpse of the little known world of Manchu soldiers in the field, in addition to being an important source for one of the most important events of seventeenth-century Chinese history.

Let me address a question that I have been asked several times, namely, whether the "authenticity" of the Diary can be tested, and what indication, if any, we have about the date and manner of composition of this work. First of all, an analysis of the internal evidence presented by the text, be it based on the content, on the language and style, or on the graphological characteristics of the script, suggests no doubts about its authenticity. Indeed, no person that has studied the text or used it as a source has expressed misgivings about it. There is also external evidence to support it. Many of the names mentioned in the account are those of actual historical figures that are amply documented elsewhere. Moreover, the dates generally tally (for what I have been able to see) with those found in official compilations, and the descriptions of specific events often provide, as we might expect, a personal interpretation that enriches and complements the official record.

As for the specific motives that led Dzengšeo to writing the diary, it would be futile to speculate, given that we know nothing about the author. What we should register is that the author's views may have been at odds with prevailing images of the Manchu Bannermen, which tend to emphasize the prowess and valor of the Manchus, bred in an environment that valued martial accomplishments and instilled a "love for war" in direct contrast with the civil virtues cultivated in Chinese society. Dzengšeo is the one Manchu voice that does not find war appealing at all but provides a grim, cynical, and absolutely credible view of it.

In addition to the tidy writing, the manuscript is well organized and the narrative polished; obviously this is a work at which the author worked for some time, reorganizing and committing to writing notes that he may have taken during the war as well as his own memories and recollections. It is possible that some of the personal comments that appear in various parts of the narrative were inserted at a later date so as to add a literary layer to it. That the author of the diary was not a Chinese, but a Manchu, has little bearing on the question of authorship since there is no evidence that writing journals or memoirs was an activity common among literate Manchu Bannermen. Since there are no works of Manchu literature comparable to the personal narrative of the diary, it is difficult to establish how widespread this "genre" might have been among the Bannermen population. The absence of evidence, while not to be taken as evidence of absence, is still an indication that it was not a common practice. Some of these questions, of course, would have probably been answered by the missing portions of the diary, and, should they ever surface in the future, we might learn more about the author's identity and the purpose of his writing.

The question of when Dzengšeo wrote the diary can also be answered only tentatively. The diary is not a day-to-day account but rather a sequence of dated entries. It is not known whether the author maintained a record of facts and dates during the campaign or recalled the events later, after his return home. Internal evidence, as slim as it may be, allows us to posit the date of 1697 as the terminus post quem for the writing of the diary, given that the honorific title mentioned for Fiyanggū in the entry dated October 29, 1682 is that of "duke" (*gong*), a title that Fiyanggū received in or soon after 1697.[74] It is therefore possible that the writing of the diary occupied the author in the latter part of his life.

A personal experience, which I will mention briefly, influenced my view on the way in which the process of writing might have occurred. Some years ago, after the death of an uncle of mine, I was permitted to see the unpublished diary he wrote of his own experience in the Second World War. He fought as a junior officer in the Italian army from 1943 to 1945 in Montenegro where his company was stranded after Italy's surrender of September 1943. His diary is also a journal in which all entries are dated but not every day is recorded. Even though I have the complete typescript, if I wished to find out how my uncle "remembered" all that he wrote in his journal I would encounter the same difficulties that I met when trying to understand the method of composition of Dzengšeo's work. My uncle does not reveal in the manuscript the sources of his narrative, saying only that the "facts narrated are true and the people mentioned have existed in reality, though the narrative itself has neither historical nor literary pretense [. . .]" Only recently I learned from his wife (my aunt) that my uncle had kept a diary during the war, and that names, dates, and events had been carefully annotated. Later in life he turned these notes into a diary that he hoped, probably, to publish one day but never did. It is not inconceivable that Dzengšeo did the same, that is, kept a rough record of dates and facts at which he worked at a later stage of his life, effectively re-writing and polishing the narrative. This may have taken place at any time after 1697 and possibly after his retirement in 1712.

What surprised me in particular is that a comparison between the two diaries, which could not be more different in terms of places, times, and cultures, reveals striking similarities that go even beyond the formal one. Some of them we might expect. Both authors, for instance, are scathing, albeit in different ways, in their criticism of superior officers, and both mention often the hunger and disease that plagued them and their comrades, and express a longing for home and family. I found it extraordinary, however, that they should both end with virtually the same image. Dzengšeo explains his feeling of being back home, surrounded by his family, as a dreamlike awakening and re-birth:

> I marveled at what seemed like being born again. Yet, recollecting with sorrow that in the flock of geese one had parted [his brother had died], I could not put an end to my thinking [of him]. Is this a dream, or is it not?

My uncle diary's last sentence describes a similar experience of re-birth. Being at a theatre surrounded by elegant people, music, and perfumes, he says: "I was there, I came back to life, but then, did nothing happen???" Surely there is nothing unique about such kind of "post-traumatic" sensations, although discovering psychological similarities between a Manchu soldier of the seventeenth century and an Italian soldier of the twentieth still gave me pause. These are perhaps revealing of what one might consider as the common humanity of war experiences across times and cultures.

Content and historical value of the text

The narrative itself contains enlightening details about field operations that would be impossible to obtain other than from an "eyewitness" account. These refer primarily, of course, to military life, and in particular to those aspects specifically related to the direct experience of war, such as combat, weapons, horses, and discipline in the field. A second theme of note is the environment in which the campaign takes place: landscape, diseases, and native people. A third aspect is the cultural background of the author. His literary references and remarks about rituals and superstitions open a window on the more general issue of the soldiers' culture. The fourth and last aspect delves with the psychology of war and the personal feelings that emerge through Dzengšeo's narrative.

Military life

Combat experience is of course a central component of a soldier's active duty in war. The diary contains several descriptions of armed encounters with enemy formations. The description is lucid but naturally limited to the action in which Dzengšeo himself was participating.[75] A few pitched battles are recorded but by 1680 the rebels were engaging the government forces mostly in guerrilla actions, which were favored by the rugged mountainous terrain. The Qing soldiers were engaged in long marches over steep mountains, thick jungle-like vegetation, and often under torrential rain. These marches resemble the descriptions of the "Long March" of the Chinese Communist Army in the 1930s blended with accounts of modern jungle warfare in Indochina. Every time the soldiers stopped for the night they had to fortify their encampment by building ramparts and digging moats around it. Eventually the time arrived when the government troops had to engage the enemy in the field, or to take a fortified stronghold, or to fight pockets of resistance as they went through villages and towns. Battles were mostly favorable to the government troops, but narrowly so, and losses seem to have been very high. On one occasion Dzengšeo confesses that losses on their side had been huge, but the commanding general had been generous and had omitted that detail from his memorial to the Emperor (see entry for June 13, 1680). Indeed, the record of this battle included in the official source only says that General Manggitu and others had pacified the region.[76]

One of the most significant descriptions of combat is the battle fought at Yunnanfu before the beginning of the siege (entry dated April 9, 1681). According to it, the infantry troops of the Green Standard army, constituting the central body of the army, rushed against a barrage of artillery and small arms' fire. The Bannermen charged on horseback towards a village in what may have been a flanking maneuver, but their assault appears to have been repelled by enemy fire, which forced them to seek cover behind nearby structures, the remains of walls probably destroyed during an earlier bombardment. Incidentally, the many Bannermen who were wounded do not seem to have received any medical treatment. Indeed, the fate of the wounded is never mentioned by Dzengšeo.

Later, the Commander-in-Chief Hife ordered the Manchu cavalry to dismount and advance on foot. With poor visibility due to the smoke and dust, and troops were scattered around, the commanders used runners to communicate with the various units. The Manchu unit in which Dzengšeo was fighting shot volleys of arrows at the enemies, forcing them to surrender, but after one of them was shot dead in cold blood by a *bayara* soldier—therefore belonging to an elite unit—the others fled fearing that they would all be killed. The subsequent action shows that Qing cavalry may not have been comfortable fighting on foot, since obviously both Dzengšeo and the other soldier mentioned, Dengse, were mounting their horses. The act of killing performed by the author is mentioned here in two ways: first, as a necessary deed to save his comrade's life, and second, in the last sentence, as a duty that he had to perform in order to reach the position assigned to him. There is no particular pleasure in it, but after ten years in the army, killing enemies in battle had become routinized and no longer a matter of moral concern. Yet the humanity of the soldier surfaces in his urging the enemy to surrender—while other soldiers had no scruples about shooting prisoners—and in rescuing a comrade in peril.

In the descriptions of combat the author is able to convey, more than a lucid account of the progress of the battle, the rush of emotions that accompany the action. In the entry for March 21, 1681, he lists the commanders and their troops, and the orders they were given. The Manchu cavalry was kept in the rear, while presumably the Green Standard soldiers were taking the front. Dzengšeo carried a flag, which probably served to mark his unit's position. Again, the general impression is that the central task in the assault is performed by the Green Standard infantry, while the cavalry executed flanking or encircling maneuvers. The enemy's resistance was largely reliant on firepower, but once the Qing troops broke through the fusilade and cannonade fire, they managed to put the enemy to flight. Banner troops appear to have been superior in close-quarter combat, probably because of the force of impact of the Manchu and Mongol cavalry. But the Green Standard fought no less chivalrously: the example of bravery performed on this occasion by a soldier called Šahūri is telling. This was probably a Manchu officer serving in the Green Standard, and in my view Dzengšeo's comment about his valor could be interpreted as a sign of admiration for the brave showing of the Green Standard.

Some elements of combat may need clarification, and in particular the extensive use of firearms, the employment of cavalry and management of the horses on a terrain that seems utterly unsuitable, and the way in which the Manchu cavalry fought against elephants. The issue of cannon is one of the most intriguing stories of the Sanfan war. Already at the beginning of the war the Kangxi emperor assigned to the Belgian Jesuit Ferdinand Verbiest the task to design and produce artillery pieces that were light and handy, easy to transport over rugged terrain, while retaining their range of fire and ability to deliver heavy projectiles.[77] Such guns were necessary because many of the rebel forces' strongholds were located on steep mountains that were all but impregnable by regular infantry and cavalry troops, especially since horses were not able to negotiate easily the mountain and forests of southern China.

Father Verbiest's work, reluctantly undertaken on moral grounds, was nevertheless highly successful. Over 500 of a total of about 900 artillery pieces cast during the Kangxi period were produced under his direction, on the basis of new designs. The first cannon that Verbiest made was the so-called wooden cannon, in which a lighter barrel was reinforced by a cover of painted wood and mounted on a carriage. The preliminary trials conducted in the capital at the presence of the emperor were successful and several of these guns were produced and used in battle against the Three Feudatories. The main advantage of this gun was that it was easily transportable, but it remained relatively weak and limited in both range and caliber. Although hastily produced, this light artillery fit the requirements and spurred the emperor to continue to invest in new and better guns, which were successfully delivered in the 1680s.[78]

Dzengšeo's own combat experience reveals that firearms were used extensively in every confrontation with the enemy. The government used cannons to bombard city walls, strongholds, and villages. The enemy's musket and artillery fire seems to be coordinated, intense, noisy, and lethal for the advancing Qing troops. On two occasions Dzengšeo tells us that the sound of the volleys of musket fire resembled the sound of frying beans. Indeed, Dzengšeo and his men may have often faced superior firepower. The presence of a large number of muskets and cannons in southwest China so many years after the beginning of the war is somewhat surprising. It is likely that the rebels had stockpiled weapons and ammunition long before the war, but they may also have been able to buy them from abroad (possibly Burma), or to manufacture them on their own, but this is an aspect that awaits further research. Answering these questions may place the war in a context larger and even more significant than that of an "internal" rebellion.

Bow and arrows were the weapon of choice of the Banner cavalry. Confronted with an elephant charge the Bannermen discharged so many arrows so quickly that they managed to repel the elephants and because of the arrows stuck in the elephant's hides, the animals "resembled porcupines" (see entry for June 11, 1680). The description of the action reveals desperation more than the confidence of superior military ability, but in general, as deep a psychological impact as the appearance of the huge beasts may have had, they did not give the rebels the advantage that they may have hoped for.[79]

How many elephants were used by the rebels at any given time is not clear. They are mentioned three times in the diary. On one occasion the Qing troops captured 4 of them, on another they captured 5, and the last mention refers to some intelligence they had obtained to the effect that the rebel leader Wu Shifan was in command of an army of 20,000 troops and 5 elephants. Because of their small number, and possibly because of the difficulties inherent to their use on the battlefield, their role may not have been decisive, but it certainly introduced an element of psychological anxiety in troops who were not used to confronting the colossal beasts. As a curiosity, we may add that, in the famous battle of Delhi in 1399 the Turco-Mongol mounted troops under Timur were extremely apprehensive of the war elephants they were about to face, but managed to defeat the Indian forces thanks again to their volleys of arrows and ability to withstand the elephant charge without breaking ranks.[80]

Being in a cavalry unit, our soldier has quite a lot to say about horses. Horses were the main form of transportation, and on more than one occasion it seems clear that they were ill-suited for the type of terrain on which they were fighting. On narrow mountain paths they easily slipped and fell to their death in deep crevices. At times they were swept away by the torrential rain, while their unprotected hooves cracked on the rocky terrain, injuring the horse, which would then die from infection. These horses normally would not be shod, but soldiers made special shoes with wooden strips or iron cleats to prevent the horses from slipping on the wet moss that covered the mountain paths. Often the soldiers had to pull horses laden with supplies or equipment that had sunken into the swampy rice paddies.

If we look at the mobility if the cavalry, we see that they are typically able to cover on average 30 *li* (Chinese miles) per day, roughly equivalent to 15 kilometers. On some days they only went 10 kilometers. But if necessary they could go faster. On one occasion, for instance, Dzengšeo's unit covered 300 kilometers (600 *li*) in 14 days, at an average speed of over 20 kilometers per day. One difficulty with the calculation is that the diary is not very clear on the size and type of the units traveling from one place to the next. It seems that the cavalry company under Dzengšeo's command was always part of a bigger unit, which probably included a supply train and servants of foot that obviously slowed it down. On the other end, on one occasion a small group of 20 soldiers, led by Dzengšeo himself, covered 50 kilometers in a single day riding at full gallop. This was probably the maximum speed that could be achieved on that terrain, and only by a small select cavalry unit.

Military discipline and the impact of war on society

The diary, while of course preeminently a testimony of the personal sensitivities of the author, provides much more than just a window to explore Dzengšeo's war experience. It is also an excellent source for the study of social violence and disorder caused by the war. The existence of a concept of military discipline, and an army's ability to police the behavior of the troops and to enforce a code of conduct are matters that determine to a large extent the impact that war can have on the civilian population. The Manchu state, even before the invasion of China, had developed a detailed, fully articulated set of regulations enforced through a system of punishments and rewards.

In the pre-conquest period, the Manchu emperors issued edicts that included, among others, the following provisions: (1) Only people who actively resisted and either fought against the soldiers or attempted to flee could be killed; (2) Those who surrendered and did not attempt to flee were to be spared; (3) It was forbidden to steal clothes and other property from the prisoners; (4) Husbands and wives could not be separated; (5) Raping women was not allowed (we should note that women were distributed among the soldiers as "booty" and therefore this prohibition applied only to random violence).[81] The latter two were capital crimes. Killing people who had surrendered and stealing their property were not regarded as capital crimes, but were punishable with beatings and fines according to the gravity and circumstances of the crime. The regulations sometimes extended beyond these general rules. For instance we find that soldiers were at liberty to butcher a pig or a chicken for their own consumption but not a sheep, goat, or larger animals such as cows and horses. Houses and temples could not be looted. In particular, the desecration of a temple and the theft of ritual objects were regarded as capital crimes. The priests could not be taken prisoners or mistreated, nor were the troops allowed to set up camp within a temple's premises. Before the invasion of a region inhabited by Chinese people, there is mention of rules issued for the protection of livestock, fruit-bearing trees, and for moderation in the use of food and alcoholic beverages requisitioned from the civilian population.

These attempts to limit violence do not originate in what we might call a "human rights" moral position. The regulations were aimed to preserve order among the troops, to avoid the wasteful loss of food and property, and, therefore, to protect the common interest of the army, which normally had to live off the land. Overriding considerations were the need to guarantee that the booty be distributed in orderly fashion, making sure that rank prerogatives be observed, and the need to avoid complete social collapse. The prohibition to separate husbands and wives and to keep together family units clearly points to a concern that goes beyond the preservation of the integrity of the spoils and directly attempts to limit the damage that troops could inflict on the civilian population. Preserving the social fabric of the conquered villages and towns was vital to the Manchus' success on political and economic grounds. The severe ethnic strife that followed the occupation of a large portion of the Liaodong peninsula—where Manchu commanders severely mistreated the local people—showed the conquerors how costly the harsh treatment of a vanquished population could be. The decision to keep the Banner garrisons physically separate from the Banner population responded to the same general principle.[82] But there is also a moral dimension that cannot be ignored. Even though the fate of the prisoners, both men and women, was grim, there were still *some* rights that were recognized to them. When respected, these rights, as limited as they were, preserved the lives of men and women who surrendered, prevented indiscriminate violence, and protected the war zone from wanton destruction.

35

The Qing army during the Sanfan rebellion seems to have been subject to similar rules, and the diary clearly shows what happened when discipline was violated, and how difficult it was to control the soldiers and the civilian laborers who accompanied the army. The most problematic disciplinary issue was the random looting perpetrated by the soldiers or their servants, as shown by the proliferation of orders forbidding brutalities against the civilian population. The soldiers were even sometimes confined to their encampment to prevent disorders, and extra policing was required to protect local people. The measures taken to enforce discipline were draconian. In one case two servants of a soldier belonging to a company subordinate to the regiment under Dzengšeo's command found a dead cow and stole a chunk of beef (entry dated April 29, 1680). As we have seen above, stealing a large animal was regarded, already in the 1620s, as a crime. After the culprits were apprehended by the general's guards, who functioned as military police, all the officers in the chain of command of the division and company to which the thieves belonged—including Dzengšeo—were summoned and criticized for the actions of their subordinates. The general apparently used "soothing words" but nonetheless all those involved were punished: the division commander was sentenced to pay 3 months of salary; the vice-commander and Dzengšeo were fined a sum equivalent to 6 months' salary; the head of the company was sentenced to 70 cane strokes; Hoošan, the master of the servants who had committed the crime, to 80 strokes; and the servants themselves to 100 strokes. Even such severe punishments, inflicted on the basis of collective responsibility, did not deter crime when the circumstances were desperate. On the eve of the fall of Yunnanfu, when the army was in great distress and occasions for looting presented themselves, it was no longer possible to maintain any discipline. Dzengšeo reports that, notwithstanding the guards placed by the various commanders at the gates of Yunannfu to prevent that people enter the city to loot and rob indiscriminately,

> soldiers and civilians stealthily entered the city, and stole and brought out a great number of starving women and children. They also stole rice and brought it into the city, to exchange it for a great quantity of silk, clothes, and other things.
>
> (entry dated December 8, 1681)

Lacking proper logistic support, the soldiers were supposed to live off the land. Once the army reached a local village, people were sent out to find rice and cereals buried in the ground by the local people. The civilians (Manchu *irgen*) mentioned in the text are probably the laborers that accompanied the army. These were salaried people enlisted to perform various non-military (or at least non-combat) tasks, but of course were equally affected by the scarcity of food. The term *irgen* can also refer, in a generic sense, to the civilian servants that accompanied the Manchu and Mongol soldiers as part of their personal belongings. Stragglers and local people may have also participated in the looting.

The equivalent of a military police was used to preserve public order. On one occasion the soldiers were enjoying themselves in some town, indulging in "rest and relaxation." So an edict was issued to the effect that those caught drunk or not wearing their swords would be punished. But aside from the loss of control and insubordination, the chief cause leading to discipline breakdowns was, simply, the abject conditions in which the war was being fought, as lack of food drove everyone to desperation.

This is not the only instance of criticism voiced by Dzengšeo. Another, more troubling aspect of military discipline concerns the egoism and self-serving attitude of various commanders, whose lust for gain was deemed excessive. When the army was demobilized and the Banner troops were on their way back to the capital, they often traveled by river. Since it is highly unlikely that animals, booty, slaves, and servants could be carried on small boats on very fast rivers and rapids, one must assume that only the officers and soldiers were able to make use of boats, while their servants proceeded by land taking care of the animals and slaves. Even so, the scramble for boats was phenomenal. Some soldiers were simply ordered to proceed by land, but the high officers who had the authority to appropriate boats in excess of what they needed tried to rent them to other soldiers, presumably at a high price (entry for June 8, 1682).

It would be otiose to seek evidence of anachronistic sensitivities in Dzengšeo's writing. Clearly, he accepted slavery, looting, and the commodification of human beings as part of the way in which his world was organized (he once sold a woman to buy horses). Yet the suffering of the common people, as widespread as it must have been throughout the war zones, was not something to which he was wholly insensitive. Terse notations of reports of cannibalism and the sale of children like those found in the entry for October 20, 1681, represent some of the most telling examples of the dehumanizing effects of war.

Famine and starvation are common enough in every war, and here, too, no one seems to be able to escape them. Food prices sky-rocketed to levels that were not sustainable even for the wealthier officers. Scavenging soldiers were able to enrich themselves selling some of the legally or illegally appropriated foodstuffs, and those who did not have enough to eat robbed and plundered, while the merchants, who performed a key role in keeping the army supplied, were killed to appropriate their merchandise (February 13, 1682). Dzengšeo implicitly suggests that the profiteering that merchants may have engaged in was one of the causes for the "extreme poverty" of the soldiers, thereby linking the instances of disorder, and even the murder of the merchants, to the merchants' own greediness. Whether this truly reflected the reality of the situation, or whether Dzengšeo's account is colored by a bias against merchants, it is difficult to say.

The only remedy that the commanding officers could find to solve the situation was to move away from an area where food had been exhausted, as is recorded for February 20, 1682. The sequence of events seems to suggest that the general could no longer contain the level of violence caused by the famine, and was compelled to move on to another area where supplies might have been more plentiful, and prices more reasonable. This passage also suggests that the length of time that a large body of troops could be stationed at a given place was closely tied to the ability of the soldiers to find or buy supplies *in loco*. In one instance Dsengšeo mentions sending some servants to search a village in order to find hidden rice stocks, indicating once again that the army was extremely dependent on whatever foodstuffs could be requisitioned.

Sieges, of course, were especially taxing on both the army and the local people, since they required that the attacking army be able to stay in a limited area until the city was taken. Once Yunnanfu fell, as mentioned above, the commanders placed armed guards around it to prevent soldiers from entering and looting it, even though this policing was unsuccessful. It may be interesting to compare this situation with the "massacre of Yangzhou."[83] According to the eyewitness report at Yangzhou the Manchu leadership allowed the troops to run wild and inflict upon the local surviving population ten days of pillage and violence without any kind of restraint or policing. This was done to punish the city for its courageous and prolonged resistance. The sack of a town, as is well known, was used widely by Inner Asian armies already at the time of Chinggis Khan as a form of psychological warfare, and had strategic relevance to the outcome of a given campaign. But the idea that the Manchu and Mongol troops practiced a type of warfare that was always or predominantly based on inflicting massive violence on the local population does not conform to the historical facts. Episodes of extreme brutality, including mass murders, can be found in every war and in every army, but the diary, as well as other sources, tell us that *unregulated* looting and killing was the exception, as it was not only contrary to stated military discipline but also, and perhaps especially, to the economic principles of the Manchu military. The Manchu army was above all an aristocratic army, and the privileges of the upper echelons had to be respected. Looting was therefore an organized exercise, conducted under close supervision, and an accountant's eye for precise allocation according to rank. We are very fortunate to have, in the entries from December 11, 1681 to January 2, 1682, a detailed description of the distribution of the spoils of war.

The author, himself a member of the middle rungs of the military hierarchy, is caustic about the behavior of his superiors. As we have already observed above with regard to the "boat-rental scheme," Dzengšeo does not hesitate to criticize those who took advantage of their position for personal gain. The highest ranking commanders and those in charge of the distribution of the booty somehow ended up with valuables in excess of what their station entitled them to. Incidentally, Dzengšeo must have done pretty well for himself, since he required over thirty horses to carry his possessions back to Beijing, which is evidence of the profitability of war even for lesser and presumably honest officers. While he must have accepted the principle of looting, he found the greediness, wanton violence, and inhumanity associated with it utterly repulsive. Even after every scrap of the rebels' properties had been distributed, the soldiers continued to chase and abduct local citizens, especially women and children, although they were not legal spoils of war. Dzengšeo's denunciation of the horrors of war does point to the belief in an *ethos* of military behavior and to an expectation of honorable conduct, and it is the breach of that ethos—not war in itself—that Dzengšeo finds objectionable, in the same way in which today a soldier may find war profiteering loathsome, may object to his own army's excessive brutality, or may castigate one's leaders for needlessly placing the troops in harm's way.

Still, the war was now over, and Dzengšeo could finally head back home. In the chaos of the demobilization (over 500,000 troops had to return to their bases), the journey back to Beijing lasted over ten months. The return journey was fraught with dangers, too, mostly because of the lack of appropriate transportation and because of the misbehavior of the troops. The boats he received were sometimes second-rate and inadequate to brave the fast currents of some rivers. On one occasion he did not receive any boats at all. His luck changed when he was assigned to the inspection and distribution of boats, at which point his problems in finding suitable transportation seem to be over. But Dzengšeo continues to be apprehensive: in the euphoria of the demobilization soldiers were drunk or careless, and accidents were frequent as some of them were shooting poorly at hares and pheasants, and sometimes hit and killed people or horses. Dzengšeo considers ironically the possibility of being hit by soldiers "who could not shoot from horseback" after having survived ten years of war (October 11, 1682).

Nature

One of the recurrent themes of the narrative is the relationship between the author and the surrounding land, including the terrain, the animals, the weather, the diseases, and the native peoples. The environment was for him the source of many dangers and constant tribulations. As a northerner and as a Manchu, he shows no enthusiasm for the southwest and evidence of a deep sense of cultural alienation can be detected in the author's description of the natural habitat. His exploration of Yunnan and Guizhou, unlike that of more famous and almost coeval travellers such as Xu Xiake, was not due to a voluntary excursion or literary pilgrimage. Dzengšeo's southwest is an inhospitable and insalubrious land, where mountains and rivers are inimical and treacherous. The landscape is wild, and signs of civilization are rare.

Among the most frequently mentioned hardships, Dzengšeo often refers to the inclement weather. The frequent torrential rains were particularly hazardous when the soldiers had to encamp in narrow ravines crossed by mountain streams. The water, coming down from the mountains with tremendous force, flooded the encampment, and the tents and their contents were swept away to the despair of the troops. Land marches are often described as utterly painful, as soldiers struggled with their animals and cargo over hills and mountains under rain and hail, which left them soaked to the bone.

Usually the land the soldiers cross is afflicted by malodorous miasmas and pests. Having arrived at a certain locality, Dzengšeo learns from local people brought in for questioning that at that time of the year the river becomes infested with snakes, worms and peacocks (feared for fouling the drinking water and making it poisonous), and the rain is so abundant that the river floods the road so that nobody can get through, not to mention the miasmatic vapors that emanate from the water, which are believed to infect and kill anyone exposed to them. For those reasons, according to the author, people built their houses on mountain tops away from the river.

More than the enemy bullets Dzengšeo seems to fear illness and disease. Fear of contagion was common among the Manchus even before the conquest of China, and especially smallpox was a source of considerable anxiety; various edicts were issued meant to protect the troops from contagion and from the spread of disease to Manchu areas.[84] But quite aside from what may perhaps be regarded as a cultural phobia, surely Dzengšeo's fears reflected a real concern, given that disease appears to be one of the major causes of death among the Qing troops, and he himself fell ill at least twice. On the first and more serious occasion he became ill with a debilitating fever or influenza that left him utterly weak and unable to stand for more than three months. A number of soldiers, including General Manggitu—one of the chief commanders of the expedition—fell ill and eventually died due to a disease that carried a high fever. Such a fever apparently lasted, as a rule, a little over a month, during which period people either died or recovered. The same illness decimated Dzengšeo's unit and as a consequence he was left with only 5 servants, the others (probably 2 or 3) having also died. On a second occasion Dzengšeo became sick with a gastric ailment (he "vomited") but this time the illness was rapidly overcome.

One of the diseases in question is almost certainly malaria, which is still endemic to Southeast Asia. Untreated malaria can be fatal, although symptoms may subside after a while and recur later in time. The northern Manchu and Mongol soldiers were probably particularly susceptible to tropical diseases, a problem that could not be countered in any ways. It may be interesting to note that European armies in tropical Asia suffered especially of fevers of one type or another and of diseases of the stomach, bowels, and liver. Such diseases accounted for 80 percent of the nonviolent and non-accidental deaths.[85] Following a time-honored Chinese idea of the south as a disease-ridden place, Dzengšeo believes that the infection is caused by "miasmatic vapors," as reported in the passage dated October 19, 1681, in which he describes the appearance of Qing soldiers returning from the front: they were sickly and emaciated, and the unhappy survivors of what appears to be an outbreak of a contagious agent that affected both men and horses.

Another aspect of the encounter with the local environment is the relationship with the natives. As is well known, the southwest was (and still is) home to various non-Chinese people, utterly alien to the northerners, and the Manchu soldiers coming to the south from Beijing must have appeared to these people and felt themselves much like a colonial army in a land inhabited by "savages." The presence of aboriginal people is mentioned only in passing, yet those cursory remarks give us a sense of their interaction with the Manchu forces. Mostly, local

40

people seem to have been caught in an uncomfortable position between the imperial forces and the rebels. The Qing troops used aborigines to gather intelligence, and at one point the chief of a certain village came to surrender. In doing so, he also reported that the chieftain of another village had associated himself with the rebels. Acting on this piece of intelligence, General Manggitu dispatched a unit of Chinese Bannermen to destroy the village with artillery. Given that the village was leveled on suspicion that its inhabitants were sheltering rebels or were collaborating with them, it would not be too far-fetched to wonder whether the chieftain who had provided the information in the first place had been moved purely by a sentiment of loyalty to the dynasty, or whether local rivalries may have played a role.

On a few occasions Dzengšeo reports that local chieftains came to submit. In one case as many as 500 of them are said to have flocked to welcome the Qing forces after an enemy stronghold had been bombarded and stormed. If these chieftains had any loyalty towards the rebels, they were quick to change sides. The few times when Dzengšeo refers to local chieftains he does not have much good to say about them, and the Miao as a people are said to have customs that are "cruel and wicked in the extreme" (see entry for May 1, 1682).

On the way back home, however, there seems to be a change in Dzengšeo's relationship to nature, and he seem to recover a sense of appreciation. Still haunted, as we have seen above, by a myriad dangers and difficulties Dzengšeo was proceeding by boat on a fast river, with shallow rocks that threatened to crash the shell of the vessel at any time, when he observes that, on top of mountains' cliffs and peaks "the monkeys were playing and, on top of the cliffs, the houses of the people, made by making frames of wooden sticks, looked like swallow nests" (June 13, 1982). Nature seems to have become much friendlier, and the change reflects a transformation in the state of mind and in the feelings of a man who, after so many years of deprivations, was slowly returning to a normal life.

Cultural aspects

Finally, let us look at an aspect of the diary that speaks to some other form of anxiety, and to the cultural background of Dzengšeo and his fellow soldiers. Superstition and belief in omens and supernatural occurrences were common among soldiers. There is no certain indication that Dzengšeo was himself superstitious, but he reports several occurrences of strange and unusual events. Let us consider the facts described in the entry for June 28, 1680. The miraculous appearance of Guandi, the God of War, who was said to have descended among the troops and taken possession of a soldier's body, is not really questioned by Dzengšeo. On the other hand, his general Manggitu takes it with extreme seriousness.[86] The contrast between those who prostrate in front of the presumed God and Dzengšeo's detached and noncommittal report seems to point to some skepticism on his side.

41

Just a few lines below another form of superstition is reported. When Manggitu killed a very large python people said that because the python was called *mang* in Chinese—thus replicating the first syllable of the general's name—bad luck was going to come to him (July 5, 1680).[87] Sure enough, a few days later the general fell ill and died shortly thereafter, thus confirming the prophecy. Again, Dzengšeo reports these facts without personal comments, but one cannot help noticing the irony of the fate of the superstitious general, who, while on the one hand venerating Guandi's apparition, had become himself the victim of a fateful disregard of superstitious logic.

Finally, a passage indicates that Dzengšeo probably believed in the interpretation of celestial phenomena, and in the identification of auspicious signs (December 25, 1680). Military prognostications have a long history in China's military culture, and in this as well as in other respects it is difficult to say whether Dzengšeo is exhibiting any trait of a specifically "Manchu" cultural identity. Indeed, his astrological notations would not be regarded as unusual or eccentric, had they come from the brush of a Chinese scholar. Likewise, we find in other passages of Dzengšeo's account, and in the behavior of the army as a whole, numerous examples of acculturation. The New Year's ceremonies, which are mentioned several times in the diary, are performed in Chinese temples. The funerary rites that accompany the funeral of General Manggitu (August 22, 1680) are performed by "priests and monks" who were presumably Taoist and Buddhist.

Perhaps more significantly, there are references in the Diary to the great epic heroes of that classic of Chinese literature: the *Romance of the Three Kingdoms*. Dzengšeo might have enjoyed reading it as a boy or teenager, since the first Manchu translation of the "Romance" was already available in the early 1650s, when Dzengšeo was presumably born.[88] Several passages testify to his personal knowledge of the book, and to the general cult of the military heroes it celebrates among the soldiers. In the entry of October 5, 1682, he recognizes the—now desiccated—river across which the hero Liu Bei once leaped with his "bucephalus." A few days later (October 10, 1682) Dzengšeo reached a temple dedicated to the legendary statesman Zhuge Liang, also celebrated in the *Romance of the Three Kingdoms*. This was clearly a place of cult for military people, who presented offerings in front of his statue.[89]

Educated Manchu soldiers were not alien to a certain accessible layer of Chinese culture, be it general education, popular literature, or religious cults. This was not the rarefied erudition of the *literati* but rather a degree of common knowledge that made them conversant with the large majority of Chinese people. This is not to say that the Manchus were "sinicized," but that many underwent a process of acculturation that blurred the line between them and other Chinese people, in particular those serving in the military.[90] Familiarity with and appreciation of Chinese culture should not be confused with assimilation, or the loss of their own Manchu identity.[91] We should also recall that Dzengšeo had been born in Beijing after the Manchus had already installed themselves as rulers of China.

He had a Manchu as well as Chinese education, and his values and beliefs as a soldier were probably shared by other military people, whether Manchu, Mongol, or Chinese, and whether they were Bannermen or Green Standard soldiers.

Only once there is an explicit reference to the Manchu "identity" of the author, when, on his way to Beijing, he recognizes that the soldiers were setting up dwellings in the shape of Manchu houses (June 26, 1682). There is a sense of recognition of something familiar in his observation that anticipates the return to his own home. But aside from this, throughout the Diary there is no indication of any deep cultural cleavage that would set a certain group of soldiers or people aside from the others.

Finally, we shall consider the emotional world of Dzengšeo, and the more personal feelings that transpire in the diary. One of the recurrent motifs is that of the separation from the family. In the opening scene Dzengšeo contrasts the revelries of the soldiers who celebrate the New Year of the nineteenth year of Kangxi (January 31, 1680), singing and dancing in the streets—some of them dressed in women's clothes!—with his wistful longing for his parents: "in my heart, I felt sad thinking about my old folks." On New Year's Day of the following year (February 18, 1681) the scene all but repeats itself: "We bought a few pints of water and spirits and one pig to celebrate the New Year. In my heart I felt sad and grieved and, longing for my old people, wept under the blanket." The New Year's celebration is obviously an occasion that is strongly associated with the unity of the family. The sorrow of separation on festive occasions that families are supposed to spend together (much like Christmas in Europe or Thanksgiving in the United States) constituted an emotional bond between the soldiers in the field and their families in Beijing.

Approaching home on June 27, 1682, a sigh of relief is almost audible as Dzengšeo meets familiar people, perhaps his own siblings, friends or servants. In turn he sends one of his servants home to inquire about his parents' health but also to announce his imminent return. Eating well is part of the elation of getting back, while his anxiety that nothing should happen while he is so close to the end of his odyssey is still perceptible in his comments about the frightening rapids of the river.

The long-awaited reunion with his family begins with the encounter with his elder brother, who comes to greet Dzengšeo (November 8, 1682) not far from the capital, and then, like brothers would do, the two spend the night talking, exchanging information, recollecting. After another march, and taking part with the rest of the returning army in the greeting ceremony performed by the Kangxi emperor in person outside the city gates, Dzengšeo is dismissed and can go home to a particularly poignant scene. Weeping is the natural reaction to the emotions that keep rushing forth, while the joy of having returned home mingles with an array of feelings as he cannot recognize his own children and learns about the death of one of his brothers. The sensation of awakening from a dream signals his final return to normal life, his "re-birth."

Conclusion

Dzengšeo's diary is a source that, more than any other I know, introduces us to the conditions under which wars were fought in seventeenth-century China. It gives us a soldier's perspective on military life, the hard business of surviving adversities and dangers, as well as killing, and the misery that war caused to the common people. One of the lessons that we can possibly learn from it is that the impact of war on society at large cannot be judged properly unless we decode the principles operating within the army. Dzengšeo's testimony points above all to the weak structure of logistic, supplies and to the escalating food prices as a major cause for disorder among the military, and for the suffering among the civilians.

Another factor that contributed substantially to the destructive nature of war was the legal right to loot, which of course included human beings. Human beings identified as enemies or the property of enemies could be legally taken away in captivity, bought and sold, and became legitimate spoils of war. The line between legitimate and illegitimate booty, however, was not easy to draw, and in the confusion of the battle it was not possible (as Dzengšeo laments in the diary) to prevent people from grabbing anyone or anything that might bring in a profit. Paradoxically, it must have been easier to punish soldiers who committed crimes against property, such as the unlawful appropriation of animals, than to punish those who committed crimes against human beings, given that certain types of legal booty were more easily identifiable than others.

A third factor contributing to disorder was the commanders' inability to keep discipline, or to alleviate the damage that soldiers could inflict on a given territory. Fighting units were reshuffled and placed under different commanders every time a new operation was planned, and presumably the "esprit de corps" of the units, as well as the troops' loyalty to their commanders, must have been more a matter of general discipline than the result of a special camaraderie or bond among soldiers and between soldiers and officers. But general discipline was brittle. As we see in the narrative, Dzengšeo seldom makes positive remarks about any of his commanding officers, infractions were punished heavily, and military police was deployed often. The lives of the rebels who were taken prisoners were often spared, although we have seen that on occasion enemies were shot after they had surrendered. This was certainly a violation of the military code of conduct, but if and how such a crime was punished in practice cannot be ascertained.

Fourth, a military campaign did not bring to the war zone just soldiers but also salaried laborers and merchants. The laborers toiled at various tasks, mainly consisting of transportation and construction. The merchants were in charge of supplying food and other items, although the army also appears to have had a logistic support structure, mainly responsible for appropriating and distributing local resources. Quite independently from the actual fighting units, these people contributed to increase the population pressure in a certain area. Although the military might try to rein them in whenever disorders occurred, in a situation of generalized chaos these non-combatant workers could easily turn to violent means, and contribute to oppressing the local population. The merchants, as we have seen, were attacked, robbed, and sometimes killed, thus requiring extra protection from the military units.

Fifth, there is no indication that people were treated differently, within or outside the army, on account of their ethnicity. Surely there was a consciousness of who was what, but whether the ethnic boundaries played a part in how Dzengšeo's related to Manchus, Mongols, or Chinese, cannot be seen from the diary. On the rare occasions when an identity is specified, this is more likely to be a military than an ethnic one, as in the case of Šahūri, described as a man of the Green Standard army, although his name is Manchu. But the disparaging remark, quoted above, about the Miao savagery may be an indication that aborigines were indeed seen as very different people, and suggests a possible ethnic bias.

One of the most graphic descriptions of the author's disillusionment with military life is a passage in which the author contrasts the "façade" of obedience and discipline with his inner feelings. As the army was approaching the enemy's main stronghold, on January 12, 1681, the commanding general assembled his officers, and in order to make sure that there would be no hesitation among the troops at the moment of the battle, he asked those who were willing to fight to step forward. All the officers—including undoubtedly Dzengšeo—answered in one loud voice: "Each and every one of us will leap forward whenever we meet city walls and battlements." After reporting this, Dzengšeo comments: "I only had four horses left. With four hundred ounces of silver I bought four [more] horses and six head of cattle. Because [my] horses and servants were so few, I was worried and distressed." The silent contrast between the rhetoric of heroism and the reality of survival captures the essence of Dzengšeo's war (perhaps of any war) and, with it, the fragile and easily broken humanity that accompanied the violence and dangers that soldiers and civilians had to live through.

1

DIARY OF MY SERVICE IN THE ARMY BY DZENGŠEO

1680

[January 31]

On the first day of the first month of the year of the Yellow Monkey,[1] nineteenth year of Kangxi [1680], General Manggitu[2] led the councilors, officers, and local officials, and gathered them at the Dongyue temple in the prefectural city of Nanning[3] in Guangxi province, where they together performed a ritual ceremony. The high dignitaries and the officers of the two wings saluted each other by kowtowing. On the occasion of the New Year all officers and soldiers of the Eight Banners drank and ate. The *bayara* guards and the armored soldiers were in the streets,[4] in women's clothes and make-up, enjoying themselves singing the song *doo yang ke*.[5] In my heart, I felt sad thinking about [my] old folks.

[March 25]

On the twenty-fifth of the second month, Field Marshal of the Second Rank, and Prince Pacifier of the South Shang Zhixin[6], Protector of the South General Manggitu, Protector of Jiangning and other places General Ecu,[7] Councilors and Lieutenant-generals Lebei[8] and Hife,[9] and Major-general[10] Ehene met in council to discuss strategies of how to enter and take Yunnan. They decided to launch the expedition in winter. I fed the horses and prepared my tent, saddle, and weapons.

[April 1]

On the third day of the third month an imperial edict was issued:

> After Sichuan province has been secured, out of all the troops of the Frugal Prince, each *niru* must leave one soldier in the city of Guilin of the Guangxi province. The Prince himself will then lead his troops to protect the city of Liuzhou. The *anda*[11] Prince Shang Zhixin, heading the troops under his command, must defend Gui county; General

Manggitu, leading the troops of Lieutenant-general Liu Yanming and those subordinated to the governor-general of the two Guang Provinces [i.e. Guangxi and Guangdong]. Jin Guangzu,[12] the Count Follower of Justice Ma Chengyin[13] and Kong Sizhen[14] XXX, who was [daughter of] the Prince Who Pacifies the South,[15] shall enter and conquer Yunnan.

I prepared all the provisions to take with me.

[April 3]

On the fifth, as we approached the day of departure, we were ordered to prepare the weapons.

[April 4]

On the sixth Ganduhai and his lower officers thoroughly checked the number of the horses. The Department Magistrate of the Binzhou[16] district reported repeatedly that Ma Chengyin had rebelled.[17]

[April 11]

On the thirteenth General Manggitu gave Lieutenant-general[18] Hife and Major-general of the Guards Ehene three *bayara* guards from each *niru*, along with 5,000 Green Standard troops from the five expeditionary battalions [of the Green Standard], bidding them to leave for Binzhou to fight against the rebellious bandit Ma Chengyin. This same day eight horses of mine were stolen.[19] I felt sad and distraught. When I reported the theft to the general [Manggitu], he informed the officers and commoners of the five battalions.[20] An investigation was carried out, but in the end I did not get [the horses] back.

[April 14]

On the sixteenth General Ecu, at the head of his troops, came by boat from Yongchun[21] county to Nanning.

[April 18]

The military horses of Yongchun arrived on the twentieth. The general [Manggitu] ordered that the government horses [that arrived] from Yongchun be requisitioned and given to the armored soldiers who had no horses. Because at the time of the requisition [the soldiers] were unwilling to give up [the horses] [the general] reprimanded the camp commanders in charge saying that they were weak. General Manggitu summoned the officers and camp commanders on duty and told them: "Why are the horses not being handed over? You are ignoring [my order].

And refusing to make even a single effort! You must give up the government horses immediately." Then the horses were requisitioned and allocated in an appropriate manner to the departing soldiers.

[April 23]

On the twenty-fifth I followed General Manggitu, Lieutenant-generals Lebei and Hife, who were leading a force made of four soldiers from each company.[22] From the city of Nanning we set out towards the prefectural city of Liuzhou[23], passed Jinchengzhai[24], and crossed the Kunlun Pass.[25]

[April 28]

Covering 170 *li* in five days, on the thirtieth we reached Binzhou. We caught up with the *bayara* troops that had set off earlier and, joining the Manchu-Mongol cavalry, we formed a squadron.

[April 29]

On the first day of the fourth month, the servants of Hoošan [a soldier] of the Booju company of my regiment,[26] brought and shared [among themselves] the meat of a cow belonging to common people that had been killed by others.[27] They were apprehended by the armored soldiers of general [Manggitu's] personal guard. The general summoned me and the camp commanders, and made us sit in [his] tent. He comforted us with good words, but we felt ashamed. After the crime was adjudicated, Ganduhai was sentenced [to a fine of] three months of salary, I and the assistant adjutant[28] Dandai to a fine of six months of salary, the corporal[29] to seventy cane strokes, the slave master Hoošan to eighty, and the servants to a 100.[30]

[May 2]

On the fourth, after the food supplies for the whole army had been used up, the general gave the order to move camp, to set up a new camp at a distance of 15 *li* from Binzhou, to search for food in every single village, and to pound the husked rice. I sent the family boy-servants to the village. Digging up pits they found the unhusked rice, and brought it [to me]. Then they dug holes into the ground, and pounded the rice.

[May 4]

On the sixth [General Manggitu] ordered the Green Standard troops to build a pontoon bridge across the river at Binzhou.

[May 6]

On the eighth a document arrived from the Ministry, which said: "The Frugal Prince and the *Anda* Prince Shang Zhixin must join [their forces] and subdue the rebellious bandit Ma Chengyin after having joined [their forces]. You, General Manggitu, must report at once about the reason why you have not yet attacked and invaded Yunnan." We heard that the localities of Haicheng county, Jinmen and Xiamen in the province of Fujian had also been taken.

[May 11]

On the thirteenth an urgent dispatch arrived ordering us to proceed with the occupation of Yunnan.

[May 14]

On the sixteenth, because the troops and servants were harming the civilian population, a legal decree was issued to the effect that nobody was allowed to leave his post.

[May 17]

On the nineteenth [we] crossed the river, marched for 15 *li*, and set up camp in a place called Taodeng on the near side of the Shamao Mountain.[31] I made a grass shelter. A dispatch sent by the *Anda* Prince read:

> Governor-general Jin [Guangzu] shall take the marines and set out by boat on the thirteenth. I myself, together with Provincial Commander-in-Chief Jelken,[32] will proceed with our troops by land on the fifteenth. Honorable General [Manggitu] [you] shall take Laibin county and, after I take Wuxuan county,[33] we shall meet in person to deliberate whether, we should wait for the Frugal Prince of the Blood before we seize the prefectural city of Liuzhou, or whether our troops should immediately [proceed to] take Liuzhou Prefecture.

I heard that the Governor-general of Yunnan and Guizhou Heroic Strategist General Zhao Liangdong[34] had secretly memorialized [as follows]:

> The rebellious bandits Wu Sangui and Wu Guogui have died. The remaining Wu Yingqi, Wu Shifan,[35] Hu Guozhu, Ma Bao,[36] and others have lost their nerve.[37] They are incompetent people. This is the time to take Sichuan. If we proceed to take Yunnan and Guizhou with a syn-chronized attack from four routes, it is possible to suppress the rebellion in one stroke.

[May 21]

On the twenty-third the consultation ended with a decision to advance towards Laibin. [Manggitu] issued an order to pound enough rice [to last] for one month. I ordered people to dig a storage pit, take the whole rice, and pound it to get husked rice.[38]

[May 26]

On the twenty-eighth some soldiers were sent to gather information about the rebels. I went, too.

[May 27]

On the twenty-ninth I became sick and vomited.

[June 1]

On the fifth of the fifth month I heard that the Peaceful Prince of the Blood was taking in person his troops back to Beijing. So, I left [my unit] to follow the Peaceful Prince, but I did not manage to be sent back with him. I felt demoralized.

[June 3]

On the seventh I heard that the soldiers of the rebels Fan Qihan and Zhan Yang who had come from Yunnan, and the soldiers of Ma Chengyin, after crossing the river at Laibin, camped at Dashiqiao. Thereupon by General Manggitu issued a universal order to fortify every encampment. I was put personally in charge of the troops to construct during the night shift a camp wall and a moat. All the soldiers complained.

[June 9]

On the thirteenth the rebels advanced, and facing us at a distance of 5 *li* they occupied the mountain top and set up camp [there]. The general ordered the Green Standard forces to combine with our troops and guard the camp wall. I wore my armor night and day and stood guard.

[June 11]

On the fifteenth the false generals Ma Chenglie and Rao Yilong, subordinate to the rebel bandit Ma Chengyin, together with the false generals Fan Qihan and Zhan Yang, who had come from Yunnan, jointly leading over 10,000 rebels, advanced forward, pressing on to attack [our] camp. In the locality of Taodeng, they arranged in good order their *chevaux-de-frise*, shields, muskets, and elephants in four rows, and came forward in an imposing manner. General Manggitu, leaving in each encampment one officer and ten armored soldiers, came out at the head of the [rest of the] whole army. He ordered Hife and Masitai[39] to take position in front with the troops of the second squadron. Then he ordered Ehene to take position on the right flank at the head of the soldiers of the first squadron. He also ordered Lebei to deploy on the left flank with the troops of the wing column. He lined up the Green Standard troops in front. [Our troops] moved forward firing cannon. The rebels immediately rushed forward breaking through [our lines]. The Green Standard troops were not able to hold [them] and vacillated. The Plain Yellow and the Plain Red [Banners] broke into two halves, creating an opening. As the rebels penetrated in one whole group [we] split into small groups and withdrew. One could see that as our western flank was being pressed on, the Bordered Blue [Banner] was being pushed up against the rebels' *chevaux-de-frise*. The rebels' musket fire sounded like frying beans. Following that, the soldiers of the first column were attacked by the elephants. The flags of Major-general of the Guards[40] Walda of the Yellow Banner, and of Lieutenant[41] Ulehi of the Manchu-Mongol cavalry were captured. As the elephants closed in on the encircled soldiers of the second column, the arrows shot by all of my men [into the elephants' hides] looked like the quills of a porcupine. The elephants fled towards the hills [but] I was greatly alarmed and had a strange feeling. The rebels withdrew from the plain and split into groups [to hide] in the thick forest of the mountain. As evening fell, they lined up *chevaux-de-frise* facing opposite [directions]. Our soldiers also did not attack but returned to the encampment, and protected [it] by strengthening the ramparts.

[June 12]

On the evening of the sixteenth General Manggitu personally rode out at the head of 200 select troops. As they drew closer to the bandits, they frightened them yelling here and blowing the conch there.

[June 13]

The false bandit generals Fan Qihan, Zhan Yang, Ma Chenglie, and others fled on the night of the seventeenth. At daybreak General Manggitu, leaving inside the camp one soldier from each company, pursued [them] with the whole army, and I went along, too. We pursued the bandits, and we did not kill, but set free all those who surrendered and the generals; we then returned to the camp in the middle of the night. General Manggitu was lenient and forgiving, and without saying anything at all about our soldiers[42] reported to the throne that [we] had defeated and killed a mass of up to 20,000 rebel soldiers, and that, when the rebels fled on the night of the sixteenth, we pursued them capturing and killing many. [He also reported that] we had captured four elephants, and standards, flags, cannon, and muskets in great quantity.

[June 23]

On the twenty-seventh, when the general mercifully sent the wounded and sick officers and soldiers to Nanning, there were a great number who went back by pretending [to be sick or wounded].

[June 27]

On the second day of the sixth month, General Manggitu at the head of the army deliberately slowed the march, advancing only 30 *li* per day, and set up the encampment after crossing the Shamao Mountain. A report arrived that the soldiers of the Frugal Prince of the Blood had reached Luorong county.[43]

[June 28]

On the third we set up camp at Da Qiao (Great Bridge). When the chieftain[44] of Shangban village came to surrender, he reported that the chief of Li village had associated himself with the rebels.[45] [General Manggitu] dispatched Green Standard troops, who bombarded [this village] with cannon and destroyed it. We were resting for a couple of days when the whole body of a *bayara* guard of the Bordered White [Banner] changed, and [he] said that the Great Ancestor Guan[46] had descended. General Manggitu came and asked the reason for [the people's] kneeling. I said that this was really extraordinary. From that moment the general carried with him an image of the god Guandi, and prostrated every day.

[July 1]

On the sixth we set out and passed Bosa. On the eighth we set up camp 20 *li* from Jiangkou.[47] Between Taodeng and Jiangkou we covered 180 *li*.

[July 4]

On the ninth Governor-general Jin [Guangzu] and Provincial Commander-in-Chief[48] Jelken reached Jiangkou. I was surprised to hear that, since the *Anda* Prince had been arrested by imperial edict on a charge of rebellion, the troops under his command had scattered and gone plundering and did not obey the order to surrender.

[July 5]

On the tenth General Manggitu killed a large python long over 10 *da*.[49] Some people said: "A python is called *mang*[50] [i.e. sounds similar to the general's name]. Evil [will come] to the general for killing it."

[July 6]

On the eleventh we advanced to the bank of the river.

[July 7]

On the twelfth, after holding consultations, it was decided that we would bombard for the whole night the rebels' encampment on the opposite bank from Jiangkou. I stood ready in the rear guard in full armor. Since nothing happened, it was decided that the general in person would cross the river and occupy Xiangzhou[51] in order to cut off the rear route of the bandits.

[July 12]

On the seventeenth each of the Eight Banners obtained its share of boats and crossed the river all together. I myself crossed in the middle of the night.

[July 13]

Having set out on the eighteenth, we camped after a march of 15 *li*. The bandits in Jiangkou were not able to hold up, and they fled towards Liuzhou.[52]

[July 14]

On the nineteenth we camped after marching for 35 *li*. The prefect[53] of Liuzhou came to surrender, and presented to the General a letter of submission from the bandit Ma Chengyin.

[July 15]

On the twentieth we marched 25 *li*, and reached Xiangzhou. There we realized that the rebels had fled earlier on. We issued regulations to pacify the local people.

[July 16]

On the twenty-first the general consulted with the high officers, then we crossed the river [again] in Xiangzhou. Once more I crossed it during the night.

[July 17]

On the twenty-second a document sent by the Frugal Prince of the Blood said: "The rebel Ma Chengyin has shaved his head in submission,[54] and handed over his seal and imperial diploma [of appointment]. General Manggitu, you must come here at once to consult [with me] and deliberate." Because General Manggitu had fallen ill, we set out on the twentieth,[55] but proceeded slowly for 135 *li*.

[July 21]

On the twenty-sixth we reached Liuzhou. Since the general was ill, he was unable to meet with the prince, but summoned the councilors and said, "If our army is to advance and capture Yunnan, Liuzhou is not a place we should care about. Discuss the matter of the boats to accommodate the soldiers." Thereupon the councilors met with the Prince and reported on the situation. I entered the city twice, and found out that, after the troops of the Prince had placed their artillery pieces into position, the soldiers of Ma Chengyin were being been pressed from above and below. Though the false generals Huang Ming and Ye Bingzhong had surrendered, they had been killed together with another forty officers, and their household properties, women, and children had been confiscated and divided up among our councilors and camp commanders. I heard this and thought that this was not the way to keep order.

[July 26]

On the first day of the seventh month the general's illness grew worse. Staying in the same boat as Governor-general Jin Guangzu, he set off by river route with 400 Manchu soldiers.

[July 27]

On the second, Hife, Lebei, and Ehene at the head of the greater part of the army set out by land.

[August 2]

On the eighth, while crossing the Sohon Turanggi[56] River, a boat of the Plain Yellow Banner capsized and over thirty *bayara* guards, armored soldiers, and servants fell into the water and drowned. We rested for two days and recovered the corpses.

[August 5]

On the eleventh we set out and, as we passed Taodeng, we saw that [our] encampment and camp walls were still there.[57] We got food in Binzhou, and then went through the Kunlun Pass.

[August 8]

On the fourteenth we reached the Prefectural City of Nanning. Between Liuzhou and Nanning we had covered 520 *li*.

[August 22]

On the twenty-eighth the general passed away. At his funeral, from the servants to the higher ranks of the Eight Banners, to the Green Standard soldiers, and to the common people, there was no one who did not grieve. When [his] remains were sent off [to the capital] the people gathered like clouds, burned paper money, and even the [Taoist] priests and [Buddhist] monks wept and read scriptures aloud.

[August–September]

In the eighth month Hoošan, Baši, and Šota died one after another. Only my servants Bayartu, Manca, Hondai, Hūijeo, and Maitu remained. Over twenty horses died. I was greatly distressed, and thought, "How am I going to go on now that the servants are few and I have no horses?" I wept in sorrow under the blanket. Since there was absolutely nothing that could be done [I] drank every day and even sold a woman to buy horses.

[September 12]

On the twentieth, since [people were] enjoying themselves spending money, drinking alcohol, and not wearing swords, Lieutenant-general Hife issued an order to the effect that those caught [in these malfeasances] would be punished.

[September 23]

On the first day of the eighth intercalary month, Hife and others held a meeting to report to the emperor that the general had died and that the troops were exhausted. They also memorialized that if they were to advance and take Yunnan, once all the army's horses had been used up, one would scarcely manage to select five soldiers out of each company.[58]

[October 3]

On the eleventh we heard of a big earthquake in the city of Beijing, and of a great drought. I became very worried.

[October 5]

On the thirteenth there was a fire inside Nanning city that extended even to the suburbs.

[October 12]

On the twentieth, in a document sent by the Ministry, it was said that Lieutenant-general Lebei was to be appointed as our new Field Marshal. The others said it was just right.

[October 20]

On the twenty-eighth, because there were too many colonels, I was discharged from that post.[59]

[October 22]

On the first day of the ninth month Ganduhai petty-mindedly decided that people would receive fodder on the basis of the [actual] number of horses. After officers and soldiers checked the number of [their] horses [it resulted that] they had decreased. Because [Ganduhai] then allotted fodder on the basis of the number of tails, everybody was very angry.[60]

[October 27]

On the sixth an urgent dispatch arrived ordering that we invade and conquer Yunnan. When officers and soldiers were about to set out, Brigadier-general[61] Masitai did not send me because my horses and servants were so few. But Baikan Age and Gioro Afan talked to Ganduhai, so that he reversed this decision and sent me [anyway].

[November 30]

On the tenth of the tenth month, in a document sent from the Board[62] it was said that Lieutenant-general[63] Laita had become Field Marshal to Wage War to the South, and was now to invade and conquer Yunnan.[64]

[December 1]

On the eleventh the Beijing troops reached Nanning but were disappointed because Lieutenant-general Maci[65] did not go out to receive them when they arrived.

[December 7]

On the seventeenth Lieutenant-general Zhao Lian ordered that the rear-guard troops continue to march divided up into squads. When we saw them enter Nanning, everyone praised them for their imposing appearance.

[December 25]

On the fifth of the eleventh month, Sub-Chancellor of the Grand Secretariat Ekuri and Field Marshal to Wage War to the South Laita appointed by imperial decree to supervise the expeditionary army reached Nanning. They divided the whole army into three squadrons and issued the following order:

On the 15th [January 4] Hife and Commissioned Brigadier-general[66] Herbu will set out at the head of the first squadron. On the 18th [January 7] Lieutenant-general Maci, Brigadier-general Hong Shilu, and Lieutenant-general of the Hanjun[67] Zhao Lian will set out at the head of the second squadron. On the 23rd [January 12] Field Marshal Laita, Lieutenant-general Lebei, Major-general of the Guards Ehene, Brigadier-general Masitai, and Brigadier-general of the Hanjun Zu Zhichun, at the head of the third squadron will set out to take Yunnan.

All the soldiers bought one or two cows. Cattle were sold at 20 ounces [of silver] per head, and horses at sixty or seventy. The Field Marshal gathered the officers, and asked that those willing to struggle on step forward. All answered in one loud voice: "Each and every one of us will leap forward whenever we meet city walls and battlements." I only had four horses left. With 400 ounces of silver I bought four [more] horses and six head of cattle. Because [my] horses and servants were so few, I was worried and distressed.

On the night of the fifth a star appeared in the west;[68] it had a white mist that spread across an area of over 20 *da*.[69] One could see that in shape it resembled a sword, and it was red at the base. Everyone said that if it advanced towards the imperial palace it would be a bad omen. [But] this was an auspicious sign for the pacification of Yunnan. Since two officers from each banner and, in addition to the Outer Mongol troops, two armored soldiers from each company who were without horses, old, or sick were to be left in Nanning, I, Yeremu, Handu, and the others left [there] thirteen armored soldiers.[70] Ganduhai made me join the first squadron.

1681

[January 4]

On the fifteenth Lieutenant-general Hife and the others, leading the first squadron, which was formed by three *bayara* guards and five cavalrymen [out of each company], left Nanning, and after a march of 20 *li* set up camp. Because I only had a few servants and horses left, I departed in a surly mood, and could only think that I would die in battle, and gain honor [in that way]. We were led into a 5 mile-long mountain pass in Wuyuan county,[71] we squeezed through it for two nights.

[January 6]

On the seventeenth we finally came out of the mountain pass. Having past Wuyuan county, then we were led in a meandering manner, stopping and going, on a narrow path through mountain passes and along the back of the mountain. Proceeding at night we covered 600 *li* in fourteen days.

[January 17]

On the twenty-eighth, when we reached Tianzhou,[72] we realized that the bandits had already fled. We heard that [our troops] had taken Zhenyuan and Guizhou.[73]

[January 18]

On the twenty-ninth we marched for 20 *li* and set up camp at Nabiao.

[January 19]

On the thirtieth we set up camp 30 *li* further on, at Zhaima. It was announced that there were bandits in Guiluo, so at night we mounted guard wearing armor.

[January 20]

On the first day of the twelfth month we marched in full armor and set up camp in Zhujiutang. The rebels of Guiluo had fled.

[January 21]

On the second Hife and others issued the following order: "Search for whole rice, and obtain and pound [enough] rice [to last] for forty days; then rest and wait for [the arrival of] the Field Marshal." Everyone in the encampment was making pounders and pestles, digging holes, and looking for whole rice to pound into husked rice.

[January 23]

On the fourth the Field Marshal sent a dispatch ordering [us] to wait.

[January 24]

On the fifth the leader of local chiefs Muwang[74] surrendered. Spies previously sent by General Manggitu came back and reported that the rebels had fled after setting the Tiesuo[75] bridge on fire, and that our Provincial Military Commander[76] Sangge[77] had [already] crossed the Lushui[78] river. The councilors, camp commanders, and the major-generals of the Guards[79] met to deliberate, and thereafter submitted the following written report:

> Our troops have obtained provisions for five days only. If [you] provide them with food for another five days, then we shall follow the Field Marshal's order as to whether we should set out or wait here for the Field Marshal.

[January 25]

On the sixth a [reply] document sent by the Field Marshal arrived. It said, "Provincial Commander Li Benshen[80] and Provincial Governor Cao Shenji[81] have surrendered, giving up Guizhou. Now, I have dispatched ten boats to you with rice. Wait for me." We rested in Zhaimadang for eleven days.

[January 31]

On the twelfth we received a written order to advance, and set out. Because the road was a cramped pass in a narrow mountain ravine, and because of the swampy rice fields, the march was extremely hard and distressing and the horses' loads fell off or got stuck. We proceeded [in this way] for eight nights, covering 290 *li*.

[February 7]

On the nineteenth we were ordered not to drink the water of the Badu river[82] because there was a bad smell. In a message sent by Hife and others it was ordered that gifts should be entrusted to the officers[83] to be delivered in person [by them] to the Field Marshal. After this order reached our Banner Ganduhai handed [the gifts] over to me and I presented them.

[February 8]

On the twentieth we set out from Yanyangtang and marched through a forest where sunlight could not be seen. After marching in close order for 15 *li* we set up camp.

[February 9]

On the twenty-first we marched for 35 *li*, reached Xilongzhou[84] and set up camp. The distance between Tianzhou and Xilongzhou exceeds 380 *li*. After Xilongzhou was captured, no walls were left and the place had a barren and desolate appearance. Longtukuan surrendered, and 500 native chiefs came to welcome [us]. We chopped wood and gave it to them to build a pontoon bridge.

[February 10]

On the twenty-second the Field Marshal met with the councilors, and decided to set out as soon as the pontoon bridge had been completed. Moreover, they issued the following order:

> Put the Green Standard troops in front, followed by a select first squadron with the Vanguard Regiment and three guards and three cavalrymen from each company; [these troops] shall be given a full complement of horses, and shall set out on the 26th [February 14] under the command of Councilors Lebei, Hife, and Ehene. A select second squadron, composed of two guards and three cavalrymen from each company, with a full complement of horses, led by the Field Marshal and by Councilors Maci, Hong Shilu, Herbu, Zhao Lian, and others, shall set out soon afterwards. The baggage column and the wing squadrons should be composed of two camp commanders [from each company] and seven captains from each banner, and by three soldiers without horses from each company, and must be provided with cattle.[85] [In addition] 500 infantry soldiers from the provincial capital must also be provided with cattle. These shall march behind at a slower pace. All the Green Standard troops under the direct command of Governor-general Jin Guangzu shall serve as rearguard.

Ganduhai made me join the second squadron. On the twenty-sixth the troops of the first squadron left.

[February 18]

On New Year's Day of the twentieth year of Kangxi, year of the White-Gray Rooster, we left Xilongzhou, and built a pontoon bridge [across the Badu River]. One could see that the river water looked greenish, the current was fast, and the track on the bank of the river, along the mountainside, was only two feet wide. Soldiers and horses were all pressed one against the other in a single row.

We had not proceeded 10 *li* when it became dark. Because it was impossible to find a [suitable] place to camp, we pitched our tents in the sand on a bend of the river. The sand was being lifted up in the wind. We bought a few pints of water and spirits, and one pig to celebrate the New Year. In my heart I felt sad and disconsolate and, longing for my old people, I wept under the blanket. The Field Marshal issued an order: "The road is narrow; there is no place to set up the encampment. Pitch the tents one after the other as you see fit." We brought in some local people and questioned them [about the road]. They replied:

> [In this place] since ancient times there has never been a road for a marching army. After the *hangsi* festival,[86] peacocks, snakes, and worms fill the river. Because the river is muddy, when the water overflows the

road becomes submerged and people cannot get through. If they are struck by foul vapors, they will die. Therefore we build our houses on the top of the mountain.

Upon observation, one could often detect movements on the riverbed and in the branches of trees.[87] On the next day we departed and, as soon as night started to fall, we filed into a place where only one or two tents could stand, and set up camp.

[February 20]

On the third we heard that [our troops] had defeated the rebels at Shimen Ridge.[88]

[February 25]

Not until the eighth we reached and set camp at Bandunteng. Squeezed tight, we stopped at Shimen Ridge for eight days. Then we were ordered to cover the road with grass when marching.

[March 4]

On the fifteenth we set out again, and because it was raining and hailing lightly, we strapped leather and iron cleats [to our shoes] and walked on foot on the narrow mountain road for 15 *li*. Then we set up camp at the foot of Shimen Ridge.

[March 5]

On the sixteenth crawling and slipping along the way, we climbed up to the first level of Shimen Ridge. We spread grass on the slippery moss, and fetching the horses one by one, we crossed with great effort that swampy and hideous place. One could see that many horses had fallen into the precipice and died. The men's feet were covered with blisters, and could not go any further. After we had walked for 3 *li* it was getting dark. Staggering and stumbling, we struggled on crossing over the rock layer of the second ridge, and set up camp. One could see one by one the bodies of the rebels who had been killed.

[March 6]

On the seventeenth we marched 20 *li* on foot. With aching feet we struggled to cross over the third level ridge, where we rejoiced for being able to ride horses [again]. So we proceeded [on horseback] until we reached Anlongsuo.[89] There one could see that the rebels who had surrendered were coming towards the city taking [with them] the common people's women and children. I thought that was just the right place to stop, and said so to Hose, who is the head of the encampment[90] that faces mine [when we camp]. We set up camp after we passed the city. Between Xilongzhou and Anlongsuo there are over 225 *li* of awful road [conditions].

[March 7]

On the eighteenth we set out. The area appeared wide and barren. We joined up with the squadron in front and, marching all night, we covered 60 *li*.

[March 8]

On the nineteenth we rested. An order was issued that we form three squadrons. Ganduhai assigned me to the first one.

[March 10]

On the twenty-first the Field Marshal said that the Bordered Blue Banner would have to endure an overnight march.[91] We were given a Chinese guide, and in two days we covered 80 *li* taking shortcuts.

[March 12]

On the twenty-third we built a pontoon bridge on the Mabie River[92] and rested. We heard that the rebels were camped at Huangcaoba,[93] and ready to resist.

[March 15]

On the twenty-sixth the bridge was completed, and we were ordered to leave one soldier without horse from each company with the entire baggage train, and to cross the river on the next day wearing armor.

[March 16]

On the twenty-seventh the Field Marshal crossed the river with the whole army, and after a march of 30 *li* over a barren territory we approached the rebels' encampment. One could see the swamp-like rice paddies. [The rebels] had set up their encampment against the mountain, and protected it with ramparts and moats. That place was a really wicked one, and could not be attacked. Therefore [the general] withdrew the army. Departmental Director Walda and others, who had come from the capital to build relay stations, arrived with an imperial dispatch, in which the emperor inquired about the well-being of officers and soldiers. The Field Marshal, leading everyone else, prostrated himself in accordance with the New Year's rites.

[March 17]

On the twenty-eighth we crossed the Mabie River and, after a 5-*li* march set up camp, mounting guard in full armor.

[March 19]

On the twenty-ninth the Field Marshal arranged the army in rows and advanced. We went through the mountain and the wilderness, and after a march of 25 *li*, feigning an attack, we closed in on the rebels' camp. We realized that it was impossible to attack it frontally. Therefore we came to the rear [of the enemy], and made fortifications and set up our camp in front of it.

[March 20]

On the first day of the second month the whole army was ordered to line up by units and ranks. We advanced, and tried to decide the place we were going to attack. Our troops looked mighty and powerful.

[March 21]

On the second day the Field Marshal ordered 400 Manchu soldiers and 1000 Green Standard soldiers who were mounting guard at the camp to make a frontal attack as a decoy. Then he ordered Councilors Ehene and Maci to lead the wing squadron; Councilors Hife, Hong Shilu, Herbu, Lieutenant-general Masitai, and Zu Zhichun, of the Hanjun, to lead the first squadron; and Lieutenant-general Lebei and Zhao Lian, of the Hanjun, to lead the second squadron. He also ordered the Green Standard troops to line up in front, and the Manchu troops in the rear, arranged in four echelons. Holding shields and spears [we] advanced along a narrow mountain road behind the enemy camp. Suddenly a thick fog rose and even men [standing] close-by could not see one another. The rebels at the entrance of the mountain pass were not ready [for our attack]. Our troops advanced, and we could hear the incessant sound of artillery. Shields that had been abandoned by our troops could be seen everywhere on the road. Carrying a flag I ran forward, entered the mountain pass, and saw rebels who, had come out of the encampment, lined up *chevaux-de-frise*, shields and elephants, and joined battle with our Green Standard troops. The fire from cannon and muskets sounded like frying beans, the earth was shaking. Šahūri, a man of the Green Standard, received a wound, but got up once again. Our first and wing squadrons advanced yelling. It was as if the earth itself was falling down. The enemy could not hold their ground and, been overwhelmed, started to flee. I was carrying a flag and, killing [rebels], came closer to the camp on the mountain side. The rebels in the camp were firing their muskets from holes in the ramparts. Hurrying down the mountain slope I pursued and killed mounted rebels for 5 *li*. When the troops were recalled and returned to the camp one could see corpses covering that wilderness in all directions. Blood was flowing on the ground. In the [enemy] camp cannons and rifles, whether in good or bad condition, had been abandoned all over the place. We captured five elephants.

When they were interrogated, the captured rebel generals Wang Yougong and Zhan Yang reported that the rebel false generals He Jizu, Wang Hongxun, Zhao Yu,

Wang Hongju, Ba Qisheng, Zhang Guangxin, Liu Shizhen,[94] and themselves, nine people in all, at the head of approximately 20,000 soldiers all together, were protecting Huangcaoba, on the strategic road to Loping,[95] in the Qujing prefecture.[96]

[March 22]

On the third day we rested. When officers and soldiers were reassigned and squadrons were formed Ganduhai assigned me again to the first squadron.

[March 23]

On the fourth we marched for 40 *li*, and then set up camp at night.

[March 24]

On the fifth we marched 40 *li* and crossed the Huangni River.

[March 25]

On the sixth we climbed over a mountain ridge and, marching overnight, covered 30 *li*.

[March 26]

On the seventh, as we were climbing on foot the great mountain ridge of Yunnanbao, a formidable wind rose, and because the sand was getting into our eyes, it became impossible to proceed. Having marched 30 *li*, it got dark for the night, and a heavy fog rose up.

[March 27]

On the eighth [still] a strong wind blew, and it was impossible to open our eyes because of the dust. We passed Yizuo county covering 60 *li*.

[March 28]

On the ninth we marched 30 *li*, then stopped at Huanghe Mountain, We were ordered to send a Banner officer, together with twenty armored soldiers, out on a mission to gather information in Qujing and Jiaoshui.[97] Ganduhai sent me.

[March 29]

On the tenth I, at the head of the armored soldiers, covered over 100 *li* [riding] at full gallop, and reached Yuezhou.[98] Upon inspection [I saw that] there were no rebels, and returned by way of the Qujing bridge.

[March 30]

On the eleventh Li Chaogui, the Prefect of Minfu[99] in the Qujing prefecture, surrendered with 1,000 men. The Field Marshal, at the head of the army, passed Qujing and camped after a march of 20 *li*. Because Jiaoshui is an important city on the routes to Yunnan, Guizhou, and Sichuan, he ordered my first squadron's soldiers to go there at night. After having proceeded for 25 *li*, we reached Jiaoshui. The rebels had run away earlier. In the city granaries there were 50,000 *hule*[100] of rice. We seized the rice and rested for three days. The Guizhou army of Jangtai Beise[101] arrived. The Field Marshal issued orders that troops be reassigned and formed into squadron, and that the army moved out on the fourth night watch[102] to take Yunnan [city]. Ganduhai assigned me to the second squadron.

[April 3]

We set out in the middle of the night of the fifteenth and, passing Malongzhou,[103] we covered 80 *li*. A single horseman of [Jangtai] Beise's guards caught up with us.

[April 4]

On the sixteenth[104] we hurried through Yilong,[105] climbed over the Guansuoling mountain ridge, and reached Yanglin after having covered 120 *li*. [There] we heard that the bandits were camped at Shangban Bridge.

[April 5]

On the seventeenth the Field Marshal ordered that the troops of three squadrons line up in [battle] formation in full armor and proceed for 30 *li*. When [we] reached Shangban Bridge [we] saw that the rebels had abandoned the camp and fled.

[April 6]

On the eighteenth an order was issued that said: "Prepare your shields. After the Green Standard troops have arrived attack the city."

[April 7]

On the nineteenth the Field Marshal, at the head of both the main army divided into three squadrons and the troops of the Beise, slowly advanced for 20 *li*, climbed the Guihuasi Mountain, and then lined up the army in formation. Looking at it, the city [of Yunnanfu] appeared strong and impregnable, then [the Field Marshal] withdrew the troops and retreated to a distance of 7 *li* from the city. [We] set up our encampment along the mountain side, and received orders to make ramparts and moats during the night. I, at the head of the regiment's[106] soldiers, worked overnight erecting ramparts and digging moats. Between the provincial city of Nanning, in Guangxi province, and the capital of Yunnan, there is a distance of 2015 *li*.

[April 9]

On the twenty-first the rebels made a sortie out of Yunnan city and attacked [our troops]. The Field Marshal gathered the whole army outside the encampment in battle formation. After having examined the battleground, he ordered the wing squadron to protect the rear of the camp. Then he pointed his finger and ordered the troops of the first squadron to advance as to outflank [the enemy]. Pointing the finger again, he ordered the troops of the Green Standard to line up in front with those of the second squadron behind them, and [both] to advance against the front [of the enemy]. The first squadron, moreover, advanced to cut off the tail of the bandits, and to seek an opening towards the city. When our Green Standard troops charged the enemy, the roaring sound of cannons and muskets was incessant, and lasted for such a long time that the ears became used to it. Half of the rebels vacillated and fled, but the other half, comprising several squadrons, did not budge, and were resolved to fight to the death. The troops of our second squadron attacked those enemies that had already been completely routed. Councilor Hife called aloud for the Bordered Red Banner and our own [Bordered Blue] Banner, and ordered: "Crush those rebel detachments that have not been routed and are still in control of the bridge and village." Our two Banners yelling went to the assault, but the [enemy's] fire of cannons, fiery arrows, and the volleys of musket was overwhelming. [Protecting themselves] in hidden spots among the ruined walls, our two Banners became all mingled into one group. I reached the bank of the river by myself, and saw that our soldiers were being continuously wounded.

Hife sent a man with the order to advance on foot, and as soon as we got within shooting range, the rearguard of the rebels was in disarray. I immediately grabbed the flag, and crossed the river, pressing forward in pursuit of the rebels' rearguard. The rebels fled. As soon as I caught up with them, I told them that they must all surrender. They all knelt down, lay down their weapons and begged me to spare their lives. Then, when a *bayara* guard shot a rebel with an arrow, they all stood up and fled. Two rebels got hold of long swords that had been abandoned, and, indifferent to death, came forward slashing [at us]. Rushing off, I whipped the horse and climbed on top of the high riverbank. Looking behind me, I saw that armored soldier Dengse could not climb onto the bank. One rebel caught up with him and hacked at him. Because Dengse was scared, he ducked, turning his body on one side, so the rebel hit the quiver and the horse's croup. As Dengse fell off the horse, I shot the rebel, and made him fall down. Who killed the other rebel, I do not know. I looked to make sure that Dengse had not been harmed, then quickly got hold of my flag, and pushing and killing reached the base of the city wall. One could see that the rebels at the base of the wall were ready [for battle], thickly lined up in a two-echelon formation. They were also firing cannons from the top of the wall. As our soldiers heard the bugle signal for the withdrawal of the troops, they immediately turned back all together. Then we interrogated captured rebels who reported: "The false prince of the resisting rebels Wu Shifan[107] sent an order to the false generals Hu Guobing, Liu Qilong, and Huang Ming, and they have come to fight with twenty thousand infantry rebel troops and five elephants."

[April 10]

On the twenty-second we advanced to Guihuasi, where [the Field Marshal] positioned half of the army in the rear, and took charge of the other half. When we had to construct ramparts and moats around the city, I went, too. Once ramparts and moats had been prepared, we moved the encampment, and we were ordered to make assault ladders.

[April 14]

On the twenty-sixth, after the ladders had been made, we dug a moat during the night around the encampment.

[April 15]

On the twenty-seventh the Field Marshal ordered that all our troops should free the women and children of the local people that they had taken with them. The Beise [Jangtai] reached Yunnan with his army.

[April 20]

On the third of the third month, we started to erect ramparts around the city. I went [to work] every day. One false rebel general and two hundred [of our] *bayara*, armored soldiers, and servants who had been cut off [and captured] during our second assault came [over to us] seeking refuge.[108] The generals and the high officials wanted to storm Yunnanfu but, after holding council for three days, Beise Jangtai, Governor-general Cai Yurong,[109] and Provincial Commander Sangge ruled it out because [they thought] it could not be done.

[April 27]

On the tenth we divided up the perimeter of the siege with the Beise's [troops], and dug a moat.

[May 12]

On the twenty-fifth the false rebel general Ma Bao opened fire against Pingyuanfu, and seized its women and children.[110]

[May 17]

On the thirteenth we completed the construction of fortifications and moats around the city, and moved the encampment again. The houses of the [local] people had been destroyed,[111] [so] we built [new] houses. After dividing up the area [among different units], we made moats and ramparts [around] the encampment.

[May 22]

On the fifth of the fourth month we erected artillery platforms.

[May 24]

On the seventh I fell ill with fever. The Generalissimo Conqueror of the South Mujan[112] came to Yunnan from Guizhou at the head of a force of two soldiers from each company.

[June 20]

On the fifth of the fifth month [we] built a two-layer wall rampart around Yunnanfu. After a very heavy rain our camp was flushed away by the water, and there was no place to pitch [our] tents. My illness grew worse. Since my servants had also taken ill, the Hanjun Adjutant[113] Li Dezan had me carried to his tent. We heard that the rebel Ma Bao had occupied the prefectural town of Chuxiong.[114] The Beise and the Field Marshal met to deliberate. They then assigned to Councilor Hife, Lieutenant-general Masitai, Commissioned Lieutenant-general Herbu, and the Lieutenant-generals of Beise [Jangtai]'s squadron Todai and Hūwase,[115] the command of a force of three *bayara* guards and three Manchu-Mongol cavalrymen from each company, 200 vanguard soldiers, and 200 Hanjun soldiers; they also assigned to Provincial Commander Sangge the command of 10,000 Green Standard troops, and sent [all of] them to Chuxiong.

[July 8]

On the twenty-third we nailed together plum trees to make a stockade around Yunnan city, and erected a three-layer rampart. The Beise thought that the places protected by his troops were many, but, after taking measurements, they turned out to be few; since he was embarrassed, he sent 5,000 of his Green Standard troops, and 400 of his Manchu troops to protect the Biji.[116]

[July 2?]

On the seventeenth[117] the Field Marshal distributed [among the troops] positions along the marshes of the Dianchi Lake.[118] He had a continuous line of fortifications

68

built in order to cut in two the waterways to Yunnanfu. Then he assigned the Green Standard troops [to this area], and withdrew the Manchu troops of the Beise.

[July 20]

On the sixth day of the sixth month it was reported that Provincial Commander Sangge had inflicted a crushing defeat on the rebel general Ma Bao. The servants of the soldiers of the Beise and the Green Standard soldiers went to the Desheng Bridge,[119] on the outskirts [of the city], to collect plum-tree stakes.[120] When they went to pull down the houses [to get the timber], over 300 of them were cut off [and captured] by the rebels inside the city. Because the people besieged had nothing to eat, over 400 men, women, and children came venturing out of the suburbs. The Field Marshal established their price, and then sold them to the wounded soldiers of the Eight Banners. On the same day a loud noise was heard from inside the ramparts. With effort [due to the illness] I got up to see [what had happened]. An enemy patrol coming down from the mountain had captured our servants who had gone out to collect grass.

[July 27]

On the thirteenth the imperial guard Nartai came from Beijing saying that the Imperial Stables requested Chinese horses. The Beise, the generals, and the councilors gave two or three horses from Sichuan each.[121] [Nartai] on behalf of the emperor inquired about the health of officers and soldiers. After having inspected for three days the locations of the siege around Yunnanfu, Nartai left. Lieutenant-general Hife and others, at the head of the troops from Chuxiong, came back on account of the fact that both soldiers and horses were exhausted. The Beise and the Field Marshal were incensed at this, and said that they would submit a memorial to the throne indicting Hife and his men, on the ground that, refusing [to follow orders] they had not pursued the soldiers of the rebel Ma Bao after these had been defeated, but simply turned back after plundering [the area]. However, they later desisted; instead, they merely replaced those officers and soldiers who were ill or had no horses, and sent [Hife and his army] back to the provincial city of Chuxiong.

[August 23]

On the tenth day of the seventh month, I felt stronger and could stand up. The rebel Mao Bao together with five other false generals and two false regional commanders came to surrender, and were sent to Beijing.[122]

[August 24]

On the eleventh the Superintendent of Provisions and Sub-Chancellor of the Grand Secretariat Foron arrived from Guizhou. The Field Marshal appointed me to the post of officer[123] in the Board of Punishments. It was my turn to fill the vacancy in place of a dead armored soldier of the Eight Banners.

[October 5]

On the twenty-fourth of the eighth month, Lieutenant-general Gargan, in command of a force of two *bayara* guards and one Manchu Cavalryman from each company, together with Brigadier-general Unggai, who was in command of two hundred provincial troops from Xi'an prefectural city, arrived in Yunnan from the prefectural city of Jianchang, in Sichuan.[124]

[October 16]

On the sixth of the ninth month, upon examination, those among the servants and the armored soldiers who were weak and could not proceed further were allowed to stop. The officers and soldiers who were ill or disabled were also examined. All the corpses of dead officers and soldiers were removed by one officer from each wing and five armored soldiers from each banner. Then [the bodies] were sent to the capital.

[October 19]

On the ninth Lieutenant-general Jihari died. Heroic Strategist General Zhao Liangdong and others, with a force of three soldiers from each company and 20,000 Green Standard troops, arrived in Yunnan from the prefectural city of Sui yi, in Sichuan.[125] Looking at them, their faces showed an emaciated complexion, and many soldiers were on foot. Asked about their condition, they replied that they had had nothing to eat, had been struck by foul vapors, and people and horses had become ill and died in great numbers.

[October 20]

On the tenth we heard that Field Marshal Tuhai[126] had returned to Beijing from Shaanxi, and the Frugal Prince of the Blood had also gone back to Beijing from Guangxi.[127] Rebels from inside the city continuously came to surrender in ones or twos. When they were interrogated, they said that [the people] inside the city were starving and eating human flesh. Everybody in our army chose the best male children as booty, and sent the adult males to the Field Marshal. As rice was becoming scarce, one needed 20 ounces of silver to buy a bushel of rice. Many people starved to death.

[October 21]

On the eleventh, because colonel[128] Fafuri had been appointed as camp commander, the Field Marshal considered me, and appointed me [to the rank of] colonel. If others have filed a complaint, I am not aware of it.

[November 19]

On the tenth of the tenth month we advanced. I went every day to Huangtupo, 5 *li* from the city, to dig moats and build ramparts along the mountainside. Once the fortifications were completed, we moved the encampments of the Bordered Red and Bordered Blue Banners, and guarded them. The rebels' artillery rounds were either hitting the camp or falling beyond it. The people all built their houses in concealed spots. With everyone having one's own idea, only I built my dwelling on a high spot in a barren area.

[November 28]

On the nineteenth it was ordered that Councilors and Lieutenant-generals Gargan, Maci, and Lebei, Major-general of the Guards Ehene, and Lieutenant-general Hong Shilu at the head of half the army should advance to the Yinding Mountain[129] [at a distance of] three miles from the city. I myself, at the head of Captains[130] Šušu,[131] Sindai, and Gelibu, Lieutenants Laisu, Margi, and Solho, and 100 soldiers, advanced during the evening. As we were digging a moat at night, I took along Solho, Margi, and Gelibu, and while they were digging after having lifted baskets [of earth], every man was crushed to death.[132] The muskets and cannons fired by the rebels inside the city continued to roar until dawn. Projectiles were falling ceaselessly in front and behind me. Many of my men and horses were injured by the shots. The next day moats and ramparts had been fully completed.

[November 30]

On the twenty-first, Green Standard troops and Hanjun officers and soldiers were ordered to move to the front.[133] Our soldiers served in the rear, and were withdrawn only at night. Then it was ordered that, since there were problems on the Yinding Mountain,[134] the Bordered Blue Banner should immediately go there to help.

[December 8]

On the twenty-ninth the false rebel general Xian Yu, He Jinzhong, Wu Guozhu, Huang Ming, and Lin Tianqing surrendered offering the city, and presented the heads of the false General-regent[135] Guo Zhuangtu and of the false prince Wu Shifan. That same night, one brigadier-general, one Major-general, one camp commander,[136] and one colonel and 400 soldiers from each banner were sent to each of the gates of Yunnanfu, and were put on guard duty in full armor. Soldiers and civilians stealthily entered the city, and stole and brought out a great number of starving women and children. They also stole rice and brought it into the city, to exchange it for a great quantity of silk, clothes, and other things.

[December 11]

On the second day of the eleventh month, in order to take care of the women, pearls, jewels, and other possessions from the palace of Wu Shifan, and of the wives, children, and valuables of the rebel generals, Lieutenant-generals Mujan and Maci, and commissioned Brigadiers[137] of the Board of War Kiyata, Beitei, Hūsibu, Jiyehan, Lanja, Fafuri, and others made an inventory, and ordered the officers of the Guards regiment to guard all the residencies.

[December 20]

On the eleventh old women, whether in poor or good condition, signed their name and were handed over to the Eight Banners' officers and soldiers. Miscellaneous silks, clothes, and other things were also awarded.

[December 29]

On the twentieth silk was bestowed. The high officials and the ministerial functionaries in charge managed to obtain wonderful riches and good women.

1682

[January 2]

By the twenty-fourth they had finished distributing even the smallest things. The brigadier-generals were withdrawn. As troops were being re-assigned, I exchanged place with captain Ilmen, was assigned to rearguard outside the city and spent ten days there. The captain of the Guards Lobi was on guard duty at one of the city gates, when a bucket of gunpowder exploded. Three houses of the eastern part of the city and ten people at a guard post went up in the air and vanished completely. Common soldiers and servants managed to get the widows and daughters of Chinese people from Liaodong who had surrendered by deceitfully telling them that they were going to marry them, and [in this way] they took many [of these women] out of the city.[138]

[January 25]

On the seventeenth of the twelfth month a dispatch arrived from the ministry that said: "Send back with priority the imperial bodyguards, officials from the Ministry and clerks. Then withdraw the soldiers who have served for a year together with the Chinese people from Liaodong who have surrendered."

[January 28]

On the twentieth the imperial bodyguards, ministry officials, and 200 soldiers who had served for a year were brought out, the bodies [of the dead] were handed over to them, and they were sent back to Beijing. The generals met in council. The Chinese people from Liaodong were over 50,000, and it was difficult to look after them. Therefore they organized the troops into eight squadrons. Upon my request I was assigned to the first squadron. It was announced that [the army] would set out on the tenth of the first month. However, since the rebel officials who had surrendered could not go, they filed a complaint, and [that order] was revoked.[139]

[February 7]

On New Year's Day of the twenty-first year of Kangxi, year of the Black Dog, generals, dignitaries, and officers gathered at Longtou Mountain, and performed the [New Year's] rites.

[February 13]

On the seventh a dispatch from the Ministry arrived, which said: "Do not give the common people's rice and wheat to the surrendered rebels, but bring them back at once together with the army." The false rebel general Xian Yu and others had already given away in bribes pearls, gold, silver, various fur coats of sable, snow rabbit, lynx, and white ermine, fine horses, swords, quivers, and many other goods, and were reduced to begging [for food]. The generals and others met in council, and submitted [to the throne] a memorial that said: "Since we are not providing rice and wheat to the people of the surrendered rebels, these cannot go together with the army. They will be entrusted to the provincial governor[140] and allowed to reach us later." The surrendered rebels inside Yunnanfu numbered 100,000 people, and, once the rice had been used up, the price for a bushel of rice went up to 70 ounces of silver, for one peck of beans to 6 ounces, and for 1 bushel of unhusked rice to 38 ounces. A cow cost 30 ounces of silver, a pig 29 ounces, a chicken or a duck 8 or 9 coppers, and a goose 2 ounces each. The price of everything went up and the soldiers were reduced to extreme poverty. Daytime plunder and nighttime crime increased greatly, and many merchants were killed. The Field Marshal wrote an official proclaim[141] that said:

> I shall send out people [on patrol], they will to arrest those who plunder and steal, will deal with those arrested in accordance with the law, will impose heavy punishments on the officers in charge, and will investigate every day each and every soldier and servant.

[February 20]

Because of the continuing violence, on the fourteenth he ordered to send a colonel, one officer of the princely bodyguards,[142] and fifteen soldiers from each Banner to the herd.[143]

[February 21]

On the fifteenth there was a council meeting. Sub-Chancellor of the Great Secretariat Foron said that food and revenues were scarce.

[February 22]

On the sixteenth it was then announced that the Beise, at the head of the troops of the first squadron, would leave for the prefectural city of Qujing.[144] I had my horses fetched [from the herd] and was about to depart, when the rebel Xian Yu and others submitted a complaint. [The order to leave] was revoked again, and I had the horses sent back to the herd. I adjudicated a case of robbery against Loosa, of the Green Standard Troops of Governor-general[145] Cai Yurong.

[February 28]

On the twenty-second a fast courier was sent to Beijing to submit a memorial. The Palace Guard of the Plain Yellow Banner Udacan and others came back [from the capital] and reported: "The Emperor issued a favorable edict which says that he greatly rejoices, and that he only wishes to meet the high officials as soon as possible." Then it was decided that Beise Jangtai and General Laita would leave together, then an announcement was issued and we were ordered to fetch our horses. Because of a complaint brought up by Xian Yu and others the departure was again revoked, and the horses sent [again] back to the herd. Everyone was angry that there was no fixed decision.

[March 5]

On the twenty-seventh a council was held, and it was announced:

> The Beise, at the head of the first squadron, will set out on the sixth. The surrendered rebels they should be divided among six squadrons and brought back. The Field Marshal will set out at the head of the eighth squadron after all these have left.

I heard say that the Beise was ashamed and said "Let us again withdraw [together], Laita and I should be departing immediately at the head of the first squadron."[146]

[March 14]

On the sixth of the second month the Beise, Commandant of the Vanguard[147] Šangnaha and Sakca, Lieutenant-general Xi Jiabao, and Colonels Hong Shilu, Zu Zhichun, Lu Chongjun, and Gong Weihei, set off at the head of [a force of] all the *bayara* guards and Manchu-Mongol Cavalry, and of one soldier from every company. I prepared my baggage, loaded it on more than thirty horses, and happily departed from Yunnan together with the Beise. We set up camp at Shangban Bridge. One could see that the women and children taken by the soldiers were several thousands. We passed Yanglin, Yilong, and Malong.

[March 18]

On the tenth I saw, in the narrow mountain pass of Guansuoling, the Kongming and Guansuo temples.

[March 20]

We passed the Qujing prefectural capital and, on the twelfth we obtained rice in Jiaoshuizhou.

[March 23]

Passed Baishuiyi, on the fifteenth we encountered hail and rain in Pingyiwei.

[March 26]

On the eighteenth, after we passed Yizikong, we left behind the treacherous roads of Jiangxipo and Duimianpo. At Pu'anzhou I saw the Cave of the Eight Immortals.[148] We climbed up and descended Sanban Slope and Luohangsong Slope.

[March 28]

Then, on the twentieth, in Xinxingsuo we received money for twenty-days' worth of fodder and food.

[March 29]

On the twenty-first Narsai and Duhai fell ill. Then I was leading the Banner, and passed Annanwei.

[March 30]

On the twenty-second using iron ropes we built a bridge across the Lushui River at Lianyuncheng. As we crossed the floating bridge, one could see that even though the [river's] water was receding, the precipitous current was fast. Since there was no drinking water, we marched 100 *li* and set up camp in Tingzan. On the twenty-second,[149] after crossing the mountain passes at Bogouling and the

Xiangbiling we climbed on foot the 7-*li*-high Guansuoling. Then we passed Jigongbei on horseback.

[April 2]

On the twenty-fifth we reached the prefectural city of Anshun, and rested for three days.

[April 6]

On the twenty-ninth we set out under a light rain. The Beise led the *bayara* guards to Guizhou to feed the horses. The Hanjun Lieutenant-generals Xi Jiabao and Gong Weihei, in command of the cavalry, intended to feed [their horses] in Pingba Garrison. Therefore after they reached the Garrison they allocated the billets and gave [each soldier] twenty days' worth of fodder for twenty-five horses; then the horses were fed. Every day I allowed [my] worries to be released and hit [me].[150] Between Yunnanfu and Guizhou there are over 1,800 *li*. The roads are steep and narrow, there are many mountain peaks, and the people are few.

[April 27]

On the twentieth of the third month, we stayed at the prefectural city of Anshun. Our Brigadier-general of the Hanjun Liu Xianzhong, and Captain Hada, together with thirty-five soldiers, came to join our troops at Pingba Garrison. The troops from the provinces of Xi'an and Mukden were in disarray, and were therefore ordered to combine with the Manchu Banners.

[April 29]

On the twenty-second we set out from Pingbawei, and passed Pingyisuo and Weiqingwei.

[May 1]

On the twenty-fourth we reached the prefectural city of Guiyang. There we rested for a day. Looking at the [various] localities in Guizhou, one can see that they are constricted,[151] and the population is scarce. There are many chieftains of the Miao, whose customs are cruel and wicked in the extreme.

[May 3]

We set out on the twenty-sixth, and passed Longliwe and Xintianwei.

[May 9]

On the third of the fourth month we reached the prefectural city of Pingyue, and visited the temple of Zhangsanfeng.

[May 11]

On the fifth we camped in a mountain valley in Qingping county. During the night suddenly a heavy rain poured in great quantity. The mountain torrents came flowing down, and water rushed into the tents up to the knees. I took my clothes, food, quilt, and mattress out of the water all dripping, and since everything was wet, we rested [there] for two days and dried [our things] by lighting fires.

[May 14]

On the eighth we forded the Zhong'an River, and saw the Cave of Flying Clouds in Xinglongwei.

[May 15]

On the ninth we reached a slanting bridge and entered the provincial border at Huguang. Because no horseshoes had been fitted on the horses, they were limping.

[May 17]

On the eleventh we reached the prefectural city of Zhenyuan, and rested for two days.

[May 19]

On the thirteenth, we crossed a pontoon bridge on the Chenhe River, and passed Qinglangwei, Pingqiwei, and Huangzhou.

[May 26]

On the twentieth we crossed [another] pontoon bridge on the same Chenhe River.

[May 27]

On the twenty-first we passed Biansuiyi, and again crossed a pontoon bridge on the Chenhe River.

[May 28]

On the twenty-second we reached the prefectural city of Yuanzhou and rested [there] for ten days. Because the horses' hooves had been grinding on the rocky terrain, they had cracked open, pus was oozing out, and many [horses] died. Between Guizhou and Yuanzhou, in Hunan province, there is a distance of over 740 *li*. The swampy and rocky terrain make the road extremely difficult.

[June 8]

On the third of the fifth month the Beise distributed 200 boats to the Eight Banners. He then ordered half of the troops to proceed by land, and those who had been given the boats to travel by river. The Beise, bondservant company,[152] and high officials obtained boats in surplus and rented them out. Officers and soldiers hired a great number of boats and set off by water. [Janagtai] also ordered that the Commissioned Commandant of the Vanguard Sakca and the Brigadier-generals of the Hanjun Zu Zhiqun and Liu Xianzhong set out on the seventh in order to fully supervise the land routes.

[June 10]

On the fifth, I found three boats and set off by river. The downstream current was very strong, and the boats, moving at dazzling speed as if flying, covered 300 *li* before stopping.

[June 11]

On the sixth I proceeded for another 300 *li*, passed Qianyang county, and stopped at a large village called Poshi, where we saw a Dragon Boat play.[153]

[June 12]

On the seventh the river current was fast, and I was afraid there might be shoals. We covered 120 *li* and then stopped in Chenzhou.

[June 13]

On the eighth we stopped after 180 *li*. Observing [the landscape], the mountains' cliffs and peaks, they were over 40 *da* high.[154] The monkeys were playing and, on top of the cliffs, the houses of the people, made by making frames of wooden sticks, looked like swallow nests.

[June 14]

On the ninth we proceeded for 180 *li*, reached the prefectural city of Changde, and rested for three days in order to change the boats [for new ones]. [But] I did not obtain a share of [new] boats.

[June 18]

We set off on the thirteenth. In places like Bull's Nose Shoal, Tiger Shoal, Blue Wolf Shoal, and other frightful shoals, as the waves lapped [the side of the boats] and water splashed into them, the boats leaned on one side, and it was hard to get through.

[June 20]

On the fifteenth we passed the Zhanmaomajin Lake,[155] and going upstream we stopped at the mouth of a river.

[June 22]

On the seventeenth, after we passed the large garrison-village of Sengshi, we had to pull boats with towropes.

[June 25]

On the twentieth there was a mild breeze, so we spread out a sail cloth,[156] and reached Hudukouf, in the Jingzhou prefecture.

[June 26]

On the twenty-first we stopped at Xiaojiawan, near the suburbs of Jingzhou. Looking at them, our troops' dwellings and army tents were fitted with doors and windows, just like Manchu houses.

[June 27]

On the twenty-second lodgings were assigned and I stayed in Caoshi. Hadafun and Sandari came from home to greet me. I sent Mancang to inquire about the health of my father and mother. The currents between Jingzhou and Yuanzhou are strong, and the fast rapids are terribly frightening. The water flows downstream for over 1,650 *li*. Playing every day, eating good food, I rejoiced to be just going back home.

[July 24]

On the twentieth of the sixth month, because, after a memorial submitted by the Sub-Chancellor of the Grand Secretariat Foron, the soldiers' overdue salary of thirteen months and forage payment of four months were forfeited, the Eight Banners' Vanguard, Guards and Cavalry regiments all complained to the Beise.

[July 30]

On the twenty-sixth Lieutenant-general Mujan, having left behind the soldiers of the second squadron and the wives and children of the rebels, reached the prefectural city of Jingzhou leading only the rebel officials.

[August 1]

On the twenty-eighth the river overflowed, the dam at Huangtan broke, and the territory of the three counties of Jiangling, Mianyang, and Qianjiang was flooded over an area 100-*li* wide and 600-*li* long. The village of Caoshi was completely flushed away by the water. I had moved to a higher spot, and could observe how the incoming water rose with a thundering noise as high as a mountain, then suddenly smashed against the only 3-*da*-high[157] small dam. The houses where we had been staying were all swept away by the water. After the Bordered Blue Banner got hold of all the boats, and luggage had been loaded [I] reported to the Beise how the houses where we were billeted had been destroyed by the flood. Thereupon he took the houses of innkeepers that Loosa had rented in the northern suburbs, and after they moved we lodged there.

[August 4]

On the second of the seventh month Field Marshal Laita, with the troops of the eighth squadron, and Lieutenant-general Hife, at the head of the third squadron and of the rebel officials, arrived in Jingzhou. Then they gathered the troops of the Guangxi squadron at Shashi. At the moment of assigning billets, the Beise did not give [them] any. Because of this, all the troops had to set up their tents, and paid to build their houses. I also built a house.

[August 26]

On the twenty-fourth the soldiers of the third squadron, under Major-general Ehene, and those of the fourth squadron, under Lieutenant-general Lasai, arrived. Because of the matter concerning our Prince,[158] Lasai, Ehene, Masitai, and Liu Xianzhong gathered the Banner officers, collected the hats' tassels, and [we] mourned for three days holding night vigils.

[August 29]

On the twenty-seventh, when they made officers and soldiers register whether [to go back] by land or water according to their preference, I requested to go by land and registered.[159]

[September 3]

On the second of the eighth month the soldiers of the fifth squadron under Lieutenant-general Gargan arrived.

[September 11]

On the tenth the soldiers of the sixth squadron under Major-general Sige arrived.

[September 21]

On the night of the twentieth, because the overdue fodder and provisions had not yet been received [someone] wrote a cursing letter of denunciation, fastened it to an arrow, and shot it at the house where the Field Marshal was staying. Some of our soldiers went to raid the tent of the surrendered rebel general He Jinzhong. Not only did they not find anything at all, but, on the contrary, suffered injuries.

[September 29]

On the twenty-eighth it was ordered that [a force of] three *bayara* guards and three cavalrymen from each company proceed by land, and that [a force of] four *bayara* guards and seven cavalrymen from each company proceed by water after them. Those going by water or land were to be selected according to [each soldier's] personal preference.

[September 30]

On the twenty-ninth the Field Marshal, at the head of all camp commanders and officers, killed eight cows, then made offerings on top of a terrace made of stamped earth. After that, he performed the sacrificial ceremony prostrating himself and blowing the conch in front of the standard, then buried the [sacrificial] flesh.[160] The army set off, and, after covering 50 *li*, we camped overnight in Wangsipo.

[October 1]

On the first day of the ninth month, we covered 70 *li* and set up camp near a bridge called Dragon's Back.

[October 2]

On the second we covered 60 *li* and stopped at Jinmenzhou (Jinmenzhou is the Nanjun or "Southern Prefecture" of old).

[October 3]

On the third we passed Shiqiaoyi, and set up camp after having covered 80 *li*.

[October 4]

On the fourth we passed Liyi, and [again] camped after having covered 80 *li*. When the Field Marshal dispatched various officials of the Board of War to the Xiangyang River in order to distribute the boats, he [also] sent me. I left that same night, proceeded for 50 *li*, and then made a stop at an inn in Yicheng county.

[October 5]

On the fifth I left on the fourth hour, and after covering 120 *li* reached the Xiangyang prefecture. There I observed that the Tanxi river, over which Xuande jumped riding his *dilu* horse,[161] had dried up. The hoof of [my] horse carved the rock [there] to make a record of it. Once I reached the bank of the river, at the local officials' [place] I inspected and requisitioned the boats. I assigned twenty-three boats to the Beise's squadron, and twenty-two to the squadron of the Field Marshal. Then I loaded my horses and luggage on a boat and crossed [the river]. Thereupon I found a house inside the city of Fancheng and lodged there.

[October 6]

The next day the bulk of the army arrived, and it took them two days to cross [the river].

[October 8]

On the eighth we set off and passed Liuyang village, then stopped after covering 80 *li*. From there onwards game was plentiful.

[October 9]

On the ninth we passed Xinye county, and camped after covering 90 *li*.

[October 10]

On the tenth we passed Wadian, marched for 70 *li*, and set up camp in the prefectural capital of Nanyang. Then [we] went to Wolonggang, birthplace of Kong Ming [i.e. Zhuge Liang]. Here one can see low hills surrounded by plains. Then [we] made an earthen statue inside the temple of Zhuge Liang.[162] All the high officials and soldiers prostrated and made offerings of silver [to it]. I prostrated and then observed a stelae inscription.

[October 11]

On the eleventh we covered 70 *li* and camped at Bowangyi. Hares and pheasants were abundant. The rank and file soldiers were shooting arrows in a careless manner, and hit over ten armored soldiers and servants. Two armored soldiers died. I and others judged the case and a monetary compensation was paid for the bodies. In a single day many horses were shot. In my heart I was frightened and, to keep myself safe, I pondered: "I have served on a military campaign for ten years, and have not lost my life in battle; I must avoid those soldiers who are incapable of shooting from horseback."

[October 12]

On the twelfth we set camp in Yuzhou after having covered 80 *li*.

[October 13]

On the thirteenth we proceeded for 85 *li*, passed Bao'anyi and then set up camp.

[October 14]

On the fourteenth the officers of the Board of War were sent to distribute the boats at the Yellow River, and since I longed more and more for home, I submitted a request to the Field Marshal and [was allowed] to go [with them]. I passed Ye county, covered 90 *li*, and then rested at an inn's room.

[October 15]

On the fifteenth I passed Shiguzhen in Xiangcheng county, proceeded for 140 *li* and stopped at the house of local people.

[October 16]

On the sixteenth I passed Guodianyi in Xinzheng county, and lodged at an inn after having covered 80 *li*.

[October 17]

On the seventeenth I passed the Zhengzhou and Xingze counties, and after covering 70 *li* reached the bank of the Yellow River. There I pitched my tent. There I saw that the river's water had [partly] dried up and [the river had] become narrow; although the current was fast, there were no terribly frightening places. At the local officials' [place] I inspected the boats and requisitioned them.

[October 18]

On the eighteenth I assigned respectively fourty-six boats for the transportation of horses to the Beise's squadron and fourty-four boats for the transportation of horses to the Field Marshal's squadron. After loading my horse and luggage on a boat I crossed the Yellow River and pitched my tent on the opposite bank.

[October 19]

On the nineteenth the bulk of the army arrived. They crossed the Yellow River [with boats] coming and going in opposite direction, and the passage was completed quickly. Then we proceeded for 25 *li* and set up camp.

[October 20]

On the twentieth we proceeded for 85 *li* and camped in Xinxiang county. From home Mancang and Gurbu came to greet me bringing foods. I was not able to sleep at night, and asked about family affairs.

[October 21]

On the twenty-first we proceeded for 60 *li* and set up camp in Weihuifu.

[October 22]

On the twenty-second we passed Qi county, covering 85 *li*, then went to see the tomb of Chengxiang Bigan of the kingdom of Zhou,[163] knelt in front of the earthen statue of the temple, and set up our camp.

[October 23]

On the twenty-third we passed Yiqiu county and, after having covered 65 *li*, set up camp in Tangyin county.

[October 24]

On the twenty-fourth, because there was not [enough] water [to navigate][164] we proceeded for 40 *li* [only] and set up camp in Zhangde prefecture.

[October 25]

On the twenty-fifth we went on for 70 *li* and camped in Cizhou.[165] I erected the encampment of the Field Marshal.[166]

[October 26]

On the twenty-sixth we covered 70 *li* and camped in the Handan county.

[October 27]

On the twenty-seventh we covered 70 *li* and camped overnight in Daliandian.

[October 28]

On the twenty-eighth we covered 40 *li* and camped overnight in Shunde prefecture.

[October 29]

On the twenty-ninth, after covering 45 *li*, we met Duke Fiyanggū,[167] proceeded for 50 *li*, and stopped at Yincun. The emperor [sent people who] greeted [us] by awarding two imperial horses each to the Beise and the Field Marshal, one regular horse each to Mujan, Gargan, Hife, and others, and all together 300 horses and thirty camels from the imperial herd to officers and soldiers. It was ordered to take the strong ones and give them to the people without horses; and I myself stayed up at night to supervise [the matter], and to distribute [the horses] among [the troops of] the Eight Banners.

[October 30]

On the first of the tenth month we covered 90 *li* and camped at Zhaozhou.

[October 31]

On the second we crossed the Potuo river, covered 80 *li*, and then set up camp.

[November 1]

On the third we covered 60 *li* and set camp at Fuchengyi.

[November 2]

On the fourth we proceeded for 60 *li* and camped at Mingyuedian. I supervised the erection of the Field Marshal's encampment.

[November 3]

On the fifth we proceeded for 90 *li* and camped in Qingdu county.

[November 4]

On the sixth we covered 90 *li* and set up camp at the prefectural city of Baoding.

[November 5]

On the seventh we covered 50 *li* and camped in Ansu county.

[November 6]

On the eighth we did 70 *li*, and camped in Dingxing county.

[November 7]

On the ninth I made a report to the Field Marshal. Then we covered 100 *li*, reached a *tokso*[168] on the Liuli River, and rested [there].

[November 8]

On the next day, at night my eldest brother[169] arrived to greet me. After we met I prostrated in front of my brother, embraced him, and wept. We went on until daybreak talking about our cherished memories and recollections.

[November 9]

On the eleventh the bulk of the army arrived, we went on for 35 *li*, and set up camp in Liangxiang county.

[November 10]

On the twelfth the emperor in person [arrived] from Beijing at the head of the chief ministers. In a wide open space at Changxindian[170] he pitched the palatial square tent and greeted the Field Marshal, high officials, officers, and soldiers. He lined up the flags and prostrated in front of the flags at the sound of the conch. Thereupon he ordered generals and soldiers to present themselves keeling down in front of him, and offered them tea. Everyone prostrated in front of his imperial grace. I went to Lugou Bridge,[171] and keeling down met my father. I heard about the matter concerning fourth brother.[172] Then, weeping, I went through the gardens, entered the city, and [still] weeping entered [my] house. I prostrated as I met my mother and the others. When I met [my] children and younger brothers I could not recognize them. Looking at them, the houses and heated beds[173] of the capital appeared even more odd, and suddenly it was like a confused, hazy dream.

The more I thought [about it] [the more] I marveled at what seemed like being born again. Yet, recollecting with sorrow that in the flock of geese one had parted,[174] I could not put an end to my thinking [of him]. Is this a dream, or is it not?

This is the true record of my, Dzengšeo's, ten-year-long strenuous service on military campaign.

Diary of [my] service in the army. Fourth book.

2

MANCHU TEXT

elhe taifin-i sohon[1] bonio juwan uyuci aniya . aniya biyai ice inenggi . jiyanggiyūn manggitu . hebei ambasa . geren janggisa . ba na-i hafasa be gaifi . guwangsi nan ning fui hoton-i dung yoo miyoo-i dolo isibufi doroloho : ambasa juwe galai hafasa iskunde[2] hengkilehe : aniyai ucuri jakūn gūsai janggin cooha gemu jeme omime . bayara uksin-i beye giyade . hehe adali miyamifi . doo yang ke ucun ba[3] uculeme efihe : mini dolo sakdasa be gūnime ališaha :

juwe biyai orin sunja de . horon be badarambure amba jiyanggiyūn . julergi be necihiyere wang šang jy sin . julergi be tuwakiyara jiyanggiyūn manggitu . giyangning ni jergi babe tuwakiyara jiyanggiyūn ecu . hebei amban gūsai ejen lebei . hife . meiren-i janggin ehene se yūn nan be gaime dosire jalin hebe acafi . tuweri dosimbi seme toktoho : bi morin be ulebume maikan enggemu . ahūra hajun be dasataha :

ilan biyai ice ilan de . dergici wasimbuha šang cuwan de sycuwan-i golo be baha be dahame . kemungge wang-ni cooha be . guwangsi-i golo hoton gui lin fude emu nirui emte be werifi . wang-ni beye cooha be gaifi . lio jeo fu be tuwakiyakini . an da wang šang jy sin ini harangga cooha be gaifi . gui hiyan be tuwakiyakini : juwe guwang-ni dzungdu gin guwang dzu . jurgan be dahaha be ma ciyang yin . julergi be oktobure wang bihe kung sy jen-i harangga gūsai ejen lio yan ming sei cooha be . jiyanggiyūn manggitu gaifi . yūn nan be gaime dosikini sehebi . mini gamara yaya jaka be gemu dasataha : ice sunja de dosire inenggi hanci oho . ahūra hajun be sadata seme selgiyehe : ice ninggun de ganduhai buyarame janggisa morin-i ton be ciralame baicaha : bin jeo-i jy jeo hafan ma ciyang yen be ubašaha seme nurhume boolanjiha : juwan ilan de jiyanggiyūn mang gūsai ejen hife . tui janggin ehene de emu nirui ilata bayara . dahame dailara sunja ing-ni sunja minggan niowanggiyan tu cooha be bufi . neneme ubašaha hūlha ma ciyang yen be dailame bin jeo baru jurambuha : tere inenggi mini jakūn morin hūlhabufi . mini dolo ališame . jiyanggiyūn de alara jakade . jiangggiyūn sunja ing-ni hafasa . irgen de selgiyafi[4] baicabuha . naranggi baha akū : juwan ninggude jiyanggiyūn ecu . cooha gaifi yung šūn hiyan ci cuwan tefi . nan ning de jihe : orin de yung šūn-i coohai morisa isinjiha : jiyanggiyūn gisun morin akū uksin sade yung šūn-i alban-i morin be tatame gaifi bu seme tatarade lak seme burakū ofi . genere kūwaran da be uhuken seme dangsifi . jiayanggiyūn

88

mang . tuwakiyara kūwaran-i da janggisa be gajifi . morin be burakūngge adarame . emke hono faššame yabuki serakū jileršembi . te uthai alban-i morin be bu seme . morin be tatame gaifi . genere cooha de icihiyame buhe : orin sunja de bi . jiyanggiyūn mang . gūsai ejen lebei . hife sebe dahame . emu nirui duite ton-i cooha be gaifi . nan ning fuci . lio jeo baru jurafi yabume . jin ceng sy be dulefi . gun luwan guwan be tucifi . sunja inenggi emu tanggū nadanju babe yabufi . gūsin de bin jeo de isinafi . neneme genehe bayara be acafi . aliha cooha be acabufi emu meyen obuha :

duin biyai ice de . mini jalan-I booju nirui hoošan-i kutule . gūwa-i waha irgen-i ihan-i yali be dendefi gajirede . jiyanggiyūn-i gocika[5] uksin de nambufi . jiyang-giyūn . mimbe . kūwaran-i da be gamafi . cacari de tebufi . sain gisun-i necihiyere de . be yertehe[6] . weile gisurefi . ganduhai ilan biyai funglu . mimne . arahai janggin dandai be ninggun biyai -funglu faitame . bošokū be nadanju . kutule-i ejen hoošan be jakūnju . kutule be tanggū tantaha : uheri coohai jetere bele lakcafi . ice duide jiyanggiyūn ing gurime . bin jeo ci tofohon bai dubede genefi ing ilifi . teisu teisu gašan de bele baisu . handu be niohu seme selgiyehe : bi booi juse be gašan de unggifi . eye fatame handu baifi gajifi . na be sangga arafi bele niohuhe : ice ninggude bin jeo-i bira be fukiyoo ca seme . niowanggiyan tu de afabuha : ice jakūn de jurgan ci unggihe bithede . ubašaha hūlha ma ciyang yen be kemungge wang . anda wang šang jy sin ni emgi acafi dailakini : jiyanggiyūn mannitu si yūn nan be dailame dosika akū babe hūdun boola sehebi : geli fugiyan-i goloi hai cing hiyan . gin men . hiya men-i jergi babe baha seme donjiha : juwan ilan de geli yūn nan be gaime dosi seme hacihiyara bithe isinjiha : juwan ninggude cooha kutule be irgen be nungnembi seme . gemu karun ci ume tucibure seme fafun-i bithe sel-giyehe : juwan uyun de bin jeo-i bira be doofi . tofohon ba yabufi . ša moo san-i ebele too deng sere babe ing iliha : bi orhoi tatan araha : anda wang-ni yabubuha bithede . dzungdu gin mukei cooha be gaifi . juwan ilan de cuwan be jurambi : mini beye . tidu jelken-i emgi cooha be gaifi . tofohon de olhon be jurambi : lai bin hiyan be wesihun jiyanggiyūn gaisu . bi u siowan hiyan be gaifi . dere acafi heb-deki . eici kemungge cin wang be aliyafi lio jeo fu be gaire : eici musei cooha uthai lio jeo fu be gaire babe ebešeki sehebi : yūn gui-i dzungdu baturu bodohonggo jiyanggiyūn joo liyang dung-ni wesimbuhengge . fudaraka hūlha u san gui . u guwe gui bucehe : funcehe u ing ki . u ši fan . hū guwe ju . ma boo se gemu silhi meijehebi : muten akū urse : ere sucuwan be baha ucuri . duin jugūn-i sasa yūn gui be gaime dosici . emgeride toktobuci ombi seme narhūšame wesimbuhe seme donjiha : orin ilan de lai bin-i baru ibembi seme gisurefi nakaha . emu biyai jetere bele niohu seme selgiyehe : by eye fetebume handu baifi . bele niohuhe : orin jakūn de hūlha-i mejige be gaime . cooha unggirede . bi genehe bihe : orin uyun de mini beye fudame nimehe :

sunja biyai ice sunja de . elhe cin wang-ni beye cooha gaifi . beging-ni baru bederehe seme donjifi . bi elhe wang be dahame tucifi . elemangga bahafi beder-erakū seme kusucehe[7] : ice nadan de yūn nan ci jihe hūlha fan ci han . jan yang-ni cooha . ma ciyang yen-i cooha lai bin-i bira be doofi . da ši kiyoo de iliha seme donjifi . jiyanggiyūn mang geren de selgiyefi ing be akdulara de . mini beye cooha

be kadalame dobori dulime keremu ulan weilehe : coohai urse gasaha : juwan ilan
de hūlha ibeme jifi . bakcilame sunja bai dubede . alin be gaime ing iliha : jiyanggiyūn . niowanggiyan tu be musei cooha de kamcibume keremu tuwakiyabuha :
mini beye dobori inenggi akū uksilehei jucelehe : tofohon de ubašaha hūlha ma
ciyang yen-i fejergi holo jiyanggiyūn ma ciyang liyei . žao i lung . yūn nan ci jihe
hūlha-i holo jiyanggiyūn fan ci han . jan yang uheri tumen funcere hūlha be
gaifi . ing be afanjime hanci latunjifi . too deng-ni bade hiyahan kalka miyoocan
sufan duin be faidafi ambarame jehe be . jiyanggiyūn mang ing toome[8] emu janggin . juwan uksin be werifi . uheri amba cooha be gaifi tucifi . cin-i dere de
hife . masitai be jai meyen-i cooha be gaifi faida . ici ergi šaksiha[9] de ehene uju
meyen-i cooha be gaifi faida : hashu ergi šaksiha[10] de lebei šaksiha[11] meyen-i
cooha be gaifi faida seme afabufi . niowanggiyan tu be juleri sindafi . ibeme poo
sindame . hūlha uthai fondolome latunjifi . niowanggiyan tu alime muterakū
aššame . gulu suwayan gulu fulgiyan juwe hontoho fakcame angga arame ba
buhe : hūlha bireme emu dalgan-i fondolofi . baksalafi bedererede . tuwaci jebele
galai baru siribume kubuhe lamun . hūlhai hiyahan-i hanci ilinaha . hūlhai
piciyang turi tashara[12] adali sindambi : tuwaci uju meyen-i cooha sufan be birebufi . kubuhe suwayan-i bayara janggin walda tu . aliha cooha-i funde bošokū
ulehi-i tu gaibuha : sufan halgime jai meyen-i cooha de nikenjihe be . meni geren-i
gabdara[13] de . sirdan sengge bula-i adali . sufan de hadara jakade . sufan burulame
alin-i baru genehe : mini dolo faijeme[14] seme gūnime tuksitehe : hūlha necin baci
ikūme . alin-i luku bujan de kurlefi[15] . yamjitala bakcilame hiyahan faidafi
bihe : musei cooha inu afahakū . ing de bederefi . keremu be akdulame
tuwakiyaha : juwan ninggun-i yamji jiyanggiyūn mang-ni beye juwe tanggū siliha
cooha be gaifi . hūlhai hanci genefi . ergide kaicame . cargide burdeme hūlha be
burgibuha : hūlhai holo jiyanggiyūn fan ci han . jan yang . ma ciyang liyei se juwan
nadan-i dobori burulaha : gereke manggi . jiyanggiyūn mang ing de emu nirui
emte cooha be werifi . amba cooha be gaifi farhade[16] . bi genehe bihe : hūlhai
amcabufi dahahangge . jiyanggiyūn gemu waha akū sindaha : dobori dulime ing de
bederehe : jiyanggiyūn mang oncoi baktambume . musei cooha be umai sehe
akū : juwe tumen isire hūlha be ambarame gidafi waha : juwan ninggun-i dobori
hūlha burulafi . fargame amcafi ambula waha : sufan duin . tu kiru poo miyoocan
ambula baha seme wesimbuhe : orin nadan de feyelehe . nimere janggin cooha
be . jiyanggiyūn gosime nan ning de unggirede holtome genehengge umesi labdu :
ninggun biyai ice juwe de . jiyanggiyūn mang cooha be gaifi jortai elhešeme .
inenggidari damu gūsin ba yabume . ša moo san be dulefi tataha : kemungge cin
wang-ni cooha be loo žung hiyan de isinaha seme boolaha : ice ilan de da kiyoo
de tatafi . šang ban hiyang ni tusy dahame jifi . li gašan-i tusy be hūlha de dayafi
bihe seme alafi . niowanggiyan tube unggifi . poo simdame efulebuhe : juwe
inenggi indehede . kūbuhe šanggiyan-i bayara emken beye kūwaliyapi[17] . guwan
mafa wasinjiha seme . jiyanggiyūn mang genefi . hengkileme turgun be fonjiha : bi
ere ganio kai sehe : daci jiyanggiyūn guwan enduri nirugan be gaifi
yabume . inenggidari hengkilembi : ice ninggun be jurafi . be sa be dulefi . ice
jakūn de giyang geo[18] ci orin bai dubede tataha : too deng . giyang keo-i siden emu

tanggū jakūnju babe yabuha : ice uyun de dzungdu gin . tidu jelken giyang keo de
isinjiha : anda wang be hesei ubašambi seme jafara jakade . fejergi cooha samsifi
tabcilame . dahabuci jiderakū seme donjifi sesulaha : juwan de jiyanggiyūn
mang . juwan da funcere amba jabjan be waha : gūwa hendume . jabjan serengge
mang kai . waci jiyanggiyūn de ehe sehe : juwan emude birai dalin de ibefi . juwan
juwe de hebešefi . giyang keo-i bakcin-i dalin-i ing-ni hūlha be emu dobori poo
sindabuha . bi uksilehei fiyanjilaha : baitakū ofi . jiyanggiyūn bira doofi siyang jeo
be gaifi . hūlhai i amargi be lashalaki seme hebdeme toktobuha : juwan nadan de
jakūn gūsa meni meni cuwan dendeme gaifi . sasari doome . mini beye dobon
dulin de dooha . juwan jakūn de jurafi . tofohon ba yabufi . tataha : giyang keo-i
hūlha alime muterakū . lio jeo-i baru burulaha : juwan uju de gūsin sunja ba yabufi
tataha : lio jeo-i jyfu dahame jifi . ubašaha hūlha ma ciyang yen-i dahara bithe
be . jiyanggiyūn de alibuha : orin de orin sunja ba yabufi . siyang jeo de isinafi
tuwaci . hūlha aifini burulahabi : irgen be toktobume fafan selgiyehe : orin emude
jiyanggiyūn . ambasa hebešefi . siyang jeo-i giyang be doorede[19] . bi geli dobori
dulime dooha : orin juwede kemungge cin wang-ni unggihe bithede . ubašaha
hūlha ma ciyang yen uju fusifi . doron ejehe benjime dahaha : jiyanggiyūn manggitu si hūdun hahilame jifi hebešeme toktobuki sehebi : jiyanggiyūn mang
nimeme ofi . orin de jurafi . elheken emu tanggū gūsin sunja babe yabufi . orin
ninggude lio jeo de isinafi . jiyanggiyūn nimeme ofi . wang de acame mute-
hekū : hebei ambasa be gajifi hendume . musei cooha yūn nan be gaime dosire be
dahame . lio jeo be musei dara ba waka : coohai tere cuwan-i babe gisure sere
jakade . hebei ambasa . wang-ni jakade acanafi turgun be alaha : bi juwe jergi
hoton de dosifi tuwaci . wang-ni cooha . poo gaifi tere jakade . ma ciyang yen-i
cooha dele fejile hafirame tehebi : dahaha holo jiyanggiyūn hūwang ming . ye
bing jung-ni jergi dehi funcere hafan be wafi . boigon be talafi . hehe juse be hebei
ambasa . kūwaran-i dasa de dendefi buhe : bi donjifi ere icihiyahangge waka
kai sehe :

nadan biyai ice de jiyanggiyūn nimeme ujelefi . dzungdu gin guwang dzu-i
emgi cuwan tefi . duin tanggū manju cooha be gaifi . muke be juraka : ice juwede
hife . lebei . ehene se amba cooha be gaifi . olhon be jurafi . ice jakūn de lai bin
hiyan-i sohon turanggi bira de doore de . tuwahai gulu suwayan-i emu cuwan
ubaliyafi . gūsin funcere bayara . uksin kutule mukede tuhefi bucehe : juwe
inenggi indefi giran baibuha : juwan emude jurafi too deng be dulerede
tuwaci . ing kūwaran keremu an-i bi : bin jeo de bele gaifi . kun luwan guwan be
tucifi . juwan duin de nan ning fude isinaha : lin jeo . nan ning fui siden sunja
tanggū orin ba be yabuha : orin jakūnde jiyanggiyūn ufarafi acanahade . jakūn
gūsai kutule ci wesihun . niowanggiyan tu . irgen gemu gasarakūngge akū : giran
benerede niyalma tugi gese isafi . irgen se hoošan jiha dejime[20] . doose . hošang
inu songgoho . ging hūlaha :

jakūn biyai dolo hoošan . baši . šota emu siran-i ufaraha : mini kutule damu
bayartu . manca . hondai . hūijeo . maitu funcehebi : morin orin funcehe bucehe : bi
ambula ališame yaburede kutule hibcan . morin akū ainara seme . jibehun-i dolo
akame songgombi : umai araha akū ofi . inenggidari omimbi . hehe be inu uncafi[21]

91

morin udaha : orin de gūsai ejen hife . jiha eifire[22] . arki nure omire . loho asharakū
oci . nambuha be tuwame weile arambi seme fafulaha :

anagan-i jakūn biyai ice de . hife se hebe acafi . jiyanggiyūn geli ufaraha : cooha
mohoho turgun be wesimbuki seme gisurefi . yūn nan be gaime dosici . coohai
morin wajifi . sonjoci arkan emu nirui sunjata ton-i cooha be bahambi seme wesimbuhe : juwan emude beging-ni hoton de ambarame na aššaha . ambula hiya
seme donjifi . bi ambula tuksitehe : juwan ilan de nan ning-ni hoton-i dorgi tuwa
dafi . guwali inu tuwa daha : orin de jurgan-i unggihe bithede . gūsai ejen lebei be
jiyanggiyūn sindaha sehebi : gūwa hendume juken sehe : orin jakūn de jalan-i
janggin fulu seme mimbe nakabuha :

uyun biyai ice de ganduhai buyarame morin be tolome orho liyoo gaimbi
seme . janggin cooha morin be baicafi ekiyefi . uncehen tolome orho liyoo gaibure
jakade . geren gemu ambula tooha : ice ninggude yūn nan be gaime dosi seme
hacihiyara bithe isinjifi selgiyefi . janggin cooha be tucibure de . meiren-i janggin
masitai mimbe morin kutule hibcan seme tucibuhekū : barkan age . gioroi
afan . ganduhai baru gisurefi mimbe murime tucibuhe :

juwan biyai juwan de . jurgan ci unggihe bithede . gūsai ejen laita be julergi be
dailara amba jiyanggiyūn obufi . yūn nan be gaime dosikini sehebi : juwan emude
beging-ni cooha . nan ning de jime . gūsai ejen maci bargiyahakū ofi useme[23] isinjiha : juwan nadan de gūsai ejen joo liyan amargi meyen-i cooha be baksan banjibufi
yabume . nan ning de dosire be tuwaci . ambula horonggo ofi geren gemu saišaha :

omšon biyai ice sunja de . hesei takūraha dailara cooha be tuwame jurambure
ashan-i da ekuri . julergi be dailara amba jiyanggiyūn laita gemu nan ning de isinjifi . uheri cooha be ilan meyen banjibufi . tofohonde hife . araha meiren-i janggin
herbu uju meren[24] be gaifi jurambi : juwan jakūn de gūsai ejen maci . meiren-i
janggin hungsilu . ujen cooha-i gūsai ejen joo liyan jai meyen be gaifi
jurambi : orin ilan de amba jiyanggiyūn laita . gūsai ejen lebei . tui janggin
ehene . meiren-i janggin masitai . ujen coohai meiren-i janggin dzu jy cun ilaci
meyen be gaifi . yūn nan be gaime jurambi seme selgiyefi . geren cooha gemu
ihan emke juwe udaha : ihan orin yan . morin ninju . nadanju yan de
uncambi : amba jiyanggiyūn . janggisa be yooni isabufi faššame yabuki serengge
tuci seme fonjiha : geren le la seme . bi bi gemu hoton . hiyahan be ucaraci
fekumbi seme . kar mir seme jabumbi : mini morin damu duin funcefi . duin
tanggū yan de duin morin . ninggun ihan udaha : kutule morin umesi hibcan
ofi . ambula ališame joboho . ice sunja-i dobori wargi ci tucike usiha . šanggiyan
sukdun sumakangge orin da funcembi . arbun loho-i adali . da-i ergi fulahūn
sabumbi : niyalma tome diyan-i baru dosici ehe seme gisurehe : tere yūn nan be
toktobure todolo bihebi : nan ning de gūsa tome janggin juwe . tulergi monggo
cooha be dabume morin akū sakda . nimekungge emu nirui juwete uksin be
werirede . bi yeremu . handu sei jergi juwan ilan uksin be werihe : ganduhai mimbe
uju meyen de banjibuha : tofohon de gūsai ejen hife se uju meyen-i ilata
bayara . sunjata aliha cooha be gaifi . nan ning ci jurafi . orin ba yabufi
tataha : minde kutule morin komso ofi . munahūn-i jurafi . damu dain de buceki
seme gūnime . gebu gaiki sembi : u yuwan hiyan-i sunja ba golmin alin-i angga de

yarubufi . cibume juwe dobori dulifi . juwan nadan de teni angga be tucike : u
yuwan hiyan be dulefi . dobori dulihai alin-i angga . alin-i jidun-i narhūn jugūn be
mudakiyame jodome yarubufi . ninggun tanggū babe juwan duin inenggi . dobori
dulime yabufi . orin jakūn de tiyan jeo de isinafi tuwaci . hūlha burulahabi : jen
yuwan . gui jeo be baha seme donjiha : orin uyunde orin bai na biyoo de tataha :
gūsin de gūsin bai je ma de tataha : gui loo bade hūlha bi seme selgiyefi . dobori
uksilehei jucelehe :

jorgon biyai ice de uksilefi orin ba yabufi . ju jio tang de tataha : gui loo-i hūlha
burulahabi : ice juwe de hife se handu baifi . dehi inenggi jetere bele niohume
gaisu . amba jiyanggiyūn be aliyame indembi seme selgiyehe : kūwaran-i tome
yooni heliyen congkišakū arafi . eye feteme handu baifi bele niohumbi : ice duide
amba jiyanggiyūn aliya seme bithe unggihe : ice sunja de tusy-i da mu wang
dahaha : nenehe jiyanggiyūn mang-ni unggihe jiyansi jifi . tiye so kiyoo de hūlha
tuwa sindafi burulaha : musei tidu sangge lu sui giyang be dooha seme
alambi : hebei amban . kūwaran da . tui bayara janggin se acafi hebdefi . meni
cooha damu sunja inenggi bele arame bahambi . jai sunja inenggi bele bufi . eici
dosire . amba jiyanggiyūn be aliyara babe . amba jiyanggiyūn-i gisun be dahame
yabuki seme bithe alibuha : ice ninggude amba jiyanggiyūn-i unggihe
bithede . gui jeo be alibume tidu libenšen . siyūn fu dzoo šen gi dahaha : ne
suwende juwan cuwan-i bele unggihe . mimbe aliya sehebi : je ma tang-ni bade
juwan emu inenggi indehe : juwan juwede dosi sere bithe isinjifi jurafi . jugūn hafirahūn alin-i holo isheliyen . handu cyse lifakū ofi . akame jobome . morin-i aciha
tuheme lifame . jakūn dobori dulime . juwe tanggū uyunju babe yabuha : juwan
uyun de ba du ho bira muke de ehe sukdun bi . ume jetere seme selgiyehe : hife sei
unggihe emu bithe de . janggin-i beye de afabume . amba jiyanggiyūn de benebu
sehebi : musei gūsa de isinjifi . ganduhai minde bufi benehe : orin de yan yang tang
ci jurafi . bujan-i dorgi be yabume . šun be saburakū . tofohon bai dubede yarume
tataha : orin emude gūsin sunja ba yabufi . si lung jeo de isinafi tataha : tiyan jeo . si
lung jeo-i siden ilan tanggū jakūnju ba funcembi : si lung jeo efujefi hoton
akū . susu-i muru bi : lung tu guwan dahafi . ba nai tusy sunja tanggū okdome
jifi . fukiyoo cabume . muse moo sacifi buhe : orin juwede amba jiyanggiyūn hebei
ambasa be isabufi . hebešefi fukiyoo šanggame juraki : niowanggiyan tu be
juleri . sirame sonjoho uju meyen-i gabsihiyan . emu nirui ilata bayara . ilata aliha
cooha be yabubuki : gemu orin sime bufi . hebei amban lebei . hife . ehene se
gaifi . orin ninggude jurakini : sonjoho jai meyen-i juwete bayara . ilata aliha
cooha de gemu morin sime bufi . amba jiyanggiyūn . hebei amban maci .
hungsilu . herbu . joo liyan se gaifi amala jurambi : nukte meyen de . gala de juwete
kūwaran-i da . gūsa tome nadan janggin . emu nirui ilata moorin akū cooha de . ihan
sime bufi . golo hoton-i sunja tanggū morin akū cooha de . inu igan[25] sime
bufi . amala elhe yabukini : dzungdu gin guwang dzu ini harangga niowanggiyan tu
be gaifi . uncehen be fiyamjilakini seme selgiyehe : ganduhai . mimbe jai meyen de
banjibuha : orin ninggude uju meyen-i cooha juraka :

elhe taifin-i šahūn coko orici aniya . aniyai ice inenggi si lung jeo ci
jurafi . fukiyoo be doofi . ba di ho bira be tuwaci . muke niowanggiyan bime . eyen

93

turgen . alin birai cikin-i jugūn juwe cy isimbi : cooha morin yarubufi cibume .
ilihai juwan ba yabuhakū yamjifi . tatara ba baharakū ofi . birai dan-i yunggan[26]
de tatafi . edun de yunggan[27] furgime . muke nure udu gin . ulgiyan emke udafi
aniya araha : bi dolori akame ureme damu sakdasa be kidume gūnime . jibehun-i
dolo songgoho : amba jiyanggiyūn jugūn narhūn . ing ilire ba akū . siran siran-i
acara be tuwame ili seme selgiyehe : bai irgen be gajifi fonjici . julgeci ebsi cooha
yabuha jugūn waka : hangsi ci amasi . tojin . meihe . meihe . beten bira de
jalufi . bira duranggi ofi . muke bisakade . jugūn uribufi . niyalma yabuci
ojorakū . ehe sukdun de guweici[28] bucembi : tuttu ofi meni boo be alin-i ninggude
arahabi seme alambi : tuwaci mukei hirgen moo-i subehe de . ašan[29] kemuni
tahabi[30] : jai inenggi jurafi ilihai yamjime . emu juwe maikan arara bade yarume
tatame . ice ilan de ši men k'an-i hūlha be gidaha seme donjiha : ice jakūn de teni
ban dun teng de isinafi tatafi . ši men k'an de cibufi jakūn inenggi indehe : jugūn
de orho sekteme yabu seme selgiyehe : tofohon de jurafi . ser seme bonome agara
jakade . tofohon ba dabagan-i narhūn jugūn be yafaga[31] šaban kūwaitafi[32]
yabume . ši men k'an-i fejile tataha : juwan ninggude ši men k'an-i uju terkin be
micume tafame . kanggarame niolhun[33] . orho sektefi . morin be emke emken-i
ganame arkan seme lifakū ehe babe dulerede . tuwaci gūlakū de morin fuhešefi
labdu bucehebi : niyalmai bethe yooni fukanafi yabuci ojorakū . ilan ba yabufi
farhūn oho : tuheme afame arkan jai k'an-i wehe terkin be dulefi tataha : tuwaci
waha hūlha emke emken-i bi : juwan nadan de yafahan orin ba yabufi . bethe
nimeme . arkan seme ilaci k'an-i terkin e dulefi . morilaci ome selafi . geneme an
lung so de isinafi . tuwaci hūlha dahafi irgen-i hehe juse be hoton-i baru gajime
jimbi : bi teni toktoho ba seme . bakcilaha kūwaran-i da hose-i baru
gisurefi . hoton be dulefi tataha : si lung jeo ci an lung so-i siden ehe jugūn juwe
tanggū orin sunja ba funcembi : juwan jakūn de jurafi . tuwaci ba šehun onco : julergi
meyen be amcame dobori dulime ninju ba yabuha : juwan uyun de indefi selgiyefi
ilan meyen banjiburede . ganduhai . mimbe uju meyen de banjibuha : orin emude
amba jiyanggiyūn kubuhe lamun dobori dulime joboho seme . gajartai[34] nikan emke
bufi . juwe inengg dokolome jakūnju ba yabuha : orin ilande ma biye ho bira be
fukiyoo came indehe : hūlha hūwang dzoo ba de ing ilifi . alime gaihabi seme donjiha : orin ninggude fukiyoo šanggafi . uheri nukte de emu nirui emte morin akū
cooha be werifi . cimari gemu uksilefi bira doombi seme selgiyehe : orin nadan de
amba jiyanggiyūn amba cooha be gaifi . bira be doofi . šehūn[35] babe gūsin ba yabufi
hūlhai ing de nikenefi . tuwaci lifakū handu cyse . alin be gaime . keremu ulan arafi
ing ilihabi : ba ambula ehe . afaci ojorakū ofi . uthai cooha be gocika : ging hecen ci
giyamun ilibume jihe icihiyara hafan walda se isinjifi . dergici . hafan coohai sain be
fonjiha . amba jiyanggiyūn geren be gaifi . aniya doroi hengkilehe : orin jakūn de ma
biye ho bira be doofi . sunja ba yabufi ing ilifi . yooni uksilehei jucelehe : orin
uyunde amba jiyanggiyūn amba cooha be gaifi . faidafi ibeme . alin bigan be sektefi . orin sunja ba yabufi . afara arame . hūlhai ing be fehufi kimcime tuwaci cin-i
dere be afaci ojorakū : fiyanjilafi akdulame bakcilame ing iliha :
  juwe biyai ice de . uheri cooha be baksan baksan jergi jergi faidabufi . ibefi
afara babe toktobume tuwaha : musei coohai hūsun ambula etuhun : ice juwe de

amba jiyanggiyūn. ing be tuwakiyara duin tanggū manju cooha. emu minggan niowanggiyan tu cooha be yarkiyabume. cin-i dere de bakcilabufi. šakšaha meyen de hebei amban ehene. maci. uju meyen de hebei amban hife. hungsilu. herbu. meiren-i janggin masitai. ujen coohai dzu jy cun. jai meyen de gūsai ejen lebei. ujen coohai joo liyan sede cooha be afabufi. niowanggiyan tu be juleri. manju cooha be amala duin ursu faidabufi. kalka gida jafabufi. hūlhai ing ni amargi narhūn alin-i jugūn be gaime iberede. gaitai talman talmafi hanci niyalma be ishunde saburakū: alin-i angga de hūlha belhehekū. musei cooha dosifi. poo jilgan be lakcarakū donjimbi: musei gamaha kalka be waliyahangge jugūn de hiyahahabi[36]: bi tu be gaifi feksime genefi. alin-i anggai dolo dosifi. tuwaci hūlha ingci tucifi. hiyagan[37]. kalka. sufan be faidafi. musei niowanggiyan tu baru afambi: poo miyoocan-i jilgan turi tashara[38] adali. na durgembi: musei niowanggiyan tu šahūri feye bahafi. emu jergi aššafi tomsoho. musei uju meyen. šaksiha[39] meyen kaicame dosirede. na ujelere gese. hūlha alime muterakū. gidabufi burulara de. bi tu be gaifi. wame alin-i ing de nikename. ing-ni hūlha keremu sangga ci miyoocan sindambi: ebšeme alin ci wasifi. moringga hūlha be sunja ba fungeme bošome waha: cooha be bargiyafi bederere de. tuwaci giran hetu undu bigan de sektefi. senggi nade eyembi: ing de poo miyoocan agūra hajun ehe sain jaka be hiyahame waliyahabi: sufan sunja baha: jafaha hūlhai jiyanggiyūn wang io gung. jan yang de fonjici. hūlhai holo jiyanggiyūn ho gi dzu. wang hūng siyūn. joo ioi. wang hūng gioi. bakišeng jang-guwang siyan. lio ši jen meni uyūn[40] nofi. uheri juwe tumen isire hūlha be gaifi. kioi jing fu. loo ping jeo-i oyonggo jugūn-i hūwang dzoo ba be tuwakiyame bihe seme alambi: ice ilan de indefi. janggin cooha be forgošome meyen ban-jibure de. ganduhai kemuni mimbe uju meyen de bibuhe: ice duide dehi ba yabufi. dobori tataha: ice sunja de dehi ba yabufi. hūwang ni ho bira be dooha: ice ninggude dabagan dabame. dobori dulime gūsin ba yabuha: ice nadan de amba yūn nan po dabagan be yafagan[41] tafarade. amba edun dame. yonggan buraki de yasa sokime[42] yabuci ojorakū. gūsin ba yabufi. dobori farhūn talman talmaka: ice jakūn de amba edun dame: buraki de yasa neici ojorakū: i dzo hiyan be duleme ninju sunja ba yabuha: ice uyun de gūsin ba yabufi. hūwang ho san de ilifi. kioi jing. giyoo sui de mejige gaime. gūsa de emu janggin. orin uksin be tucibu seme selgiyehe: ganduhai mimbe tucibuhe: juwan de bi uksin sabe gaifi. feksime tanggū ba funceme yabufi. yuwai jeo de isinafi. tuwaci hūlha akū. kioi jing kiyoo ci bederehe: juwan emude kioi jing giyūn min fu-i jyfu coo gui minggan funcere hūlha be gaifi dahaha: amba jiyanggiyūn cooha be gaifi. kioi jing be duleme. orin ba yabufi tatafi. giyoo sui jeo. yūn nan. gui jeo. sycuwan-i jugūn hafunjiha oyonggo hoton seme. dobori meni uju meyen-i cooha be unggihe: orin sunja ba yabufi. giyoo sui de isinaci. hūlha aifini burulahabi: hoton-i dzang de sunja tumen hule bele bi: bele gaime ilan inenggi indehe gui jeo jangtai beisei cooha isinjiha: amba jiyanggiyūn meyen forgošome banjibu. duici ging-ni erinde yūn nan be gaime jurambi seme selgiyehe: ganduhai mimbe jai meyen banjibuha: tofohon-i dobon dulin de jurafi. ma lung jeo ba[43] duleme. jakūnju ba yabuha: beise-i bayara kaidu moringga amcanjiha: juwan

uyun de hahilame i lung ba[44] dulefi. guwan so ling-ni dabagan ba[45] dabame
emu tanggū orin ba yabufi. yang lin de isinjiha: donjici hūlha šang ban kiyoo de
ing iliha bi sembi: juwan nadan de amba jiyanggiyūn ilan meyen-i cooha be
uksilebufi faidafi. ibeme gūsin ba yabufi. šang ban kiyoo de isinafi tuwaci. hūlha
ing be waliyafi burulahabi: juwan jakūn de kalka ara. niowanggiyan tu isinjiha
manggi. hoton be afambi seme selgiyehe: juwan uyun de amba jiyanggiyūn ilan
meyen-i amba cooha. beise-i cooha be gaifi. elhe ibeme orin ba yabufi. gui hūwa
sy alin de wesifi. cooha be faidabufi. tuwaci hoton akdun afaci ojorakū: cooha be
gocifi bedereme. hoton ci nadan bai dubede. alirame ing ilifi. dobori dulime
keremu ulan weile seme selgiyefi: bi jalan-i cooha begaifi. dobori keremu
sahame. ulan fetehe: guwangsi goloi nan ning fu. yūn nan-i hoton-i siden juwe
minggan tofohon ba funcembi: orin emude hūlha dobori yūn nan-i hoton ci tucifi
afanjiha be. amba jiyanggiyūn uheri amba cooha be gaifi: okdome ingci tucifi
faidabufi ibeme. afara babe tuwafi. šaksiha[46] meyen be ing be fiyanjilabuha:
uju meyen-i cooha be šaksilame[47] dosi seme joriha: niowanggiyan tu-i cooha
be juleri. jai meyen cooha amala cin-i dere be dosi seme joriha: uju meyen
elemangga hūlhai uncehen be meitame[48]. hoton-i baru untuhun be baime
dosika: musei niowanggiyan tu. hūlhai baru afame. poo miyoocan-i jilgan tur
seme lakcarakū. šan ureme ambula goidaha: hūlha emu dulin aššafi. jai emu udu
kuren aššarakū teng seme bucetei afambi: meni jai meyen-i cooha yooni aššaha
bata be gidame dosika: hebei amban hife. kubuhe fulgiyan. musei gūsa be
hūlafi. tere aššara unde udu kuren-i kiyoo gašan be ejelehe bata be gida seme
joriha: meni juwe gūsa kaicame afame dosifi. poo. cu niru. paiciyang de hami-
rakū: efujehe fu-i dalda de. juwe gūsa emu bade fumerefi bisirede. bi emhun
birai dalin de ilifi. tuwaci musei cooha niyalma emdubei feye bahambi: hife
niyalma takūrafi. yafahan dosi seme jing sirdan jafara burgin de. hūlhai
amargi baksan sumburšambi: bi uthai tu be gaifi. bira be doofi. hūlhai amargi be
sundalame dosirede. hūlha burulaha. bi amcanafi. geren hūlha de daha
serede. gemu niyakūrafi. agūra waliyafi. ergen be guwebu sembi: bayara emu
hūlha be gabtara de. gemu ilifi sujuhe: juwe hūlha. waliyaha jangkū be
gaifi. buceki seme sacime dosinjiha. bi ekšeme morin be dabkiyame[49] šusi-
šame[50]. den ekcin de tafaha: amasi tuwaci uksin dengse ekcin be tafame muterakū , hūlha amcame jifi sacirede. dengse golofi beye haidarara jakade. sirdan
jebele. morin-i karhama sacibuha: dengse tuheke: bi tere hūlha be gabtame
tuhebuhe: geli emu hūlha be we waha be sarkū: tuwaci dengse hūwangiya-
hakūbi. ebšeme mini tu be gaifi. bošome wame hoton dade isinafi tuwaci. hūlha
hoton dade jursu fik seme faidafi belhehebi: hoton-i ningguci poo
sindambi: cooha bargiyara buren-i jilgan be donjime. musei cooha uthai yooni
amasi bederehe: jafaha hūlha de fonjici. fudaraka hūlhai holo wang. u ši fan juwe
tumen isire hūlha. sunja sufan. holo jiyanggiyūn hū guwe bing. lio ki
lung. hūwang ming sede afabufi afanjiha seme alambi: orin juwe de gui
hūwa sy de ibefi. hontoho cooha be fiyanjilabufi. hontoho cooha be gaifi
hoton be kara ulan keremu weilerede bi genehe: ulan keremu šanggafi
ing gurifi. afara wan ara seme selgiyehe: orin ninggude wan arafi. dobori

dulime ing-ni keremu sahaha : orin nadan de amba jiyanggiyūn musei coohai gajiha . irgen-i hehe juse be gemu sinda seme selgiyehe : beise cooha be gaifi yūn nan de isinjiha

ilan biyai ice ilade . hoton be akūmbume kara ulan feteme deribuhe : bi ineggidari genehe : hūlhai holo jiyanggiyūn emke . jai musei afarade meitebuhe bayara . uksin . kutule juwe tanggū baime jihe : jiyanggiyūn ambasa yūn nan-i babe tabcilaki seme . ilan inenggi hebešefi . beise jangtai . dzungdu dzai ioi žung . tidu sangge ojorakū ofi nakaha : juwan de beise-i emgi kara ba be dendefi . ulan fetehe : orin sunja de hūlhai holo da jiyanggiyūn ma boo . ping yuwai fu be tuwa sindafi : ini hehe juse be durifi gamaha : gūsin de hoton be kara keremu ulan šanggafi . geli ing gurihe : irgen-i boo be efulefi . boo aranuha : ba dendefi . ing-ni ulan keremu weilehe :

duin biyai ice sunjade . poo tai sahaha : ice nadan de bi harkasi nimeme : julergi be dailara jiyanggiyūn mujan . gui jeo ci emu nirui juwete cooha be gajime yūn nan bade jihe :

sunja biyai ice sunja de . yūn nan-i hoton be kara ulan jursu fetehe : ambarame ahafi[51] ing mukede gaibufi . tatara ba akū : mini beye numere ujen . kutule se gemu nimeme ofi . ujen coohai janggin li de dzan mimbe . inu tatan de gamaha bihe : hūlha ma boo cu hiong fu be gaiha seme donjifi . beise . amba jiyanggiyūn acafi hebešefi . bayara emu nirui ilan . aliha cooha emu nirui ilan . gabsihiyan juwe tanggū . ujen cooha juwe tanggū . uheri be hebei amban hife . meiren-i janggin masitai . araha meiren-i janggin herbu . beise meyen-i meiren-i janggin todai . hūwase sede afabufi . tidu sangge de niowanggiyan tu cooha emu tumen be afabufi . cu hiong ni baru unggihe : orin ilade yūn nan be kara mei hūwa juwang hadahan hadaha . ilan ursu ulan fetehe : beise ini coohai tuwakiyaha ba labdu seme futalafi . komso ojoro jakade . yoktakū ofi . ini niowanggiyan tu cooha sunja ming-gan . manju cooha duin tanggū ba[52] . bi gi guwan-i bade tuwakiyabume ung-gihe : amba jiyanggiyūn juwan nadan de diyan cy hu-i bilten dalirame babe dendefi . yūn nan-i muke jugūn be lashalame keremu ulan weilefi . niowanggiyan tu de afabufi . beise-i manju cooha be gocika :

ninggun biyai ice ninggude . tidu sangge . hūlhai jiyanggiyūn ma boo be ambarame gidaha seme boolaha : beise-i coohai kutule . niowanggiyan tu se guwali-i de šeng kiyoo de mei hūwa juwang hadahan ganame . boo be efuleme genefi . hoton-i hūlha de ilan tanggū fungeme meitebuhe : horibuha irgen jeterengge akū ofi . guwalici baime duin tanggū funcere haha hehe juse jifi . amba jiyanggiyūn jakūn gūsai feyengge cooha niyalma de . hūda salibume buhe : ineku inenggi keremu dorgi de kaicara jilgan be donjifi . bi katunjime[53] ilifi tuwaci . hūl-hai karun alin ci wasifi . musei orho ganaha kutule be jafafi gamahabi : juwan ilan de nartai hiya . beging ci isinjiha . dolo nikan morin baimbi seme . beise . jiyang-giyūn . ambasa gemu juwete ilata cuwan ma morin buhe : dergici . hafan coohai sain be fonjiha : nartai ilan inenggi yūn nan-i šurdeme kaha babe tuwafi genehe : gūsai ejen hife se cuhiong ci cooha be gaifi . coohai morin mohoho seme bederere jakade . beise . amba jiyanggiyūn se jifi banjifi . hife sei marame gid-abuha hūlha ma boo-i cooha be fargarakū tabcilafi bederehe turgunde . wakalame wesimbumbi seme gisurefi . amala nakafi . damu numere morin akū janggin cooha be teile halafi . amasi cuhiong fude unggihe :

nadan biyai juwan de mini beye mangga ofi iliha : hūlha maboo jergi holo jiyanggiyūn sunja . dzung bing juwe dahame jihe be . beging de benehe : juwan emude gui jeo ci bele ciyangliyang be uheri tuwame icihiyara . ashan-i da foron jihe : amba jiyanggiyūn . mimbe beidere jurgan-i jangin sindaha : jakūn gūsai ufaraha uksin-i oron de . etubure be anaha :

jakūn biyai orin duin de . gūsai ejen gargan . sycuwan-i giyan cang fuci . bayara emu nirui juwete . aliha cooha emu nirui juwete . si an fui meiren-i janggin unggai golo cooha juwe tanggū be gaifi . jime yūn nan de isinjiha :

uyun biyai ice ninggude . kutule uksin-i eberi ojorakūngge be baicame nakabufi . nimekulehe edelehe hafan cooha be baicafi . ufaraha janggin coohai giran be . gala de emte janggin . gūsa de sunja uksin be tucibufi . ging hecen-i baru jurambuha : ice uyun de gūsai ejen jihari ufarafi . baturu bodohonggo jiyanggiyūn joo liyang dung se sycuwan-i goloi sui i fuci emu nirui ilata cooha . niowanggiyan tu juwe tumen be gaifi . jime yūn nan de isinjiha : tuwaci cira boco wasifi . yafahan niyalma labdu . fonjici jeterengge akū bime . ehe sukdun de kūwaifi[54] . niyalma morin ambula bucehe nimehe sembi : juwan de amba jiyanggiyūn tuhai šansi ci beging de bederehe : kemungge cin wang-ni guwangsi ci beging de bederehe be donjiha : yūn nan-i hoton-i dorgi hūlha emu juwe-i dahame jiderengge lakcan akū : fonjici hoton-i dorgi yuyume niyalma-i yali jembi sembi : gemu musei coohai urse sain haha juse be sonjome gidame . amba haha be amba jiyanggiyūn de benembi : bele lakcafi . emu hule udarade orin yan bumbi : irgen ambula yuyume bucehe : juwan emu de jalan-i janggin fafuri be kūwaran-i da sindara jakade . mimbe . amba jiyanggiyūn tuwafi . jalan-i janggin sindaha : gūwa habšaci donjiha akū :

juwan biyai juwan de ibefi . hoton ci sunja ba-i hūwang tu po-i emu girin-i alirame . ulan fetefi keremu sahame . bi inenggidari genehe : ulan keremu šanggafi kubuhe fulgiyan . kubuhe lamun-i ing gurifi tuwakiyaha : hūlhai sindaha poo ing de tuhebi dababi : niyalma gemu dalda de boo araha : bi emhun meni meni giyan bi seme šehun bai den bade boo araha : juwan uyun de hebei amban gūsai ejen gargan . maci . lebei . tui janggin ehene . meiren-i janggin hungsilu se hontoho cooha be gaifi . hoton ci ilan bai in ding san alin de ibembi seme selgiyehe : mini beye . janggin šušu . sindai . gelibu . funde bošokū laisu . margi . solho . tanggū cooha be gaifi . yamji ibehe : dobori ulan feterede . bi solho . margi . kelibu be gaifi . šoro ilibufi ulan feteme . niyalma tome bucetei hacihiyambi : hoton-i hūlha poo miyoocan geretele[55] šorgime sindame . muhaliyan juleri amala emdubei tuhebi : musei niyalma . morin poo miyoocan de ambula kokiraha : jai inenggi ulan keremu uthai šanggaha : orin emude niowanggiyan tu-i cooha . ujen coohai janggin . cooha be hūnggi ibebume . musei cooha fiyamjilafi . dobori teni gocika : kubuhe lamun be yen ding san de baita bici . uthai dame gene seme selgiyehe : orin uyun de hūlhai holo jiyanggiyūn siyan ioi . ho jin jung . u guwe ju . hūwang ming . lin tiyan king se hoton be alibume dahafi . holo lio šeo jiyanggiyūn g'u juwang tu . holo wang u ši fan-i uju be alibume jihe : dobori uthai

yūn nan-i hoton-i duka tome meiren-i janggin emte . tui janggin . kūwaran-i da
emte . gūsa tome jalan-i janggin emte . cooha duin tanggū tucibufi uksilefi
tuwakiyabuha : cooha kutule se holtome hoton de dosifi . yuyuhe hehe juse be hūlhame ambula tucibuhe : gelibele hūlhame dosimbufi . suja[56] etuku-i jergi jaka be
ambula hūlašanuha :

omšon biyai ice juwede . u ši fan-i gung-ni hehesi . niocuhe tana . boobai jergi
jaka . ulin nadan . hūlhai jiyanggiyūn-i hehe juse ulin nadan be icihiyame gūsai ejen
jergi mujan . maci . araha coohai jurgan-i galai da kiyata . betei .
hūsibu . jiyehan . lanju . fafuri se tuwame talame . boo se de gemu bayara janggisa
be tuwakiyabuha : juwan emu de jukūn gūsai hafan cooha de gebu arame . ehe sain
sakda hehe buhe : geli buyarame suje etuku-i jergi jaka buhe : orin de suje
buhe : icihiyaha amban . jurgan-i janggisa ferguwecuke ulin . sain hehe
bahanuha : orin duin de narhūn jaka be icihiyame wajifi . meiren-i janggisa be
gocifi . cooha halaburede . bi janggin ilmen be halafi . hoton-i tulergi fiyamji
seme . juwan inenggi bihe : duka be bayara janggin lobi tuwakiyaha : poo-i okto
emu hunio fushufi . hoton-i dergi ilan giyan-i boo . juce-i niyalma juwan baran akū
deyehe : coohai urse . kutule se . dahaha liyoo dung-ni nikan-i anggasi hehe . sargan
juse be holtome sargan gaimbi seme gainufi . hoton ci ambula tucibuhe :

jurgon[57] biyai juwan nadan de . jurgan ci unggihe bithede . hiya . jurgan-i
hafasa . baitangga be neneme unggi : aniya goidaha cooha be gocire be
dahame . dahaha liyoo dung-ni nikasa be sasa gajikini sehebi : orin de hiyasa . jurgan-i hafasa . aniya goidaha cooha juwe tanggū tucibufi . giran be afabufi . beging-
ni baru jurambuha : jiyanggiyūn sa hebe acafi . liyoodung-ni nikan-i anggala sunja
tumen funcembi . gamara de mangga seme . cooha be jakūn meyen banjibuha
de . bi gisurefi . uju meyen oho . aniyai biyai juwan de jurambumbi seme selgiyefi . dahaha hūlhai hafasa geneme muterakū seme habšara jakade nakaha :

elhe taifin-i sahaliyan indahūn orin emuci aniya . aniyai ice inenggi . aniyai
doro . jiyanggiyūn ambasa hafasa . lung deo[58] san de ifasi hengkilehe : ice nadan
de jurgan ci unggihe bithe de . dahaha hūlha de anggala bele . fu ume bure . uthai
coohai sasa gajime jio sehebi : hūlhai golo jiyanggiyūn siyan ioi
se : niocuhe . tana . aisin menggun . seke . cindahan . silun . šanggiyan ulhu-i dahū
kurume . sain morin . loho . jebele-i jergi jaka ambula sime benjifi baire
jakade . jiyanggiyūn sa hebešefi . dahaha hūlhai anggala de fu bele burakū
oci . coohai sasa geneci ojorakū : siyun fu de afabufi . amala isibukini seme
wesimbuhe : yūn nan-i dorgi dahaha hūlha juwan tumen anggala ofi . bele
wajifi . bele emu hule de nadanju yan . turi emu hiyase de ninggun yan . handu
emu hule de gūsin jakūn yan menggun bufi udambi : igan[59] emke de gūsin
yan . ulgiyan emke de orin udu yan . coko niyehe jakūn uyun jiha de emke . niongniyaha juwe yan de emke uncame . yaya jaka gemu hūda wesifi . cooha umesi
mohofi . inenggi durime . dobori hūlharangge der seme dekdefi . hūda-i niyalma
ambula wabuha : amba jiyanggiyūn g'oši bithe arafi . bi niyalma tucibufi durire
hulgara[60] be jafabumbi . nambuci fafan-i gamambi . kadalaha hafasa be ujeleme
weile arambi . meni meni uksin kutule be inenggidari baica seme selgiyehe : jing

facuhūn ofi.juwan duin de gūsa tome jalan-i janggin emte.sula janggin emte.cooha tofohon be adun de unggi seme selgiyehe:tofohon de hebe acahade.ashan-i da foron jeku ciyanliyang hafirahūn seme gisurefi.juwan ninggude beise uju meyen-i cooha be gaifi kioi jing fude genembi seme selgiyefi.mini morisa be ganabufi jurambi serede.hūlha siyan ioi se habšafi.geli nakaha.morin be adun de benebuhe:bi dzungdu dzai ioi žung-ni niowanggiyan tu coohai loosa hūlhaha baita be beidehe:orin juwede beging de wesimbume feksihe.gulu suwayan-i gocika hiya udacan se bederefi.dele ambula urgunjembi.damu ebšeme ambasa be acaki sembi seme.sain hese wasimbuha seme alaha:beise jangtai.jiyanggiyūn laita sasa juraki seme gisureme toktofi.meni morisa be selgiyefi ganabuha:siyan ioi se habšara jakade.geli jurara be nakafi.morin be adun de unggihe:geren gemu toktohon akū seme gasaha:orin nadan de hebe acafi.beise be uju meyen be gaifi.ice ninggude jura.dahaha hūlha de ninggun meyen de dendefi gamame.gemu jurambuha manggi.amba jiyanggiyūn jakūci meyen be gaifi.jurambi seme selgiyehe:donjici beise be geli goci.laita mini beye uthai uju meyen be gaifi.jurambi seme girubuha sembi :

juwe biyai ice ninggun de.beise.galai amban šangnaha.sakca.gūsai ejen sijiyaboo.meiren-i janggin hungsilu.dzu jy cun.lu cung giyūn.gung wehe.bayara aliha cooha gemu emu nirui emte be gaifi juraka.bi aciha be dasatafi.gūsin isire morin be ilibufi.urgunjeme beise-i sasa yūn nan ci jurafi.šang ban kiyoo de tataha:tuwaci coohai gajiha hehe juse udu minggan bi:yang lin.i lung.ma lung be dulefi.juwan de ajige guwan so ling dabagan de kungming.guwan so-i miyoo be tuwaha:kioi jing fu be dulefi.juwan juwe de giyoo sui jeo de bele gaiha:be sui i be dulefi.tofohonde ping i wei de bono aga be ucaraha:i dzi kung be dulefi.juwan jakūnde giyang si po.dui miyan po-i ehe babe tulefi.pu an jeo de ba siyan dung be tuwaka:san ban po.lo han sung po be wesime wasime.orin de sin hing so de orin inenggi orho liyoo-i menggun be gaiha:orin emude narsai.duhen nimeme tutaha.bi gūsa be gaifi.an nan wei be dulefi.orin juwe de liyan yūn ceng-ni lo sui giyang-ni sele futai kiyoo efujefi.fukiyoo be doofi.tuwaci muke gocicibe haksan eyen turgen.jetere muke akū ofi.tanggū be yabufi ting dzan de tataha:be geo ling.siyang bi ling dabagan be dulefi.orin juwede den nadan ba-i guwan so ling dabagan de yafahan tafafi.morilafi gi gung bei be dulefi.orin sunja de an šun fude isinjifi.ilan inenggi indehe:orin uyun de ser sere aga de jurafi.bayara be beise gaifi gui jeo de morin ulebumbi:aliha cooha be.ujen coohai gūsai ejen sijiyaboo.gung wehe gaifi.ping ba wei de ulebumbi seme.wei de isinafi boo dendefi.orin inenggi orin sunja morin-i orho liyoo gaifi morin ulebuhe:bi inenggidari tanggilame ališara be tokobuha:yūn nan.gui jeo-i siden emu minggan jakūn tanggū ba funcembi:jugūn haksan hafirahūn.alin dabagan labdu:irgen komso :

ilan biyai orin de.an šun fude tehe.musei ujun coohai meiren-i janggin lio hiyan jung.janggin hada.gūsin sunja cooha be gajime.ping ba wei de meni cooha de kamcime jihe:si an.mukden-i goloi cooha be facuhūn seme manju gūsa de kamcibuha:orin juwede ping ba wei ci jurafi.ping i so.wei cing wei be dulefi.orin duin de gui yang fude isinafi.emu inenggi indehe:gui jeo-i babe

tuwaci hafirahūn bime . irgen komso . miyoose tusy labdu . tacin umesi oshon
ehe : orin ninggude jurafi . lung li wei . sin tiyan wei be dulefi[61] :

duin biyai ice ilade . ping yuwai fude isinafi . jang san fung-ni miyoo be
tuwaha : ice sunja de cing ping hiyan-i alin-i holo de tatafi . dobori gaitai amba aga
hungkereme agafi . alin-i muke wasinjifi . maikan be dobgiya gese muke
birefi . mini etuku . bele . jibehun sisehe gemu muke ci sekiyeme gaifi . usihiyere
jakade . juwe inenggi indefi . tuwa de walgiyame olhobuha : ice jakūn de cung an
giyan be doofi . hing lung wei de . fei yūn dung be tuwaha : ice uyun de piyan
kiyoo de isinafi . hūguwang-ni jecen de dosika : morin de tagan[62] belhehekū
ofi . dohošome juwan emude jen yuwan fude isinafi . juwe inenggi indehe : juwan
ilade cen ho birai fukiyaoo be doofi . cing lang wei . ping ki wei . hūwang jeo be
dulefi . orin de ineku cen ho-i fu kiyoo be doofi . orin emude biyan sui i be
dulefi . geli cen ho birai fu kiyoo be dooha : orin juwe de yuwan jeo fude isinjifi . juwan inenggi indehe : morin-i wagan[63] wehe de nijarabufi jakanafi . niyaki
tucime ambula waliyaha : gui jeo . hūnan-i yuwan jeo-i siden . nadan tanggū dehi
funcere ba bi . lifakū bime . wehe jugūn hon ehe :

sunja biyai ice ilade . beise jakūn gūsa de . juwe tanggū cuwan dendeme
bufi . olhon de genere hontoho cooha . cuwan bahara niyalma muke be genekini
seme selgiyehe : beise . boo niru . ambasa cuwan eleme gaifi turime . janggin cooha
ambula cuwan turifi muke be juraka : araha gabsihiyan-i galai amban sakca . ujen
coohai meiren-i janggin dzu jy cun . lio hiyan jung olhon de . uheri be kadalame . ice
nadan de jurambi seme selgiyehe : ice sunja de . bi ilan cuwan baifi . cuwan giyan be
jurafi . wasihūn muke eyen turgen . cuwan geri geršeme[64] . deyere gese ilan tanggū
babe yabufi iliha : ice ninggude inu ilan tanggū ba yabufi . kiyan yang hiyan be
dulefi . po ši sere amba gašan de ilifi . lung cuwan-i efire be tuwaha : ice nadan de
mukei eyen hahi . tan bi seme sengguweme . emu tanggū orin babe yabufi . cen jeo
de iliha : ice jakūn de emu tanggū jakūnju ba yabufi iliha : tuwaci alin-i fiyeleku
hada den dehi da funcembi : monio efime . hadai fiyeleku de irgen moo sisime
giyaselame araha boo . cibin-i feye adali sabumbi : ice uyun de emu tanggū jakūnju
ba yabufi . cang de fude isinjifi . cuwan halame ilan inenggi indehe : bi ubu-i cuwan
gaiha akū : juwan ilan de jurafi . nio pi tan . lao hū tan . cing lang tan-i jergi gelecuke
tan de . mukei boljon calgime . cuwan de muke dosime . cuwan haidarafi yabume
arkan dulembi : tofohon de jan mao ma gin hū be dulefi . wesihun mukei birai angga
de iliha : juwan nadan de seng ši amba jen-i gašan be dulefi . kiyan fuda[65] cuwan be
ušame . orin de ijishūn edun be bahafi . pen tatafi ging jeo fu-i hū du keo de
iliha : orin emude ging jeo-i gūwali-i siyoo giya wan de iliha : tuwaci musei coohai
boo musei coohai tatan . manju booi adali uce fa sindahabi : orin juwe de dzoo ši de
boo dendefi tehe : booci hadafun . sandari okdoho . mancang be takūrafi ama eniyei
elhe be fonjime unggihe : ging jeo . yuwan jeo-i siden muke hahi bime . hargi . turgen . ambula sengguwecuke : wasihūn muke eme minggan ninggun tanggū susai ba
funcembi : inenggidari efime sain jaka jeme . damu boode genembi seme urgun-
jembi :

ninggun biyai orin de ashan-i da foron . wesimbufi . coohai edelehe juwan ilan
biyai ciyanliyang . duin biyai orho liyoo be faitaha turgunde jakūn gūsai

gabsihiyan bayara. aliha cooha gemu beise de habšaha: orin ninggude gūsai ejen mujan jai meyen-i cooha. hūlhai hehe juse be werifi. hūlhai hafan be teile be gaifi. gingjeo fude isinjiha: orin jakūn de giyang-ni muke biltefi. hūwang tan dalan efujefi. giyang ling. miyang yang. ciyang giyang ilan hiyan-i ba. tanggū ba onco. ninggun tanggū ba golmin. muke be birebufi. dzoo ši gašan yooni muke de gaibuha: bi jidere muke be den bade genefi tuwaci hūwanggar seme. alin-i gese den mukdefi. ilan da den ajige dalan be dartai birefi. meni tehe boo gemu mukede gaibuhabi: kubuhe lamun gemu cuwan jafafi. aciha tebufi. tehe boo mukede gaibuha turgun be beise de alafi. amargi guwali-i loosa turire diyan-i irgen-i boo be gaifi gurifi tataha:

nadan biyai ice juwe de. amba jiyanggiyūn laita. jakūci meyen-i cooha. gūsai ejen hife sei ilaci meyen-i cooha. hūlhai hafan be gaifi gingjeo de isinjifi. guwangsi meyen-i cooha be ša ši de bargiyafi boo gaire de. beise burakū ofi. cooha gemu maikan arafi. menggun tucibufi boo aranuha: bi inu boo araha: orin duide tui janggin ehene-i ilaci meyen. gūsai ejen lasai-i duici meyen-i cooha isinjifi. musei wang-ni baita-i turgunde. lasai. ehene. masitai. lio hiyan jung se gūsai janggisa be isabufi. boro-i sorson be gaifi. ilan inenggi gasame dobori duliha: orin nadan de muke olhon-i hafan cooha be cihangga be tuwame tuciburede. bi olhon be genembi seme anggalafi tucike:

jakūn biyai ice juwe de gūsai ejen gargan sei sunja ci meyen-i cooha isinjiha: juwan de tui janggin syge-i ningguci meyen-i cooha isinjiha: orin-i dobori edelehe orho liyoo-i baharakū jalin. amba jiyanggiyūn-i tataha boo be. toome[66] giye tiye bithe arafi. sirdan de hūwaitafi gabtaha: musei coohai urse dahaha hūlhai jiyanggiyūn ho jin jung-ni tatan be gidanafi umai jaka baha akū. elemangga koro baha: orin jakūn de olhon be emu nirui ilata bayara. ilata aliha cooha genembi muke be emu nirui duite bayara. nadanta aliha cooha amala genembi: muke olhon be generengge gūnin cihangga sonjokini seme selgiyehe: orin uyūn de amba jiyanggiyūn. geren kūwaran-i da. janggisa be gaifi. jakūn igan[67] be wafi. boihon mutubume araha terkin de dobofi. tu de hengkileme burdeme wecefi. yali be umbuha: cooha jurafi susai ba yabufi. wang sy po de ing iliha:

uyun biyai ice de. nadanju ba yabufi. lung bei sere kiyoo de ing iliha: ice juwe de ninju ba yabufi ging men jeo de iliha: (ging men jeo julgei nan giyūn)[68]. ice ilade ši kiyoo i be dulefi. jakūnju ba yabufi ing iliha: ice duide li i be dulefi. jakūnju ba yabufi ing iliha: amba jiyanggiyūn. siyang yang giyang de. cuwan dendebume coohai jurgan-i janggin sabe unggirede. mimbe tucibuhe: tere dobori jurafi. susai ba yabufi. i ceng hiyan-i diyan fang de tataha: ice sunja de. duici ging de jurafi. emu tanggū orin ba yabufi. siyang yang fude isinjifi. hiowande-i dilu morin-i fekuhe tan-i bira be tuwaci fahabi. wehe be morin–i wahan forofi ejehebi: giyang-ni dalin de jifi. bai hafan de cuwan be baicame gaifi. beise meyen de orin ilan cuwan. amba jiyanggiyūn meyen de orin juwe cuwan dendefi. mini morin. aciha be cuwan de tebufi doofi. fan ceng-ni hoton-i dolo boo baifi tataha: jai inenggi amba cooha isinjifi. juwe inenggi dooha: ice jakūn de jurafi lioi yang i be duleme. jakūnju ba yabufi iliha: ereci

julesi gurgu elgiyen : ice uyun de sin ye hiyan be duleme. uyunju ba yabufi ing
iliha : juwan de wa diyan be duleme. nadanju ba yabufi nan yang fude ing
iliha : kungming-ni susu o lung k'ang de genefi. tuwaci alin ajige alarame ba
necin. jug'oliyang-ni miyoo de. boihon-i oren arahabi : ambasa cooha geme
hengkilehe. menggun buhe : bi hengkilefi bei bithe be tuwaha : juwan emu de
nadanju ba yadufi bo wang i de ing iliha : gūlmahūn ulhūma elgiyen coohai urse
balai niyamniyara de. juwan funceme uksin kutule gabtabuha. juwe uksin
bucehe : be baidefi[69] beye hūda bubuhe : emu inenggi ududu morin
gabtabumbi : mini dolo geleme gūnime. bi juwan aniya afame yabufi funcehe
ergen. dain de gaibuhakū. ere niyamniyame bahanarakū coohai urse de guweke
seme olhošome. juwan juwede jakūnju ba yabufi. ioi jeo de ing iliha : juwan ilan
de jakūnju sunja ba yabufi. boo an i be dulefi ing iliha : juwan duin de hūwang ho
bira de cuwan dendeme. coohai jurgan-i janggin be unggirede. bi boo be ele
kidume ofi. amba jiyanggiyūn de anggalafi genehe : yei hiyan be duleme. uyunju
ba yabufi. diyan fang de tataha. tofohonde siyang ceng hiyan-i ši gu jen be
duleme. emu tanggū dehi ba yabufi. irgen-i boode tataha : juwan ninggude sin
jeng hiyan. k'o diyan i be duleme. jakūnju ba yabufi. diyan fang de tataha : juwan
nadan de jeng jeo. hingje hiyan be duleme. nadanju ba yabufi. hūwang ho birai
dalin de isinafi. maikan arafi tataha : tuwaci birai muke fafi isheliyan. eyen udu
turgen seme. ambula olhocuka ba akū : bai hafan de cuwan be baicame
gaifi. juwan jakūn de. beise meyen de morin-i cuwan dehi ninggun. amba jiyanggiyūn-i meyen de. morin-i cuwan dehi duin dendefi. mini aciha morin be. cuwan
de tebufi doofi. hūwang ho-i cargi dalin de maikan arafi tataha : juwan uyūnde[70]
amba cooha isinjifi. hūwang ho bira be jurcenjeme doome. dartai wajifi. orin
sunja ba yabufi ing iliha : orin de jakūnju sunja ba yabufi. sin hiyang hiyan de ing
iliha : booci mancang. gurbu jetere jaka gajime okdoko : bi dobori amgaci ojorakū
booi baita be fonjiha : orin emude ninju ba yabufi. wei hūi fude ing iliha : orin
juwe de ki hiyan be duleme. jakūnju sunja ba yabufi. jeo gurun-i cenghiyang bi
g'an-i eifu be tuwanafi. miyoo-i boigon-i oren de hengkilefi. ing iliha : orin ilade
i kio i be duleme ninju sunja ba yabufi. teng in hiyan de ing iliha : orin duide
muke akū seme. dehi ba yabufi. jang de fude ing iliha : orin sunjade nadanju ba
yabufi. tsi jeo de ing iliha : bi amba jiyanggiyūn-i kuwaran be ilibuha : orin ninggun de nadanju ba yabufi. han dan hiyan de ing iliha : orin nadan de nadanju ba
yabufi. da liyang diyan de ing iliha : orin jakūn de dehi ba yabufi šun de fude ing
iliha : orin uyun de dehi sunja ba yabufi. fiyanggū gung be acafi. susai ba yabufi
in dzun de iliha : dergici. beise de gocika morin juwe. amba jiyanggiyūn de gocika
morin juwe. mujan. gargan. hife sede morin emte. uheri janggin. cooha de amba
adun-i morin ilan tanggū. temen gūsin okdoko : gemu morin akū niyalma de. hūsun
gaisu seme. mini beye dobori dulime baicafi. dendeme jakūn gūsa de buhe :

juwan biyai ice de. uyunju ba yabufi. joo jeo de ing iliha : ice juwe de po to ho
bira be doome. jakūnju ba yabufi ing iliha : ice ilan de ninju ba yabufi. fu ceng i
de ing iliha : ice duin de ninju ba yabufi. ming yuwei diyan de ing iliha : bi amba
jiyanggiyūn-i kūwaran be tuwame ilibuha : ice sunja de uyūnju[71] ba yabufi king
du hiyan de ing iliha : ice ninggun de uyūnju ba yabufi boo ding fude ing iliha : ice

nadan de susai ba yabufi . an so hiyan de ing iliha : ice jakūn de nadanju ba yabufi . ding hing hiyan de ing iliha : ice uyūn de bi amba jiyanggiyūn de alafi . tanggū ba yabufi . lio li ho-i tokso de genefi indehe : jai inenggi dobori amba age okdome jifi . acafi . bi age de hengkilefi tebeliyefi songgoho : kiduha jongko be gisureme gerembuhe : juwan emu de . amba cooha isinjifi gūsin sunja ba yabufi . liyang hiyang hiyan de ing iliha . juwan juwe de . ging hecen ci han-i beye . ujulaha ambasa be gaifi . amba jiyanggiyūn . ambasa . janggin cooha be cang sin diyan-i šehūn bade . cacari cafi okdofi . tu be faidafi . burdeme tu de hengkilefi . jiyanggiyūn cooha be hengkileme acabuha . cai omibuha : geren kesi de hengkilehe : bi lu keo kiyoo de genefi . ama de hengkileme acaha : duici deo-i baita be donjifi . songgome yafan de derifi . hoton de dosifi . songgome boo de dosika . eniye sede hengkileme acaha : juse deote be acaci takarakū ohobi : tuwaci ging hecen-i boo nagan ele encu ofi . uthai buru bara tolhin-i[72] adali : ele gūnici dasame banjiha beye seme ferguwehe : ai damu niongniyaha feniyen emke fakcaha seme kidume nasame . gūniha seme wajirakū : ere kemuni tolhin[73] wakao semeo :

ere dzengšeo mini juwan aniya . dain de faššame yabuha . yargiyan baita be ejehengge : cooha de yabuha be ejehe bithe duici debtelin

APPENDIX

Military ranks used in the translation

Manchu	Chinese	English
amba jiyanggiyūn	da jiangjun 大將軍	Field Marshal
bayarai jalan-i	hujun canling 護軍參領	Colonel of the Guards
janggin(bayarai)	hujun tongling 護軍統領	Major-general,
tui janggin		Commandant of the Guards
bošokū	lingcui 領催	Corporal
funde bošokū	xiaoqixiao 驍騎校	Lieutenant
galai amban	qianfeng tongling 前鋒統領	Commandant of the Vanguard
galai da	yi zhang 翼長	Brigadier
gūsai ejen	dutong 都統	Lieutenant-general (Commander of a Banner)
jalan-i janggin	canling 參領	Colonel
jiyanggiyūn	jiangjun 將軍	General
kūwaran-i da	yingzong 營總	Camp Commander
meiren-i janggin	fu dutong 副都统	Brigadier-general (Deputy Commander of a Banner)

GLOSSARY

This glossary includes only Chinese personal names, place name, and words mentioned in the Introduction and in the Translation whose characters could be identified. To facilitate the task of identifying some of the Manchu names, I have also introduced the Chinese characters commonly used to transcribe them, when known.

Ajige	阿濟格	Changsha	長沙
Anlongsuo	安籠所	Changxindian	長辛店
Annanwei	安南衛	Chengxiang Bigan	承相比干
Anshun	安順	Chenhe	辰河
Ansu	安肅	Chenzhou	辰州
		Chongqing	重慶
Ba Qisheng	巴啓生	chuanma	川馬
Baishuiyi	白水驛	Chuxiong (fu)	楚雄府
Bandunteng	班敦騰	Cizhou	磁州
Bao'anyi	保安驛		
Baodingfu	保定府	Daliandian	褡褳店
Baoning	保寧	daoyangge	蹈秧歌
Baqi	八旗	Desheng	德勝
Batu	八渡	Dianchi	滇池
Biansuiyi	邊綏驛	dilu	的盧
Biji	碧雞	Ding nan wang	定南王
Binzhou	賓州	Dingxing	定興
Bo Wenxuan	白文選	Dodo	多鐸
Bogouling	波溝嶺	Dongyue	東岳
Bosa	伯撒 伯撒	Dorgon	多爾袞
Bowangyi	博望驛	Duimianpo	對面坡
Cai Yurong	蔡毓榮	Ecu	額楚
Cao Shenji	曹申吉		
Caoshi	草市	Fan Qihan	范齊韓
Changde	常德	Fancheng	樊城

106

Feiyun	飛云	Hudukou	虎渡口
Fiyanggū	費揚古	*hujunying*	護軍營
Fu Honglie	傅弘烈	*huoqiying*	火器營
Fuchengyi	福城驛	Hūwase	花色
Fulin	福臨	*jalan*	扎攔 or 甲喇
Geng Jimao	耿精忠	Jangtai	彰泰
Geng Jingzhong	耿精忠	Jelken	哲爾肯
Geng Zhongming	耿仲明	*jia*	家
Giyešu	傑書	Jianchang	建昌
Gong Weihei	公委黑	Jiangkou	江口
Guandi	關帝	Jiangling	江陵
Guangxi	廣西	Jiangxipo	江西坡
Guansuo	關所	Jianzhou	建州
Guansuoling	關索嶺	Jiaoshui (zhou)	交水州
Guihuasi	歸化寺	*jie*	街
Guilin	桂林	Jiezhou	階州
Guiluo	貴羅	Jigongbei	雞公背
Guiyang	貴陽	Jin	金
Guizhou	貴州	Jin Guangzu	金光祖
Guodianyi	郭店驛	Jincheng Temple	金城寺
Haicheng	海澄	Jingnan wang	靖南王
Han Daren	韓大任	Jingzhou	荊州
Handan	邯鄲	Jinhua	金華
Hanjun	漢軍	Jinmen zhou	荊門州
Hanzhong	漢中	Jirgalang	濟爾哈朗
He Jinzhong	何進忠	Kangxi	康熙
He Jizu	何繼祖	Kong Sizhen	孔四真
Hife	希福 (?)	Kong Youde	孔有德
Hong Chengchou	洪承疇	Kongming	孔明
Hong Shilu	宏世祿	Kunlun	昆侖
Hong Taiji	洪太極 or 黃台吉	Kunming	昆明
Hu Guobing	胡國柄	Laibin	來賓
Hu Guozhu	胡國柱	Laita	賴塔
Huang Ming	黃明	Lebei	勒貝
Huangcaoba	黃草壩	*li*	里
Huangni	黃泥	Li	里
Huangtan	黃潭	Li Benshen	李本深
Huangtu	黃土	Li Bu	吏部
Huangzhou	晃州	Li Chaogui	李朝貴
Huangzhu	黃柱	Li Dezan	李德贊

Li Dingguo	李定國	Nabiao	那標
Li Fan Yuan	理番院	Nanjun	南郡
Li Zicheng	李自成	Nanning	南寧
Liangxiang	良鄉	Nanyang	南陽
Lianyuncheng	連云城	Ningyuan	寧遠
Liaodong	遼東	Nurhaci	努爾哈赤
Lin Tianqing	林天擎	Pengcun	朋春
Liu Bei	劉備	Pingbawei	平壩衛
Liu Qilong	劉起龍	Pingnan Wang	平南王
Liu Shizhen	劉世真	Pingqiwei	平溪衛
Liu Xianzhong	劉賢忠	Pingxi dajiangjun	平西大將軍
Liu Yanming	劉延明	Pingxi wang	平西王
Liuli	琉璃	Pingyisuo	平義所
Liuyang	瀏陽	Pingyiwei	平夷衛
Liuzhou (fu)	柳州府	Pingyuanfu	平遠府
Liyi	麗驛	Pingyue	平越
Longchuan jie	龍船節	Poshi	坡石
Longliwei	龍里衛	Potuo	坡沱
Longtou	龍頭	Pu'anzhou	普安州
Longtuguan	龍圖關	Qi	淇
Loping	羅平	*qianfengying*	前鋒營
Lu Chongjun	盧崇軍	Qianjiang	潛江
Lugou	盧溝	Qianyang	黔陽
Luohangsong	羅漢松	Qingdu	慶都
Luorong	雒容	Qinglangwei	清浪衛
Lushui	瀘水	Qingming	清明
Ma Bao	馬寶	Qingping	清平
Ma Chenglie	馬承烈	*qinjunying*	親軍營
Ma Chengyin	馬承廕	Qinwang	亲王
Mabie	馬別	Qujing (fu)	曲靖府
Maci	馬齊	Rao Yilong	饒一龍
Malongzhou	馬龍	Raozhou	饒州
mang	莽	*San Guo zhi yanyi*	三國志演義
Manggitu	莽依圖	Sanban	三板
Masitai	馬錫泰	Sanfan	三藩
Mianyang	沔陽	Sengshi	僧石
Mingyuedian	明月店	Shamao	紗帽
Mujan	穆占	Shang Kexi	尚可喜
Muwang	姆王	Shang Zhixin	尚之信

108

Shangban	尚板	Wu Shifan	吳世璠
Shanhaiguan	山海关	Wu Yingqi	吳應麒
Shashi	沙市	Wu Yingxiong	吳應熊
Shiguzhen	石固鎮	Wuxuan	武宣
Shimen	石門	Wuyuan	武緣
Shun	順	Xi Jiabao	錫嘉寶
Shunde	順德	Xia Guoxiang	夏國相
Shunzhi	順治	Xiamen	廈門
Sige	斯格	Xian xing zeli	現行則例
Songgotu	索額圖	Xian Yu	腺紆
Suiyi	綏義	Xiangbiling	象鼻嶺
Sun Kewang	孫可望	Xiangcheng	襄城
Sun Sike	孫思克	Xiangyang	襄陽
Sun Yanling	孫延齡	Xiangzhou	象州
Šušu	舒恕	Xiaojia	肖家
Taiping	太平	xiaoqiying	驍騎營
Tangyin	湯陰	Xilongzhou	西龍州
Tanxi	檀溪	Xinglongwei	興龍衛
Taodeng	陶登	Xingning	興寧
Taotun	陶屯	Xingze	滎澤
Tianzhou	田州	Xintianwei	新添衛
Tiesuo	鐵索]	Xinxiang	新鄉
Tingzan	庭贊	Xinxingsuo	新興所
Tuhai	圖海	Xinye	新野
Wadian	瓦店	Xinzheng	新鄭
Wang Fuchen	王輔臣	Xu Xiake	徐霞客
Wang Hongju	王宏舉	Xuande	玄德
Wang Hongxun	王宏勛	Xuanye	玄燁
Wang Jinbao	王進寶	Yanglin	楊林
Wang Pingfan	王屏藩	Yangzhou	揚州
Wang Yougong	王有功	Yanyangdang	延陽塘
Wangsipo	王西坡	Ye	葉
Wannianxian	萬年縣	Ye Bingzhong	嘩秉忠
Weihuifu	衛輝府	Yicheng	宜城
Weiqingwei	衛青衛	Yilong	易龍
Wolonggang	臥龍崗	Yincun	尹村
Wu Guogui	吳國貴	Yinding	銀丁
Wu Guozhu	吳國柱	Yiqiu	宜丘
Wu Sangui	吳三桂	Yizikong	亦資孔
Wu Shicong	吳世琮	Yizuo	亦佐

Yolo	岳樂	Zhanmaomajin	展茂馬金
Yongchun	永淳	Zhao Lian	趙璉
Yongli	永历	Zhao Liangdong	趙良棟
Yuanzhou	沅州	Zhao Yu	趙玉
Yuezhou	越州	Zhaozhou	趙州
Yunnanbao	雲南堡	Zheng Chenggong	鄭成功
Yuzhou	裕州	(Koxinga 國姓爺)	
Zeng-shou	曾壽	Zhengzhou	鄭州
Zhaima	砦馬	Zhenyuan	鎮遠
Zhaimadang	砦馬塘	*zhizhou*	知州
Zhan Yang	詹養	Zhong'an	重安
Zhang Guangxin	張廣新	Zhu Youlang	朱由榔
Zhang Xianzhong	張獻忠	Zhuge Liang	諸葛亮
Zhang Yong	張勇	Zhujiutang	朱久塘
Zhangde	彰德	Zu Zhichun	祖志春
Zhangsanfeng	張三風	*zuoling*	佐領

110

NOTES

INTRODUCTION

1 On the Southern Ming see the definitive work by Lynn A. Struve, *The Southern Ming, 1644–1662*, New Haven: Yale University Press, 1984.

2 Lawrence Kessler, *K'ang-hsi and the consolidation of Ch'ing Rule, 1661–1684*, Chicago: The University of Chicago Press, 1976, p. 83; Pierre Joseph d'Orléans, "History of the Two Tartar Conquerors of China," New York: B. Franklin, 1971 [Rpt], pp. 56–57.

3 Dzengšeo [Zeng-shou] (1987) *Beye-i cooha bade yabuha babe ejehe bithe. Sui jun ji xing yizhu*. Translated and annotated by Ji Yonghai, Beijing: Zhongyang minzu xueyuan.

4 Mark Elliott, *The Manchu Way: The Eight Banners and Ethnic Identity in Late Imperial China*, Stanford: Stanford University Press, 2001, pp. 187–191.

5 I have retained the term "Feudatory" following current usage. However, this is a less than felicitous translation or even rendering of the Chinese term *fan*. The most reader-friendly translation into English would probably be "satrapy" or "satrap." The main meaning of *fan* is that of a region (usually remote or peripheral), rather than the person governing it. Satrap or satrapy would also more correctly indicate the relationship between the provinces ruled by the three autonomous, but still formally dependent and centrally appointed, governors and the emperor. The provinces of Southern China were not "vassal states" in the sense that there was no formal recognition of the kind of wide-ranging powers that the head of a "vassal state" would enjoy. They were regular provinces that had grown more independent and harder to control from the center, like a satrapy would be perceived by a Western readership.

6 The name Jin is a reference to the dynasty of Manchurian origin that ruled northern China from 1115 to 1234. Founded by a people known as the Jurchen, which was the ethnonym of the Manchus before the official adoption of the name "Manchu," in 1634. Reference to this dynasty, which conquered northern China replacing the rule of the Chinese native Song dynasty, is a clear indication of the extent of Nurhaci's ambitions.

7 Ray Huang, "The Liao-tung Campaign of 1619," *Oriens Extremus*, vol. 28, no. 1, 1981, pp. 30–54.

8 For an assessment of Hong Taiji's rule see Gertraude Roth Li, "State Building Before 1644," in *The Cambridge History of China, Vol 9, Pt. 1, The Qing Dynasty to 1800*, ed. Willard J. Peterson, Cambridge: Cambridge University Press, 2002, pp. 51–72; Pamela K. Crossley, "A Translucent Mirror: History and Identity in Qing Imperial Ideology," Los Angeles and Berkeley: University of California Press, 1999, pp. 177–215.

9 Fourteenth son of Nurhaci, he had been a favorite brother of Hong Taiji, raised by him to the highest aristocratic ranks, placed in command of the important Plain White Banner at the age of 15 (1627) and entrusted with key military positions throughout Hong Taiji's reign. He was favored by many as successor to the throne, but out of loyalty to the former emperor he never challenged nor allowed others to challenge the decision to make the Young Fulin emperor. As co-regent during the minority of the Shunzhi emperor, he undermined the role of the other co-regent Jirgalang, and tried to concentrate control of various Banners in his hands. He died in 1650, still young, of illness. He was posthumously denounced as a usurper and stripped of his former charges, while some of his followers were tried, condemned, and some executed. Only over a century later his name was cleared again, by the Qianlong emperor, in recognition of his enormous merits and contribution to the Manchu conquest. See Arthur W. Hummel, *Eminent Chinese of the Ch'ing period (1644–1912)*, Taipei, Ch'eng-Wen Pub. Co., 1975, pp. 215–219.

10 He was the sixth son of Nurhaci's brother Šurhaci, and became soon a key military figure. In 1630 he took command of the Bordered Blue Banner, and the following year obtained a concurrent post as head of the Board of Punishment. As co-regent, he clashed with the more powerful Dorgon, who proceeded to reduce his ranks and responsibilities. After Dorgon's death he was instrumental in the campaign that led to the denunciation of Dorgon and his supporters. Interestingly, he also appealed the court to request that the princely titles accorded to Wu Sangui and Geng Zhongming be withdrawn. Had he been listened to, there probably would not have been a "War of the Three Feudatories" twenty years later. He died in 1655 of an illness, and received the highest honors. See Hummel, *Eminent Chinese*, pp. 397–398.

11 Lynn A. Struve, *Voices from the Ming-Qing Cataclysm: China in Tiger's Jaws*, New Haven and London: Yale University Press, 1993, pp. 28–48.

12 Their biographies can be found in Hummel, *Eminent Chinese*, respectively on pp. 435–436, 416–417, and 635–636.

13 Struve, *The Southern Ming*, pp. 147–149.

14 Frederic E. Wakeman, *The Great Enterprise: the Manchu Reconstruction of Imperial Order in Seventeenth-Century China*, Berkeley, University of California Press, 1985, vol. 1, p. 501.

15 Struve, *The Southern Ming*, p. 149.

16 On Sun see Hummel, *Eminent Chinese*, p. 683.

17 Wakeman, *The Great Enterprise*, vol. 2, p. 1017.

18 Wakeman, *The Great Enterprise*, vol. 1, p. 223, note 197.

19 Angela Hsi, "Wu San-kuei in 1644: a Reappraisal," *Journal of Asian Studies*, vol. 34, no. 2, 1975, pp. 443–453.

20 Wakeman, *The Great Enterprise*, p. 296. For the argument that Wu Sangui had always meant to defeat the Qing eventually, see Deng Zhongmian, "Lun Wu Sangui," *Beifang luncong*, 1987, no. 6, pp. 74–75. A general appraisal of Wu Sangui and summary of different opinions expressed by Chinese scholars with respect to attitude towards the Qing can be found in Xiu Pengyue, "Guanyu Wu Sangui pingjia de jige wenti," *Beifang luncong*, 1988, no. 1, pp. 86–91.

21 Fang Chao-ying, "A Technique for Estimating the Numerical Strength of the Early Manchu Military Forces," *Harvard Journal of Asiatic Studies*, vol. 13, no. 1–2, 1950, p. 204 and Table II, p. 208.

22 Eric Hauer, "General Wu San-kuei," *Asia Major*, vol. IV, no. 4, 1927, pp. 569 ff., Hummel, *Eminent Chinese*, pp. 877–880.

23 Struve, *The Southern Ming*, pp. 167–170.

24 On Wu's pacification of local leaders in Yunnan and Guizhou see Zuo Shu'e, "Shun Kang zhi ji Wu Sangui pingding Yun Gui tusi shulun," *Guizhou shehui kexue* (wenshizhe), 1988, no. 8, pp. 60–64.

25 Struve, *The Southern Ming*, pp. 175–178.

26 David H. Shore, "Last Court of Ming China: The Reign of the Yung-li Emperor in the South (1647–1662)," PhD Dissertation, Princeton University, 1976, p. 209.

27 Ts'ao Kai-fu, "The Rebellion of the Three Feudatories Against the Manchu Throne in China, 1673–1681: Its Setting and Significance," PhD Dissertation, Columbia University, 1965, p. 65; Id., "K'ang-hsi and the San-fan War," *Monumenta Serica*, no. 31, 1974–1975, p. 109. Chang Jen-chung, "The Nature of the 'Three Feudatories Rebellion' and the Causes for Its Failure," *Chinese Studies in History*, vol. 15, no. 1–2 (Fall–Winter 1981–1982), p. 11, estimates Wu's Green Standard troops at 16,000. According to yet another and much lower estimate, Wu Sangui has at his disposal 53 Banner companies and 12,000 Green Standard troops, and Geng and Shang together had fifteen Banner companies and 6–7,000 Green Standard troops. If a company force is calculated also, as mentioned above, at roughly 100 men per company, Wu had only 5,300 Bannermen, and Shang and Geng 1,500; see Xing Yulin, "Cong pingding 'Sanfan' panluan kan Kangxi de junshi sixiang" in Kang Yong Qian San di pingyi, ed. Zuo Buqing, Beijing, 1986, p. 88.

28 On the social basis of the rebellion, and in particular on the support that Chinese civil servants and common laborers gave to the rebellious leaders, see Fengyun Liu, "Shilun Qing chu San Fan fan Qing de shehui jichu," *Beifang luncong*, 1986, no. 3, pp. 62–67. On the motives of the rebellion see also Shi Song, "Ping Wu Sangui cong tou Qing dao fan Qing," *Qingshi yanjiu tongxun*, 1985, no. 5, pp. 14–19; Yang Hongpo (1988) "Lun Wu Sangui pan qing" *Liaoning daxue xuebao*, no. 6, pp. 73–76.

29 Kessler, *K'ang-hsi and the Consolidation*, p. 80; and Su Heping (1984) "Shilun Qingchu San Fan de xingzhi ji qi panluan shibai de yuanyin," *Shehui kexue* (Lanzhou), no. 5, pp. 107–112.

30 This account of the rebellion is based mainly on the studies by Kai-fu Ts'ao, namely, his dissertation and an article. See Ts'ao, *The Rebellion*; Id., *K'ang-hsi*, pp. 108–130. The most comprehensive Chinese-language work is Liu Fengyun, *Qingdai Sanfan yanjiu*, Beijing: Renmin Daxue chubanshe, 1994.

31 Hummel, *Eminent Chinese*, p. 879.

32 Ts'ao, *The Rebellion*, pp. 83–85.

33 For an overview of the Kangxi emperor's strategy, see Kong Deqi, "Luelun Kangxi di pingding Sanfan zhanzheng zhanlue zhidao shang de jige wenti," *Qingshi yanjiu tongxun*, 1986, no. 3, pp. 14–18.

34 On the question of the lower standards of training after the conquest of China and on military discipline, see Xing, "Cong pingding," pp. 90–92.

35 On Giyešu, see Hummel, *Eminent Chinese*, pp. 270–271.

36 Hummel, *Eminent Chinese*, pp. 439–440; Kessler, *K'ang-hsi and the Consolidation*, pp. 88–89.

37 On the role of Chinese general in the suppression of the rebellion in the northwestern provinces (Shaanxi, Gansu, and Sichuan) see Shang Hongkui, "Kangxi pingding Sanfan zhongde Xibei san Han jiang," *Beijing daxue xuebao* (zhexue shehui kexue), 1984, no. 1, pp. 55–62.

38 Ts'ao, *The Rebellion*, p. 120; Elliot, *The Manchu Way*, p. 129.

39 Zahiruddin Ahmad, *Sino-Tibetan Relations in the Seventeenth Century*, Roma: Istituto Italiano per il Medio ed Estremo Oriente, 1970, p. 218. Deng Ruiling, "Wu Sangui pan Qing qijian tong diwu bei Dalai Lama tongshi shimo,", *Zhongguo Zanxue*, 1998, no. 4, pp. 16–25.

40 We may note that the family feuds among Shang Kexi's descendants continued at least into the nineteenth century. According to a document preserved in the Harvard-Yenching Library and studied by Professor Yoshio Hosoya, the Shang family branch residing in Haicheng (Liaodong) and the branch residing in Beijing had a legal dispute in 1876, regarding costs for the maintenance of the ancestral family temple.

See Yoshio Hosoya, "A Document of Shang Ke-xi in the Harvard-Yenching Library," paper presented at the Second North American International Conference on Manchu Studies, Harvard University, 27–29, May 2005.

41 Hummel, *Eminent Chinese*, p. 880.

42 Ts'ao, *The Rebellion*, p. 140.

43 Jonathan Spence, *Emperor of China: Self-Portrait of K'ang-hsi*, New York: Vintage Books, 1975, pp. 42–43.

44 Chang, *The Nature*, pp. 7–18.

45 Spence, *Emperor of China*, xvii, p. 37.

46 Ch'en Wen-shih, "The Creation of the Manchu Niru," *Chinese Studies in History*, 1981, vol. XIV, no. 4, p. 25.

47 Before the conquest the Bordered Yellow Banner had 31 companies, of which 25 were hereditary, 5 non-hereditary, and 1 originally controlled by a whole clan and then made into a hereditary one. The Plain Yellow Banner had 27 companies, of which 20 were hereditary, 6 non-hereditary, and 1 belonging to a clan and latter turned to hereditary. The Plain White Banner had 39 companies, of which 37 were hereditary and 2 non-hereditary. The Plain Red Banner had 29 companies, divided into 23 hereditary and 6 non-hereditary. The Bordered White Banner had altogether 37 companies, of which 33 were hereditary and 4 non-hereditary. The Bordered Red Banner had 33 companies, of which only 1 was non-hereditary. The Plain Blue Banner had 36 companies, divided into 26 hereditary and 10 non-hereditary ones. Bordered Blue Banner had 33 companies, of which 1 was non-hereditary and the rest hereditary. On the formation of the *nirus* see Ch'en, "The Creation," pp. 33–36.

48 There has been some discussion in the field about the way in which this term should be rendered in translation. The literal meaning of the Chinese term Hanjun is "Chinese Army," which corresponds to (although it does not translate) the Manchu term *ujen cooha*, meaning "heavy troops" and understood as soldiers armed with heavy weaponry, that is, artillery. Since this was a Banner army that had the same eight banners as the Manchu and Mongol Banners, and its members were set apart from the rest of the Chinese populace, I have retained the term Hanjun in its attributive form, as in "Hanjun Banners" or "Hanjun Bannermen" as it strikes me as simpler and more direct than translations like Chinese-martial or Chinese Army Banners, both of which of course remain just as valid.

49 On the creation of the Mongol and Chinese Banners, see Liu Chia-Chü, "The Creation of the Chinese Banners in the Early Ch'ing," *Chinese Studies in History*, 1981, vol. XIV, no. 4, pp. 61–64; Elliot, *The Manchu Way*, pp. 71–72, 75. On the Hanjun see also Li Yanguang, "Qingdai de Baqi Hanjun," *Manxue Yanjiu*, no. 1, Changchun, 1992, pp. 91–103; Chen Jiahua and Ketong Fu, "Baqi hanjun kaolue" in Wang Zhonghan ed., Manzu shi yanjiu ji, Beijing: Zhongguo shehui kexue, 1988, pp. 281–306.

50 Evelyn Rawski, *The Last Emperors: a social history of Qing imperial institutions*, Berkeley: University of California Press, 1998, pp. 27 and 100.

51 On the Banner garrisons see Elliot, *The Manchu Way*, pp. 89–132; Kaye Soon Im, "The Rise and Decline of the Eight Banner Garrisons in the Ch'ing Period (1644–1911): A Study of the Kuang-chou, Hang-chou, and Ching-chou Garrisons," PhD Dissertation, University of Illinois, 1981, pp. 12–16.

52 Fang, "A Technique for Estimating," *Harvard Journal of Asiatic Studies*, vol. 13, nos 1–2, pp. 198–199, Elliot, *The Manchu Way*, p. 81, Edward J.M. Rhoads, *Manchus and Han: ethnic relations and political power in late Qing and early republican China, 1861–1928*, Seattle: University of Washington Press, 2000, p. 27. Thomas F. Wade, "The Army of the Chinese Empire: its two great divisions, the Banners or National Guard and the Green Standard or Provincial Troops: their organization, location, pay, condition &c.," *Chinese Repository*, vol. 20, no. 5, May 1851, p. 264.

53 On this see Li Yanguang and Guan Jie, eds, *Manzu Tongshi*, Shenyang, Liaoning minzu chubanshe, 2003, pp. 424–425.

54 Chen Qun, *Zhongguo bingzhi jianshi*, Beijing: Junshi kexue chubanshe, 1989, p. 381.

55 Xie Lihong, "Hongyi dapao yu Manzhou xingshuai," *Manxue Yanjiu*, ed. Yan Chongnian, Beijing 1994, vol. 2, p. 110.

56 Fang, "A Technique for Estimating," pp. 201–202.

57 Ergang Luo, *Lüying bing zhi*, Beijing: Zhonghua shuju, 1984, pp. 61–62; Kessler, *K'ang-hsi and the Consolidation*, pp. 108, 198 n. 190, Wakeman, *The Great Enterprise*, p. 480.

58 Kessler, *K'ang-hsi and the Consolidation*, pp. 108–111.

59 Elliott, *The Manchu Way*, pp. 136, 168.

60 James Millward, *Beyond the Pass: Economy, Ethnicity, and Empire in Qing Central Asia: 1759–1864*, Stanford: Stanford University Press, 1988, p. 23.

61 *Baqi tongzhi*, juan 29, vol. 8, p. 5218.

62 Giovanni Stary, "A Dictionary of Manchu Names: A Name-Index to the Manchu Version of the 'Complete Genealogies of the Manchu Clans and Families of the Eight Banners," *Aetas Manjurica* 8, Wiesbaden: Harrassowitz, 2000, p. 475.

63 See *Baqi Manzhou shizu tongpu* (1744) 32:9b, 32:18a; 25: 9b, 47:4a, 23: 22a.

64 *Man ming chen zhuan*, Taipei 1970, vol. 4, p. 2949. On Pengcun see Hummel, *Eminent Chinese*, p. 621.

65 I assume this to be the age at which Manchu Bannermen entered the regular military service, based on the regulations issued in 1629; see Nicola Di Cosmo and Dalizhabu Bao, *Manchu-Mongol Relations on the Eve of the Qing Conquest*, Leiden: E. J. Brill, 2003, pp. 66–67.

66 On the juvenile ranks in the Eight Banners, and the young age of the draftees, see C.R. Bawden, "A Manchu Military Relic from the First Opium War," *Journal of Turkish Studies*, no. 9, 1985, pp. 7–12.

67 Elliot, *The Manchu Way*, p. 187.

68 *Qinzheng pingding shumo fanglüe*, eds Wenda *et al.*, rpt. Beijing 1994, p. 16.26a.

69 Wei-ping Wu, "The Development and Decline of the Eight Banners," PhD Dissertation, University of Pennsylvania, 1969, p. 153.

70 See Note 3.

71 Jonathan Spence in *The Death of Woman Wang*, New York: Penguin Books, 1979 makes use as one of the chief sources of the personal memoir of a local magistrate in Shandong. Lynn A. Struve, in *Voices from the Ming* presents a series of personal memoirs.

72 Alfred de Vigny, "Servitude and Grandeur of Arms," trans. Roger Gard, London: Penguin Books, 1996, p. 9.

73 See Peter C. Perdue, *China Marches West. The Qing Conquest of Central Eurasia*, Cambridge, MA: Harvard University Press, 2005, p. 463.

74 Hummel, *Eminent Chinese*, pp. 248–249.

75 Keegan discusses eloquently the issue of the "personal angle of vision." Many of the conditions that impeded or altered vision at Waterloo, such as the preoccupations of duty, topographic features, smoke, and dust, would also apply to Dzenšeo's narrative. See *The Face of Battle*, New York: Penguin Books, 1978, pp. 128–134.

76 *Pingding sanni fanglü e* (1970), p. 414.

77 Fu Lo-shu, *A Documentary Chronicle of Sino-Western Relations (1644–1820)*, Tucson: University of Arizona Press, vol. I, p. 48.

78 On Verbiest's cannons see: Shu Liguang "Ferdinand Verbiest and the Casting of Cannons in the Qing Dynasty," *Ferdinand Verbiest (1623–1688) Jesuit Missionary, Scientist and Diplomat*, ed. John W. Witek, S.J., Nettetal: Steyler Verlag, 1994, pp. 227–244; and Ma Chujian "The introduction of western artillery by the Jesuit Missionaries and the consequent changes in the wars between the Ming and the Qing,"

Martino Martini: A Humanist and a Scientist in Seventeenth Century China, ed. Franco Demarchi and Riccardo Scartezzini, Trento: Università di Trento, 1994, pp. 307–321. On the general issue of Qing artillery see Hu Jianzhong "Qingdai huopao," *Gugong Bowuyuan kan*, no. 2–4, 1986, pp. 49–57, 87–94.

79 War elephants, as is well known from Indian military history, are risky for those who use them, as they are temperamental animals, which can get easily frightened. Musketry, fire, or a hail of arrows could scare them, with the result that they would "run amuck," and crush friends and foes alike. In India the elephants were therefore primarily used as battering rams to demolish the gates of fortresses. On this see Gayatri N. Pant, *Horse and Elephant Armour*, Delhi: Agam Kala Prakashan, 1997, pp. 87–104. According to Erich Hauer these elephants were imported from Burma; see Hauer, *General Wu San-kuei*, p. 604, n. 10.

80 Gérard Chaliand, ed., *The Art of War in World History*, Berkeley and Los Angeles: University of California Press, 1994, pp. 486–488.

81 Nicola Di Cosmo, "Military aspects of the Manchu-Čaqar Wars," *Warfare in Inner Asian History (500–1800)*, ed. Nicola Di Cosmo, Leiden: E. J. Brill, 2002, p. 346.

82 See Im, "The Rise and Decline," p. 12.

83 On the "massacre of Yangzhou" see Struve, *Voices from the Ming*, pp. 28–48.

84 On the Manchu fear of smallpox and related policies, see Chiang Chia-feng, "Disease and Its Impact on Politics, Diplomacy and the Military: The case of Smallpox and the Manchus (1613–1795)," *Journal of the History of Medicine*, no. 57, 2002, pp. 177–197.

85 Peter Coclanis, "Military Mortality in Tropical Asia: British Troops in Tenasserim 1827–36," *Journal of Southeast Asian Studies*, vol. 30, no. 1, 1999, p. 29.

86 On the cult of Guandi see Presenjit Duara, "Superscribing Symbols: The Myth of Guandi, Chinese God of War," *Journal of Asian Studies*, vol. 47, no. 4, 1988, pp. 778–795.

87 In Yunnan these large pythons, called *mang* by the people, were associated with local myths and legends. See Mark Elvin, *The Retreat of the Elephants: An Environmental History of China*, New Haven, CT: Yale University Press, c2004, pp. 17–18.

88 The Manchu translation of the History of the Three Kingdoms (*Sanguo zhi*) was published in 1647 and the translation of the Romance of the Three Kingdoms (*Sanguo yanyi*) was published in 1650. See Stephen Durrant, "Sino-Manchu Translations at the Mukden Court," *Journal of the American Oriental Society*, vol. 99, no. 4, 1979, p. 656. See also Martin Gimm (Mading Jimu), "Manzhou wexue shulüe" in *Manxue yanjiu*, ed. Yan Chongnian, Changchun, 1992, vol. 1, p. 205.

89 Zhuge Liang (181–234), the venerated Prime Minister of the Kingdom of Shu of the Three Kingdoms period, is said to have lived near Nanyang, where he was thrice visited by Liu Bei. A memorial temple was built in his honor in the Wolong district of the Nanyang Prefecture, which surely is the one visited by the soldiers. Less famous than the memorial temple erected in Chengdu, this is still regarded as a valuable tourist destination.

90 On the banner school education see Han Damei, "Qingdai baqi zidi de xuexiao jiaoyu," *Liaoning Shifan Daxue Xuebao*, 1996, no. 2, pp. 73–75.

91 John R. Shepherd, "Rethinking Sinicization: Processes of Acculturation and Assimilation," *State, Market and Ethnic Groups Contextualized*, ed. by Bien Chiang and Ho Ts'ui-p'ing, Taipei: Academia Sinica, 2003, pp. 133–150.

1 DIARY OF MY SERVICE IN THE ARMY BY DZENGŠEO

1 In Manchu the year is marked by a combination of colors and animals according to a sexagesimal cycle that corresponds to the Chinese cycle of stems and branches. In the text the year is given, mistakenly, as *sohon bonio*, that is, "yellow monkey," instead of

šanyan bonio, meaning "white monkey" and corresponding to the Chinese seventh stem and ninth branch *gengshen*, which is the correct designation for the year 1680.

2 General Manggitu was a Bannerman of the Bordered White Banner who started his career as commander of the city garrison of Taiyuan. In 1658 he fought against southern Ming forces and defeated General Li Dingguo. In 1663 he fought under Mulima against the rebel Li Laiheng in Hunan. In the wars against Wu Sangui he was at first subordinate to Niyahan, and fought at Youzhou, and then took part in the expedition to Canton, where he was appointed commander of Zhaoqing city. During the rebellion he was besieged in the city but managed to break out and reach Jiangxi. In 1677 he was appointed Lieutenant-general, and in 1678 he fought against Wu Shizong in Guilin, Wuzhou, and Nanning; in 1680 he fought against Ma Chengyin. As we shall see below in diary's account, he died in the same year while in the field after contracting an illness. See Erich Haenisch, "Bruchstüke aus der Geschichte Chinas Unter der Mandschu-Dynastie," *T'oung-pao* 1913, p. 90; Hummel, *Eminent Chinese*, p. 271.

3 *The Historical Atlas of China. Zhongguo lishi ditu ji* (1982) [hereafter, *Historical Atlas*], ed. Tan Qixiang *et al.*, Shanghai: Cartographic Publishing House, vol. 7, map 74–75, 5–5.

4 In the Manchu text "giya de." Giya is a common Manchu transcription for Chinese *jia* and other similar sounding words. The Chinese translator renders it with *jie* "streets," therefore emendating the text. However, it could also render the word *jia* "house," in which case the translation would read "in the houses."

5 The meaning of this song is not clear. Given that the manuscript is not immune from scribal errors, one might conceivably read the Manchu *ke* as *ge*. The reading *doo yang ge* may point to some variant of the *yangge* style of folk song and dance particularly popular in north China and among the Manchus. These dances, of which many different types still exist, are associated with New Year celebrations. The word *doo* (*dao*) could either stand for the character, as in *wudao* (dancing), or it might stand for another unidentified character (perhaps *tao*, a variant reading of *tiao*?) indicating a local or special type of *yangge* style. Since *yangge* dances are performed often by heavily made-up women or men dressed up as women, this is probably what the soldiers were doing; the characters therefore could be rendered with *daoyangge* "dancing the yangge" and the whole phrase could be translated as "singing *yangge* songs" or "singing songs in the *yangge* style." We may also note the extremely interesting picture published in Wu Hung's article on the photography of Liu Zheng, which portrays a contemporary old man (1995) performing *yangge* dances and songs with a group of other men; he is dressed in women's clothes and wears heavy make-up. The soldiers described by Dzengšeo may have been dressed somewhat like him. See Wu Hung (2001) "Photographing deformity: Liu Zheng and His Photo Series 'My Countrymen'," *Public Culture* 13.3, pp. 410–411. For the *yangge* dances among the Manchus see Shen Lijuan (1998) "Man Han wudao de ronghe", *Manzu yanjiu* no. 1, pp. 82–85.

6 Shang Zhixin (1636–1680) was a Hanjun Bannerman of the Bordered Blue Banner, and the second son of Shang Kexi, the governor of Guangdong. He became the heir to his father's title after the death of the elder brother in 1654. Sent to Beijing to be in attendance of the Shunzhi emperor, he distinguished himself in the service of the emperor, and was also favored by the Kangxi emperor upon his accession to the throne. In 1671 and on account of his father's poor health, he was assigned to Guangdong to assist the ailing parent and to take charge of military affairs. In this position he appears to have behaved badly, and was prone to violence and cruel mistreatment of others due to a fierce temper. In 1673 his father petitioned the Emperor for permission to retire to his native Liaodong. This request, which suggested a hereditary succession to the post of governor of Guangdong for Shang Zhixin, precipitated

the Sanfan rebellion. Although Shang Kexi remained loyal to the dynasty, Shang Zhixin wavered, and in 1676, as his father's health continued to deteriorate, Wu Sangui's forces appeared to gain strength. When his younger brother Shang Zhixiao was sent by the emperor to settle the situation in Guangdong, Shang Zhixin, piqued at having been given a rank lower than his brother's, arrested his own father and joined Wu Sangui's forces. He then went with an army to Meiling, in order to prevent the standing imperial army of Jiangxi from entering his province. However, he lost various battles and the following year he surrendered to General Manggitu, thus allowing the province of Guangdong to be recovered by the imperial forces. He was also allowed to keep his title and Governorship. Urged to undertake further military operations against the rebels, he did nothing until after the death of Wu Sangui in 1678, when he began military operations in Guangxi. Meanwhile, accusations against him, brought up mainly by his own brother Shang Zhixiao, were accumulating, and he was finally arrested in the spring of 1680, after he had taken the city of Wuxuan in northern Guangxi. Moved to Canton, he was ordered by the emperor to be executed after he had tried to protect himself by having one of his accusers murdered. Other family members were also executed, and the title of Prince Who Pacifies the South (Pingnan Wang) held by Shang Kexi and Shang Zhixin was abolished. Hummel, *Eminent Chinese*, pp. 634–635; Haenisch, "Bruchstüke," pp. 94–95.

7 Ecu was a Manchu Bannerman of the Bordered Yellow Banner. During the Shunzhi period he participated in the war against the Southern Ming and against Koxinga, whom he defeated in the battle to take Jiangning. He was then based at Jiangning, gradually rising to the ranks of vice-commander and then, in 1668, commander of the local garrison. When Wu Sangui attacked Hunan in February 1674, Ecu received the order to join with his troops General Niyahan, who had been assigned to the protec-tion of the city of Anqing. Later in the same year he participated in operations against the rebel feudatory Geng Qingzhong, recovering various prefectures that had fallen into enemy hands. In 1675 the rebels again attacked Raozhou, and Ecu again defeated them. During the same year he defeated a 40,000-strong enemy force in Wannianxian, and subsequently joined the forces of General Labu as military advisor. During a counteroffensive of Wu Sangui's forces Ecu was defeated in three battles by the rebel general Han Daren. The emperor ordered the vice-minister of the Ministry of the Interior Bandi to investigate the matter, and proposed that Ecu together with others be removed from office, but the order was reversed. After the rebels attacked the Prefecture of Shaozhou in Guangdong, Ecu joined the army of General Manggitu and defeated the rebels, liberating the city. In 1678 he fought under General Fu Honglie in Guangxi against Wu Shizong. He died in the tenth month of the twentieth year of Kangxi (November 1681). *Baqi tongzhi* v. 6, pp. 3755–3756.

8 Lebei was a Manchu Bannerman of the Plain White Banner of the Gorlo clan. He received subsequent appointments until he achieved the rank of Banner Commander (*dutong*) of the Plain Blue Banner. In 1676 he led troops from Guangxi against Wu Sangui's army. Following the death of Manggitu, Lebei was appointed Zhennan Jiangjun (General Who Pacifies the South). In 1680 and 1681 we led operations together with General Laitai against He Jizu and other rebel leaders. Crossing over the dangerous pass of Shimen Ridge, he recovered Anlongsuo. In the third month of 1681 he again defeated the rebels at Huangcaoba, and captured the rebel leader Zhan Yang. Riding fast, he attacked Yunnan, joined with the armies that were converging from Sichuan and Guizhou, and attacked Yunnanfu. See *Baqi tongzhi* v. 6, p. 4085.

9 Hife recurs often in the text, and is accompanied by the title of Councilor or Lieutenant-general. Since this is relatively common name, a firm identification eludes me. Two Hife who fought against Wu Sangui, neither of whom is likely to be this Hife, can be found on *Baqi tongzhi* vol. 6, p. 4018, and vol. 7, p. 4695.

10 The Manchu rank of *tui janggin*, Chinese *hujun tongling* was that of Commandant of the Guards (*bayara*) Regiment. It was a rank limited to the Manchu and Mongol Banners (see Charles O. Hucker, "A Dictionary of Official Titles in Imperial China," Taipei: Southern Materials Center, Inc., 1985, no. 2780; Elliot, *The Manchu Way*, p. 366). According to H.S. Brunnert and V.V. Hagelstrom, "Present Day Political Organization of China," Taipei: Ch'en Wen Publishing Co., 1978, no. 734, however, this rank indicated the commander of one of the eight sections (each corresponding to one of the eight Banners) of the Guards Division.

11 A Mongolian loanword, meaning "sworn brother."

12 Jin Guangzu was a Chinese Bannerman of the Plain White Banner. In 1659 he became first secretary (*shilang*) of the Ministry of the Interior (Li Bu). Soon afterwards he rose to the rank Treasurer of the provinces of Fujian and Guangxi, in 1664 to Governor of Guangxi, and in 1670 to Governor of Guangxi and Gunagdong. When the Guangxi General Sun Yanling joined the rebels in 1674, Jin Guangzu held for a long time the eastern part of the province for the government side. The following year he fought together with Šušu in Jiangxi, but defected to the Shang Zhixin's rebels. In 1677 he agreed on the terms of his capitulation with General Manggitu, and subsequently served in the imperial army in Guangxi and Yunnan. But because of his earlier betrayal he did not escape punishment, and after the completion of the campaign he lost his post and rank. He died a few years later. Haenisch, "Bruchstüke," p. 75; *Baqi tongzhi*, vol. 7, 4587–4588.

13 Ma Chengyin, son of Ma Xiong, the Provincial Governor of Guangxi, joined Wu Sangui's revolt. After the death of his father in the eighteenth year of Kangxi he submitted and was raised to the rank of Count and entrusted with a military command. But he defected again the following year, and suffered then several defeats at the hands of Generals Fu Honglie, Jin Guangzu, and Manggitu, and finally surrendered in the sixth month of the following year after the capture of the city of Liuzhou by Prince Labu. He was then sentenced to death and executed. Haenisch, "Bruchstüke," p. 89.

14 Princess Kong Sizhen was born in *c*.1641 in a prominent Liaodong family. Her father Kong Youde joined the Manchus in 1633, at a time when several other protagonists of our story, such as Geng Zhongming and Shang Kexi, also defected to the Manchu side. He belonged to the Plain Red Banner, and received several honors from the Manchus, the most important being the title of Prince Who Pacifies the South (Dingnan Wang), mentioned in our text, which was bestowed upon him in 1648. He committed suicide in 1652 when he found himself besieged in Guilin (Yunnan) by the anti-Manchu forces of Li Dingguo and was subsequently greatly honored as a martyr. Taken to Beijing as the sole survivor of the family, Kong Sizhen married Sun Yanling, also of the Plain Red Banner in 1660. Kong Sizhen was given the extremely high title of Imperial Princess (*hošoi gege*) and her husband raised accordingly to a high aristocratic rank, and later given the title of Military Governor of Guanxi, after Kong Sizhen successfully petitioned the throne to return to Guanxi, where her father's troops had originally been assigned. Sun Yanling was disliked by his subordinates and denounced repeatedly on various charges. At the time of Wu Sangui's uprising he joined the rebellious forces, but in 1676 he was forced by his subordinates to relinquish military command to his wife, who had remained loyal to the Manchus. Sun Yanling was subsequently murdered by Wu Sangui in 1677. This text shows that Kong Sizhen remained involved in the military leadership of the Qing forces until the end of the rebellion. See Hummel, *Eminent Chinese*, p. 683, and Priscilla Ching Chung, "Kong Sizhen, Princess" *Biographical Dictionary of Chinese Women*, pp. 104–105.

15 That is, Kong Youde (d. 1652), one of the first Chinese generals from Liaodong to defect to the Manchus. He received the title of Dingnan Wang (Prince who Pacifies the South) in 1648. See Hummel, *Eminent Chinese*, pp. 435–436.

16 *Historical Atlas*, vol. 7, map 74–75, 4–5.

17 Manchu *jy jeo hafan* translated Chinese *zhizhou*, that is, a Department Magistrate within a prefectural bureaucracy. See Brunnert and Hagelstrom, no. 855, Hucker, no. 965.

18 Manchu *gūsai ejen*, Chinese *dutong*. Brunnert and Hagelstrom, no. 719; Hucker no. 7321. The holder of this title was in command of a Banner. There is no standard translation for this title. I prefer to translate the commander of a Banner as Lieutenant-general and its second in command (Chinese *fu dutong*, Manchu *meiren-i janggin*) as Brigadier-general, rather than follow Brunnert and Hagelstrom's translation of the first as Lieutenant-general and the second as Deputy Lieutenant-general, which seems to me inappropriate to a western military rank.

19 It is also possible to translate this as "my eight horses."

20 Given that the "five battalions" were Green Standard troops, this may indicate that only Chinese people were investigated for the theft.

21 In Manchu *yung šun*, but this must surely be (as indicated by Ji Yonghai) Yongchun. See *Historical Atlas*, vol. 8, map 46–47, 5–5.

22 Given that, according to Fang Chaoying, the total number of companies in 1679 (which is the year that we should use for this calculation) was 844, the number of soldiers was 3,376.

23 *Historical Atlas*, vol. 7, map 74–75, 3–6.

24 In Manchu this is rendered as *gin ceng sy*, but there is no doubt that this is Jinchengzhai. See *Historical Atlas*, vol. 7, map 74–75, 4–5.

25 *Historical Atlas*, vol. 7, map 74–75, 4–5.

26 Judging from this episode, Dzengšeo at this point may have held a high regimental rank, which was possibly that of *jalan-i janggin* in Manchu (Chinese *canling*), a rank usually translated also as Lieutenant Colonel or Regimental Commander. See Brunnert and Hagelstrom, no. 659; Hucker, no. 6888.

27 This sentence is ambiguous, because it is unclear whether the cow belonged to civilians who had been killed, and therefore had no owner, or the cow itself, owned by civilians, had been killed by others.

28 Manchu *araha janggin*; this may correspond to Chinese *wei yinwu zhang-jing*. Brunnert and Hagelstrom, no. 725.

29 Manchu *bošokū*, the lowest officers rank in the military hierarchy.

30 Following the Manchu conquest, the number of strokes in every degree of beating was substantially reduced, although the nominal number of blows remained the same. According to the first Qing compilation of sub-statutes, the *Xianxing zeli*, issued in 1679, and later in the Qing code (1740) seventy nominal blows corresponded to twenty-five actual ones, eighty to thirty, and one hundred to forty. See Derk Bodde and Clarence Morris, *Law in Imperial China: Exemplified by 190 Ch'ing Dynasty Cases*, pp. 77, 80–81 Cambridge, Mass.: Harvard University Press, 1967.

31 Taodeng and the Shamao Mountain could not be identified.

32 Jelken was a member of the *Hanjun* Bordered Red Banner. See *Baqi tongzhi*, 7, p. 4637.

33 For both locations see *Historical Atlas*, vol. 8, map 46–47, 4–6.

34 Zhao Liangdong (1621–1697) joined the Manchus in 1645 and campaigned in Shanxi against Li Zicheng, then two years later he fought the Muslims in Gansu, and moved to Yunnan in 1654 under Hong Chengzhou. In 1662 he distinguished himself as General Major in Yunnan in the campaigns against the Prince of Shuixi and against the Lolo tribesmen. During the Wu Sangui rebellion he was recommended as Commander in Chief of the forces in Ningxia, and in this capacity stabilized Ningxia and Northern Gansu and trained an army of 5,000 men. In 1679 he volunteered to lead these men in the recovery of Yunnan and Szechwan. He led one of four armies under the general command of Tuhai. In 1680 he and Wang Jinbao advanced to

Szechwan and pacified it. Zhao was then given title of Governor-general of Yunnan and Guizhou. Blamed by jealous generals, he was not rewarded further but participated in the campaign to re-conquer Yunnan. In 1681 he advanced to the outskirts of Yunnanfu, and after a siege of several months the city fell under the assault of Zhao's men. After the city was taken the spoils were divided among all the generals except Zhao, who remained outside the city. Hummel, *Eminent Chinese*, pp. 77–78; Haenisch, "Bruchstüke," pp. 73–74.

35 This was the grandson of Wu Sangui, son of Wu Yingxiong (d. 1674). He continued to lead the anti-Qing rebellion until, besieged in Yunnanfu for months, he committed suicide on December 7, 1681.

36 Ma Bao was originally a rebel leader, who later followed the Ming Prince Gui, and in 1650 fought on his side in Guandong against Shang Kexi. After the flight of Prince Gui, Ma Bao hid in the mountains, but continue to cause unrest in the areas of Guangxi, southern Hunan, and Northern Guangdong in association with Li Dingguo. In 1659 he surrendered to Governor Wu Sangui and became his favorite lieutenant. In Wu's army Ma Bao attained the rank of Lieutenant-general, and when Wu rebelled he sent Ma Bao to fight Hunan, where he was successful in the occupation of various cities. In 1676 he assisted the city of Changsha, which was threatened by the imperial armies. In 1677 and 1678 he undertook raids in Guangxi and northern Guangdong. After the death of Wu Sangui he withdrew to Sichuan through Guizhou, and there in every way he tried to harass the invading imperial troops. When Yunnan city was besieged in 1681, he went to help Wu Shifan, but was attacked by General Hife and finally forced to admit defeat. He was executed in the autumn of the same year. Haenisch, "Bruchstüke," pp. 90–91.

37 Lit., they broke their gallbladder, that is, they are frightened.

38 The process of pounding, or flailing, the rice probably means that they were polishing it, cleaning off the husks.

39 This is probably Masitai, a Manchu Bannerman of the Bordered Blue Banner. In 1675 he participated in the war against the Čaqar rebel Burni. In 1677 he campaigned against Wu Sangui, and led troops to Ji'an. During this campaign he was promoted to Mongol Vice-Commander and then to Manchu Vice-Commander. In 1680 he joined General Manggitu on his march from Guangxi to attack Wu Shifan, and reached the locality of Taotun in Binzhou, where he defeated the false generals Fabn Qihan and Zhan Yang. The following year, in February 1681, he followed General Laita in the march across Shimen Ridge, and the attack on Huangcaoba. Thereafter, he marched against Yunnan and joined in the operations of the three armies for the pacification of Yunnan. *Baqi tongzhi*, 6, p. 4121.

40 Manchu *bayara janggin*, could be either *bayarai tui janggin* or *bayara jalan-i janggin*.

41 Manchu *funde bošokū*, in Chinese *xiaoqixiao*, a rank of level 6a.

42 I imagine this refers to the defeat suffered the previous day, and to the lost soldiers and standards.

43 *Historical Atlas*, vol. 8, map 46–47, 3–6.

44 In Manchu this is *tusy*, a Chinese loanword for "local functionary," a title given to native ruler or chief.

45 I could not identify the names of these villages, but they must be located in the same general area as Luorong.

46 That is, the God of War Guandi.

47 *Historical Atlas*, vol. 7, map 74–75, 3–6.

48 In the text this title is rendered with the Manchu transcription of the Chinese *tidu* instead of the regular Manchu title *fideme kadalara amban*.

49 This corresponds to about 16 meters, or fifty Chinese feet.

50 The name of General Manggitu in the text is often abbreviated to Mang.

51 *Historical Atlas*, vol. 7, map 74–75, 4–6.

52 *Historical Atlas*, vol. 7, map 74–75, 3–6.

53 The title is *zhifu* rendered in Manchu transcription in the text.

54 Of course this refers to the Manchu law that all males shave their forehead and let their hair grow in the back, braided into a queue.

55 This must be an error for the twenty-second.

56 The name of this river is given in Manchu in the text. *Sohon* means yellow, but the meaning of *turanggi* is unclear, although it is likely to be related to fast-flowing or muddy waters. From the location, it could be the Dunijiang (*Historical Atlas*, vol. 7, 74–75, 4–4,4–6). The name could be related to a river in the same general region, which is, however, less likely from a geographic point of view given its northern location, the Huangyuanshui (*Historical Atlas*, vol. 7, 74–75, 2–6).

57 This probably refers to a camp where they had stopped previously.

58 Since there were only 844 companies, this would put the total number of estimated available Banner forces in this expeditionary army at 4220.

59 Manchu *jalan-i janggin*. See Brunnert and Hagelstrom, nos 658, 659.

60 Most likely this means that the distribution of provisions for the horses was not made on the basis of the theoretical number of horses that officers and soldiers were allowed to take with them, but on the basis of the actual number they had. Since these provisions were in effect a part of the soldier's salary, the reduction was probably seen as a cut in pay.

61 In Manchu *meiren-i janggin*, the second in command of a Banner, in Chinese *fu dutong*.

62 Probably the Board, or Ministry, of War.

63 In Manchu *gūsa-i ejen*, in Chinese *dutong*.

64 Laita was a Manchu Bannerman of the Plain White Banner, from the Namdulu clan, fourth son of Kanggūri. He entered military service as a boy fighting at Jinzhou against the Ming army, and participated under Abatai to the invasion of Shandong. In 1644 under Dodo he joined the campaign against Li Zicheng in Henan and Shanxi. The same year he also went to Jiangnan, conquered Yangzhou and Nanjing, and attacked the Ming Prince Fu at Wuhu. In 1647 he fought with Bolo against the Ming Prince Tang, and the following year against Prince Gui. From 1654 to 1660 he campaigned in Guangdong against Li Dingguo and in Jiangning and Fujian against Zheng Chengkong (Koxinga). Having attained to a high military rank by this time, he was however demoted to the rank of Staff Officer in 1662 because of a defeat he had suffered in the campaign against Koxinga. He soon recovered from this setback distinguishing himself in battle, and in 1667 was promoted to the rank of Lieutenant-general of the Mongol Plain White Banner. In 1674 he received the command of the army against the rebellious governor of Fujian Geng Jingzhong. Until Geng's capitulation in 1676 he fought in the south and in particular on the coast of the province of Fujian against remaining pockets of rebels and sea pirates. In 1680, after the conquest of Amoy, he moved to Canton, where he rendered an important service by suppressing the mutiny of the army of Shang Zhixin as soon as he arrived. Still in the same year he marched on Nanningfu and entered Yunnan. After the conquest of Yunnanfu he turned back to Beijing and took over again his post with the White Banner. He died in 1684 and was posthumously rewarded with a dukedom in 1727 for his exploits in the Sanfan War. Haenisch, "Bruchstüke," pp. 86–87; Hummel, *Eminent Chinese*, pp. 271, 410; *Baqi tongzhi* vol. 6, pp. 3867–3873.

65 Maci (Maqi), a Manchu Bannerman of the Manchu Bordered Yellow Banner, was born in 1650 and a member of the Fuca clan. In 1669 he was appointed Assistant Deputy Director of the Board of Works. In 1672 he was promoted to a captaincy in his Banner, and in 1675 was transferred to the Board of Revenues. After the Sanfan

War he was appointed to bureaucratic positions in the Board of Works and later the Grand Secretariat. In 1686 he became Governor of Shanxi, and in later years he acquired a reputation as an able financial administrator and incorruptible official. For these merits he was raised to the Censorate in 1688. He then served in important positions and had key roles in the negotiations with the Russians leading to the Treaty of Nerchinsk and in the preparations for the war against Galdan. He later met with the Kangxi Emperor's displeasure for supporting Yinsi as heir to the throne. Having showed discourtesy to the emperor, he was sentenced to death, and then pardoned, but his family members and Maci himself lost their official positions. Having been placed under house arrest in 1708, he was freed two years later to be employed in negotiations with Russian embassies. From there his career was resurrected, and he was restored to the rank of Grand Secretary in 1716. He died in 1739. See *Hummel, Eminent Chinese*, pp. 560–561; *Man Ming Chen Zhuan, juan* 26, p. 51.

66 Manchu *araha meiren-i janggin*.
67 As mentioned in the Introduction, these are the Chinese Banners, Manchu *ujen cooha*.
68 This is certainly the "Great Comet" sighted in the European skies in December 1680 that caused such a stir among astronomer and the general public. It was described by Gottfried Kirch and Thomas Brattle, and studied perhaps most famously by Isaac Newton. It also inspired a voluminous work by Pierre Bayle. It is worth quoting a few lines from A. Prat's introduction to his critical edition of Bayle's work:

> En décembre 1680, vers la fête de Noël, le *Mercure Galant* annonçait l'apparition d'une Comète: '[…] On voit tout les soirs sur les cinq heures une trainée de lumière qui ressemble à celle que réfléchit une petite nuée éclairée du soleil et qui approche de la couleur du chemin de lait […]'

This description is remarkably close to the "white mist" seen by Dzengšeo. See Pierre Bayle, *Penss diverses sur la Com*, ed. A. Prat, Paris: Librairie E. Droz, 1939, p. i.
69 Twenty *da* corresponds approximately to 32 meters.
70 This seems to indicate that at this stage Dzengšeo is in command of a company.
71 *Historical Atlas*, vol. 7, map 74–75, 4–5.
72 The locality of Tianzhou had been occupied by Wu Sangui forces early on, and seals with the reign titles adopted by Wu Sangui were given to the local officials, as showed by seals of the Tianzhou and Zhen'an counties dated respectively to the first year of the Zhou (1674) and to the first year of the Honghua period found in Guangxi; see Jiang Tingyu "Guangxi suojian 'San Fan' tuguan yin," in *Gugong bowuyuan yuankan*, 2003, no. 3, pp. 71–74. For the location see *Historical Atlas*, vol. 7, map 74–75, 4–3.
73 Zhenyuan is a prefecture located in eastern Guizhou. The term Guizhou may refer to the whole of the province or to its northwestern part, which in Ming times was called Guizhou Xuanweisi (Guizhou Pacification Office).
74 This would also be "Prince Mu."
75 Lit. "iron rod."
76 Manchu *fideme kadalara amban*, Chinese *tidu*. Brunnert and Hagelstrom, no. 750 translates it as Provincial Commander-in-Chief. Hucker, no. 6482, translates it as Provincial Military Commander.
77 A Manchu Bannerman of the Plain White Banner. In 1673 Sangge joined General Hirgen's campaign in Jiangxi, as Chief of the General Staff. In 1675 he acted as assistant to General Niyahan in Guangdong. Thereafter Sangge stayed in Nanchang to wait for the new Commander-in-Chief for Jiangxi, Prince Yolo. Under Yolo he fought in this province and in 1679 he participated in the conquest of Changsha in Hunan. He then took part in the campaign into Yunnan, going through southern Hunan, and in 1681 was recalled to Beijing. He later took part in the campaign against Galdan and died in 1699. See Haenisch, "Bruchstüke," p. 94, no. 47.

78 I could not identify this river. A Lushui river is located in Jiangxi province, but that is clearly not the one to which Dzenšeo is referring.

79 In our text this is *tui bayara janggin*, in Chinese *hujun tongling*, who was the Commandant of the Guards (one per banner), rendered by Brunnert and Hagelstrom, no. 734, with the rank of Captain-general.

80 Originally from Gansu, under the Ming dynasty he attained the rank of Brigadier-general, and later under Prince Fu the rank of a provincial general. In 1645 he served in General Gao Jie's army. When Gao Jie was murdered, and the army's crossing of the Yangtse River was cut off, he capitulated to the Manchus. He went into the Plain Yellow Banner and took part in the military operations in the south. In 1657, serving under Hong Chengchou, he campaigned in Guizhou, where he was made Provincial Military Commander in 1659. He remained in this post for the following thirteen years, and performed important services in the repression of the Miao tribesmen in this province. In 1673 he was one of the first generals to join Wu Sangui. With the Qing capture of the city of Guiyang in 1680 he fell in the hands of the imperial troops and moved to Beijing, where he was executed the following year. Haenisch, "Bruchstüke," pp. 87–88.

81 A native of Shandong, in 1657 he was appointed a member of the Hanlin Academy and of the Historiography Bureau. Afterwards he served as Daotai (Circuit Intendant) in the provinces of Huguang and Hunan. In 1667 he became Vice-President in the Ministry of Rites and three years later he went over to the Ministry of War. In 1671 he was appointed Governor of the province of Guizhou. At the outbreak of the rebellion he joined Wu Sangui and fought on his side in Sichuan. What happened to him is not known. Haenisch, "Bruchstüke," pp. 101–102.

82 Probably one of the two rivers near Baduxu. *Historical Atlas*, vol. 8, map 46–47, 3–2.

83 Manchu *janggin*, a generic term for officers.

84 *Historical Atlas*, vol. 8, map 46–47, 3–2.

85 That is, pack animals.

86 That is, the *qingming* Festival, which is celebrated on the fifth or sixth of April.

87 This notation may refer to the presence of snakes.

88 Haenisch, "Bruchstüke," pp. 52–53.

89 *Historical Atlas*, vol. 7, map 74–75, 2–2.

90 In Manchu *kūwaran-i da*.

91 As we can see from this passage, Dzengšeo is attached to the Bordered Blue Banner.

92 I could not identify this river.

93 Haenisch, "Bruchstüke," p. 52.

94 The characters of the names of these officers are unclear.

95 *Historical Atlas*, vol. 8, map 48–49, 5–10.

96 *Historical Atlas*, vol. 8, map 48–49, 6–10.

97 *Historical Atlas*, vol. 7, map 78–79, 2–7.

98 *Historical Atlas*, vol. 8, map 48–49, 4–9.

99 The location of this place is unclear.

100 A *hule* is equivalent to a Chinese bushel, *shi*, corresponding to 103.5 liters. The volume indicated here therefore amounts to 5,175 cubic meters of rice. On the shi during the Qing dynasty see Carol H. Shiue "Local Granaries and Central Government Disaster Relief: Moral Hazard and Intergovernmental Finance in Eighteenth- and Nineteenth-Century China," *The Journal of Economic History*, vol. 64. 1, n. 14, March 2004, p. 105.

101 Jangtai (1636–1690) was a great-grandson of Nurhaci, son of Bohoto. At the outbreak of the Wu Sangui's revolt he was appointed Assistant Commander in Šangšan's army, serving in Hubei from 1674 to 1678. Under Šangšan he was not very effective, possibly because his views could not prevail. After Šangšan's death in 1678 Jangtai was given the title of Fuyuan Jiangjun (General who Soothes Distant Places). In 1679 Yolo

was recalled to the capital and Jangtai succeeded him as Field Marshal. In 1681 Jangtai entered Yunnan, combining his forces with the army under Laita and the forces from Szechwan under Zhao Liangdong. He participated in the capture of Yunnanfu on December 8. Hummel, *Eminent Chinese*, p. 396; Haenisch, "Bruchstüke," pp. 81–82. *Beise* was one of the highest Manchu titles of nobility, below *qin wang, jun wang* and *beile*.

102 About two hours before day-break
103 *Historical Atlas*, vol. 8, map 48–49, 4–9.
104 In the text we have 19, *juwan uyun*, but this must be a mistake for 16, juwan *ninggun*.
105 *Historical Atlas*, vol. 8, map 48–49, 4–9.
106 Here I have translated Manchu *jalan* with "regiment." This is evidence that Dzengšeo at this point is in command of a *jalan*.
107 He was the eldest grandson of Wu Sangui, son of Wu Yingxiong. After the death of Wu Sangui he had his power base and court in Yunnanfu, although his authority extended to Yunnan, Kweichow, parts of Hunan, Sichuan and Kwangsi. In 1679 Kwangsi went over to the Qing side. In 1680 Sichuan was taken by Zhao Liangdong while Jangtai advanced from Hunan, and Laita from Kwangsi. Defeated in Yunnan, he resisted in his besieged capital Yunnanfu for several months until he eventually committed suicide on December 7, 1681, thus ending the rebellion. Hummel, *Eminent Chinese*, pp. 879–880.
108 The meaning of *baime jimbi* is "to come seeking refuge."
109 Cai Yurong (1633–1699), was a native of Liaotong, whose father had joined the Manchus in 1642 and had then joined the Hanjun Plain White Banner. At the time of Wu Sangui's rebellion Cai had risen to the rank of Governor-general of the provinces of Sichuan and Huguang (i.e. Hubei and Hunan). His efforts in the defense of Hunan were not sufficient to stop Wu Sangui's offensive, and he was therefore demoted. Having lost his rank, he continued to serve in a military capacity and was put in charge of Green Standard troops, until in 1679 when he was promoted to General in charge of all the Green Standard troops of Hunan. After the rebellion was put down he was promoted again to the rank of Governor-general of Huguang in 1681 and in 1682 to Governor-general of Yunnan and Guizhou. Later in life he was found guilty of several crimes and sentenced to death, a sentence later commuted to confiscation, flogging, and banishment. He was pardoned and allowed to return in Zhili from Heilongjiang a few years before his death. See Hummel, *Eminent Chinese*, pp. 734–735.
110 The only place that I could identify is Pingyuanfu in Guangxi province. See *Historical Atlas*, vol. 8, map 46–47, 3–7.
111 This may refer to the aforementioned bombardment of Pingyuanfu.
112 Mujan was a Manchu Bannerman of the Plain Yellow Banner who served in the military throughout his life. In 1659 he distinguished himself in the suppression of the native Prince Nasung, and for this he was appointed Brigadier-general of his Banner. In 1673, when Wu Sangui rebelled, Mujan was appointed Chief of General Staff of the army, with the task of invading Sichuan and Yunnan from Shaanxi. In 1674 he fought under Warka and was engaged in operations against Wang Fuchen. In 1676 he was appointed Field Marshal of the Hunan army. At the beginning of 1677 he arrived in Jinzhou and immediately set out to advance south. In southeastern Hunan his operations were hindered by differences of opinion with Prince Labu. In 1680 he joined the invasion of Yunnan under Jangtai as his Chief of Staff. He died in 1683, shortly after the end of the campaign. Haenisch, "Bruchstüke," pp. 92–93; *Baqi tongzhi* vol. 6, pp. 3848–3856.
113 Manchu *janggin*, which is generic for "officer," but is likely to be of an adjutant rank. See Brunnert and Hagestrom, no. 734.

114 *Historical Atlas*, vol. 8, map 48–49, 4–7.
115 Hūwase, a Bannerman of the Manchu Bordered Red Banner, of the Nara clan. At the beginning of the rebellion he served under Prince Lorjin. He fought in various theatres throughout the war. In 1679 he joined Labu in the attack and conquest of the Xingning county in Hunan. In the summer of 1681 together with Mujai he attacked Pingyuanfu. *Baqi tongzhi* vol. 6, pp. 4080–4082.
116 *Historical Atlas*, vol. 8, map 48–49, 5–8.
117 This date is out of sequence, and might be a mistake for the twenty-seventh day, in which case it would correspond to July 12.
118 *Historical Atlas*, vol. 8, map 48–49, 5–8.
119 The bridge over the Panlong River, now in the center of Kunming.
120 The word for "stake" is rendered in the text with two words, *juwang hadahan*. The first transliterates Chinese *zhuang*.
121 In Manchu *cuwan ma*, that is, *chuanma* or horses from Sichuan.
122 On this episode see also *Donghua lu*, by Jiang Liangqi, rpt. Beijing: Zhonghua shuju, 1980, ch. 12, p. 196.
123 It is hard to say what this means, since *janggin* is a generic term for officer, without any rank specified. See also Elliot, *The Manchu Way*, n. 54, p. 446.
124 This is the Ming city of Jianchangwei, which changed its name under the Qing to Ningyuanfu. *Historical Atlas*, vol. 7, map 62–63, 8–2.
125 I have not been able to locate this place. Ji Yonghai supposes that it could be a scribal error for Zunyi, which during the Qing was a prefectural city in northern Guizhou (*Historical Atlas*, vol. 8, map 39–40, 8–11).
126 Tuhai was a Manchu Bannerman of the Plain Yellow Banner. During the Shunzhi period he was active first as Ministerial Secretary and later as an officer in the Historiography Office and other scholarly institutes. Towards the end of the Shunzhi period he was made head of the Board of Punishments, but in 1659 ran into political turmoil because of a disagreement with the emperor, and was sentenced to death, but this sentence was commuted into the loss of his rank and titles. He joined government service again only three years later, in the capacity of *jalan-i janggin* (colonel) of his own banner. In 1663 he led the campaign against Li Laiheng in Xiangyang and Yunyang, with the title of Dingxi Jiangjun (General who Pacifies the West). At the outbreak of the Sanfan rebellion in 1673 he was in charge of the Ministry of Finance. In 1675 he took the field against the rebellious Chahar Prince Burni, where he distinguished himself for his brilliant victory. In 1676 he received the command of operations against the rebel leader Wang Fuchen in Gansu, forced him to hand over Pingliang and recovered the entire province for the government. After an audience with the emperor in 1979 he went back to Shaanxi. He conquered Xing'an and Hangzhong and stayed in the latter city until he went back to Peking in 1681 because of illness. He died in the winter of the same year. Haenisch, "Bruchstüke," p. 102; Hummel, *Eminent Chinese*, p. 784. See also *Donghua lu*, ch. 12, p. 196.
127 The genitive particle *ni* after "*cin wang*" may indicate a missing word.
128 Manchu *jalan-i janggin*.
129 Spelled in Manchu *in ding san alin*. I have not been able to identify this location. See also the following entry.
130 In Manchu *janggin*. I believe this is an abbreviation for *nirui janggin* (Ch. *zuoling*) that is, a company captain, a 4a level rank.
131 There are several people by this name involved in the suppression of the Three Feudatories. The most likely is a Manchu Bannerman of the Bordered Red Banner. In 1676 he followed Tuhai as a lieutenant of the Imperial Guards in the campaign in Shaanxi against Wang Fuchen, and defeated the rebels in the locality of Ishanba, to the north of Pingliang. In 1677 he followed General Mujan in the campaign against Wu Sangui. In 1678 he continued to fight in various localities, and in 1680 reached

Guangxi. In the locality of Taotun near Liuzhou he acquired merit in battle. The following year he entered Yunnan and defeated rebel troops at Huangcaoba, then again fought victoriously outside Yunnan city and at Wumushan (*Baqi tongzhi*, vol. 7, p. 4844). A similar biographic sketch is reported also under Basan, the father of another Šušu (see *Baqi tongzhi*, vol. 6, 3742). Although the near-identical biographies make it certain that we are dealing with one and the same person, we should note that in the latter entry Šušu appears to be assigned, like his father, to the Bordered Yellow Banner, and that he would also be a member of the Gūwalgiya clan. Haenisch provides information on a different Šušu, who may also be one to whom Dzengšeo is referring, whose biographical sketch is found in the *Man Ming Chen Zhuan*. This was a Manchu general who belonged to the Plain White Banner. In 1669 he was promoted to Vice-Minister of War and two years later to Minister of the Interior. On the occasion of the rebellion of Governor Geng Jingzhong he went to Jiangxi as Chief of the General Staff under Hirgen in 1674. In 1675 he received the order to march to Guangdong and to assist Provincial Governor Shang Kexi. At Gaozhou, however, he suffered a defeat at the hands of the rebel general Ma Xiong and had to withdraw to Zhaoqing. The following year the situation worsened because of the Shang Zhixin's rebellion in Guangdong, and Šušu had to withdraw further in Ganzhou (Jiangxi). In 1677 he moved from Nan'an to Shaozhou, and then to Wuzhou, in Guangxi. With the general advance westward he received the order to march with Manggitu to Nanning, but because of illness he asked to be recalled. Either on account of a false report of illness or because of his earlier defeats, he was demoted. Hence it may be that he is here a mere *janggin* on account of that. He was later reinstated to a high rank and in 1695 he served as Banner General in Ningxia and participated to the campaign against Galdan as Chief of General Staff under Fiyanggū. See Haenisch, "Bruchstüke," pp. 59, 99–100.

132 I take this to mean that the earth removed collapsed burying them.

133 The meaning of *hūnggi* is unclear to me.

134 Spelled in Manchu *yen ding*. These are the same mountains to which he referred above.

135 Chinese *liushou jiangjun*. See Hucker, no. 3813.

136 The rank of camp commander (*kūwaran-i da*) was probably an operational one, assigned to a colonel (*jalan-i janggin*) who was temporarily put in charge of the soldiers of a camp and thereby raised above other colonels.

137 Manchu *galai da*, Chinese *yi zhang*. See Brunnert and Hagelstrom, nos 571, 737.

138 Like Wu Sangui, many of the Chinese soldiers who had come to south China and had settled in Yunnan were originally from Liaodong province.

139 I take this to mean that some surrendered rebel officers complained that they had not been included in the priority withdrawal plan, together with the Chinese people from Liaodong.

140 In Manchu *siyūn fu*, that is, Chinese *xunfu*. Brunnert and Hagelstrom, no. 821.

141 In Manchu *g'osi*, for Chinese *gaoshi*.

142 In Manchu *sula janggin*, Ch. *san ji lang*. Hucker, no. 4835, translates it as Gentleman Cavalier Attendant, and describes it as a hereditary retainer on the staff of a princely establishment.

143 This indicates an imminent departure. The soldiers sent to the herd were in charge of fetching the horses and distributing them to the various units.

144 Dzengšeo had previously requested to be assigned to the first squadron, and is therefore leaving with it.

145 Chinese *zongdu*. See Hucker no. 7158.

146 This sentence, which is grammatically complex, refers to the Beise's embarrassment about the change of plans, which now would make Laita return last, while it had been earlier decided that he would leave with the first column together with Jangtai.

147 In Manchu *galai amban*, Chinese *qianfeng tongling*. See Brunnert and Hagelstrom, no. 735.

148 In Manchu *ba siyan* for Chinese *ba xian*. The many legends connected to the popular worship of the Daoist Eight Immortals must have been known to Dzengšeo.

149 This must be an error for twenty-third or twenty-fourth.

150 There is no precise way to render this image, which I take as a metaphor of being shot and hit by one's own worries. The verb *tanggilambi* means to make a flicking move-ment with the finger, hence to shoot an arrow by flicking the finger to release it, or to play a string instrument by plucking. This qualifies adverbially the factitive/passive form *tokobumbi*, to be stung, stabbed, or pricked.

151 This is mountainous terrain and therefore there are not many open spaces.

152 The bondservant companies formed part of the personal retinue of Manchu aristo-cratic families. See Elliot, *The Manchu Way*, p. 83.

153 The Dragon Boat Festival took (and still takes) place on the fifth day of the fifth month of the lunar calendar. According to legend Qu Yuan, the famous poet of the ancient kingdom of Chu, committed suicide by drowning in the River Meilo as an act of protest against the corruption of his government. Fishermen raced on the river to try to save him, but did not succeed. The Dragon Boat festival is said to having begun in ancient times to commemorate the poet, but is also meant to propitiate a good har-vest. It is celebrated by racing boats on the river, and eating special rice cakes and dumplings. On this see E.T. Chalmers Werner, *Myths and Legends of China*, London: George Harrap, 1922, p. 44. Since the River Meilo was located in Hunan, it is possible that the reference made to the Dragon Boat festival was also meant to evoke a literary topos related to the area he was crossing, as Dzengšeo does in other parts of the diary.

154 About 60 meters, above the river.

155 I have not identified this place; judging by the itinerary, this might be a branch of Dongting Lake or another lake close to it.

156 In Manchu *pen*, for Chinese *peng*.

157 That is, about 15 Chinese feet, or 5 meters.

158 According to Ji Yonghai, this may refer to the fact that they had received news about Prince of the Blood Labu, who had gone back to Beijing on the eighth month of the previous year, and had died on the tenth month. See Dzengšeo, n. 1, p. 21.

159 The verb *tucimbi* means to come out, go out, and similar meanings, with an even wider range in the passive/causative form *tucibumbi*. From the context we cannot assume that Dzengšeo or the other soldiers were moving out at this stage, and there-fore I translated it as "register" in the sense that the soldiers were asked to express (thus "coming out") their preference as to whether they wanted to proceed by land or by water. This translation remains tentative.

160 Animal sacrifice in connection with military enterprises was a common Manchu, and generally Inner Asian, ritual. The Kitan sacrificed a white horse and a gray bull when the troops returned from an expedition. See Karl A. Wittfogel and Fg Chia-shg, "History of Chinese Society: Liao, 907–1125," Philadelphia: American Philosophical Society: distributed by Macmillan Co., New York, 1949, p. 268.

161 A reference to an episode in the Romance of the Three Kingdoms. Xuande is, of course, Liu Bei, the famous hero. The term *dilu* describes a horse with a white spot on the forehead. *Hanyu Da Cidian*, vol. 2, 4833. *Morohashi*, vol. 8, p. 70 [52] cites the episode to which the author refers. On the Manchu translation of the Romance of the Three Kingdoms, see note 88 of the Introduction.

162 See note 89 of the Introduction.

163 *Chengxiang* is an ancient bureaucratic title meaning "Prime Minister." Here Dzengšeo refers to the historical character Bigan, and assigns him to a *jeo gurun*, that is, the kingdom of Zhou or Zhou dynasty. This is incorrect because Bigan served

under the Shang king Zhou. According to the *Historian's Records* of Sima Qian, Bigan is a figure we meet in both the annals of Yin (*Shiji*, chapter 3) and the Annals of Zhou (*Shiji*, chapter 4); he is an aristocrat under King Zhou of the Shang, by whom he was eventually killed (see Ssu-ma Ch'ien (1994), *The Grand Scribe's Records*, vol. 1, ed. William H. Nienhauser *et al.*, pp. 51, 60). Later his example came to represent the ideal of the loyal functionary who chooses to provide sound advice to his foolish and cruel sovereign even at the risk of his own life. It is possible that Dzengšeo is confusing the Shang king Zhou with the Zhou dynasty. One might also, at the risk of overinterpreting, wonder whether there might be here an oblique reference to the "Zhou" that Wu Sangui chose as the dynastic name when he rebelled. To ascribe loyalty to the doomed servant of an evil Zhou emperor might have been more fitting to the times, and the ceremony of prostration in front of Bigan's image might have carried political overtones.

164 This sentence may also mean that there was not enough water for the army.

165 *Historical Atlas*, vol. 9, map 57–8, 1–7.

166 The word for encampment here is *kūwaran*, and this note may indicate that Dzengšeo has been promoted to the rank of Camp Commandant, or *kūwaran-i da*. See also the entry for November 2.

167 Fiyanggū (1645–1701), is an extremely important military figure of the Kangxi period. He began his career in the war against Wu Sangui, rising to the rank of Commander of the Imperial Bodyguard in 1679. He is especially famous, however, for being the Field Marshal and main military commander in the wars against Galdan, the powerful ruler of the Oirats who engaged the Kangxi emperor in a long war from 1690 to 1697. Fiyanggū is credited with the main victory obtained by the Qing army, in June 1696 at Jao Modo, in Outer Mongolia. See Hummel, *Eminent Chinese*, pp. 248–249.

168 The *tokso* is a village that is a part of a land grant, or estate, endowed by the emperor to Manchu nobles and high-ranking officers.

169 In Manchu *amba age*.

170 This is today a township in southwestern Beijing. In the early twentieth century it gave the name to the railway station on the Peking-Hankow line. See L.C. Arlington and William Lewisohn, *In Search of Old Peking*, Peking: Vetch, 1935, p. 314.

171 Also known as Marco Polo Bridge, this is located just outside Beijing. Dzengšeo's father has come to greet him at the entrance of the city. For its location in relation to the city see the map in Susan Naquin, *Peking: Temples and City Life, 1400–1900*, Berkeley: University of California Press, 2000, p. 12.

172 This indicates the death of his brother.

173 In Manchu *nagan* or *nahan*, these are the Chinese *kang*, heated brick beds.

174 A reference to the previously mentioned death of his brother.

2 MANCHU TEXT

The transliteration reflects the Manchu text as it appears in the original reproduced in Ji Yonghai's publications. I have provided in the notes the standard readings of words that differ from the standard dictionary form due to orthographic variants or scribal errors.

1 This should be *šanyan*.
2 ishunde
3 be
4 selgiyefi
5 gociha
6 yerdehe
7 gusucuhe

8 tome
9 šakšaha
10 šakšaha
11 šakšaha
12 tasgara
13 gabtara
14 faijume
15 kurelefi
16 fargade
17 kūwalapi
18 keo
19 doorade
20 deijime
21 oncafi
22 efire
23 usame
24 meyen
25 ihan
26 yonggan
27 yonggan
28 goici
29 aššan
30 takahabi
31 yafahan
32 hūwaitafi
33 niolmon
34 gajarci
35 šehun
36 hihahabi
37 hiyahan
38 tasgara
39 šakšaha
40 uyun
41 yafahan
42 sohime
43 be
44 be
45 be
46 šakšaha
47 šakšalame
48 meiteme
49 dabkime
50 šusihašame
51 agafi
52 be
53 katunjame
54 goifi
55 geretere
56 suje
57 jorgon
58 teo
59 ihan
60 hulhara

61 duleke
62 tahan
63 wahan
64 gerišeme
65 futa
66 tome
67 ihan
68 The section in parentheses is added in the text in smaller script at the bottom of the line, as an explanatory addition.
69 beidefi
70 uyunde
71 uyunju
72 tolgin
73 tolgin

REFERENCES

Ahmad, Zahiruddin, *Sino-Tibetan Relations in the Seventeenth Century, Roma*: Istituto Italiano per il Medio ed Estremo Oriente, 1970.

Arlington, Lewis Clark and William Lewisohn, *In Search of Old Peking,* Peking: Vetch, 1935.

Baqi tongzhi (chuji) (八旗同志（初集）, ed. Ortai, originally published in 1739, 250 + 3 *juan*. Chinese edition reprinted in eight volumes, Changchun: Dongbei shifan daxue, 1985.

Bawden, Charles R., "A Manchu Military Relic from the First Opium War," *Journal of Turkish Studies: An Anniversary Volume in Honor of Francis Woodman Cleaves*, vol. 9, pp. 7–12, 1985.

Bayle, Pierre, *Pensées diverses sur la Comète*, ed. A. Prat, Paris: Librairie E. Droz, 1939.

Bodde, Derk and Clarence Morris, *Law in Imperial China: Exemplified by 190. Ch'ing Dynasty Cases*, Cambridge, Mass.: Harvard University Press, 1967.

Brunnert, H.S. (Ippolit Semenovich) and V.V. Hagelstrom (V.V. Gagel'strom), *Present Day Political Organization of China*, Taipei: Ch'eng Wen Publishing Co., 1978 [Shanghai: Kelly and Walsh, Limited, 1912].

Chaliand, Gérard, ed., *The Art of War in World History*, Berkeley and Los Angeles: University of California Press, 1994.

Chang, Jen-chung, "The Nature of the 'Three Feudatories Rebellion' and the Causes for Its Failure," *Chinese Studies in History*, vol. 15, nos 1–2, pp. 7–18, 1981–1982.

Ch'en, Wen-shih, "The Creation of the Manchu Niru," *Chinese Studies in History*, vol. 14, no. 4, pp. 11–46, 1981.

Chen Jiahua 陳佳華 and Fu Ketong 傅克東, "Baqi hanjun kaol 芫" 八旗漢軍考略 in Wang Zhonghan 王鐘翰, ed., *Manzu shi yanjiu ji* 滿族史研究集, Beijing: Zhongguo shehui kexue, pp. 281–306, 1988.

Chen Qun 陈 群, *Zhongguo bingzhi jianshi* 中國兵簡史, Beijing: Junshi kexue chubanshe, 1989.

Chiang, Chia-feng, "Disease and Its Impact on Politics, Diplomacy and the Military: The Case of Smallpox and the Manchus (1613–1795)," *Journal of the History of Medicine*, vol. 57, pp. 177–197, 2002.

Ching Chung, Priscilla, "Kong Sizhen, Princess," in *Biographical Dictionary of Chinese Women: The Qing Period, 1644–1911*, Armonk, NY: M.E. Sharpe, pp. 104–105, 1998.

Coclanis, Peter, "Military Mortality in Tropical Asia: British Troops in Tenasserim 1827–36," *Journal of Southeast Asian Studies*, vol. 30, no. 1, pp. 22–37, 1999.

Crossley, Pamela K., *A Translucent Mirror: History and Identity in Qing Imperial Ideology*, Los Angeles and Berkeley: University of California Press, 1999.

de Vigny, Alfred, *Servitude and Grandeur of Arms*, trans. Roger Gard, London: Penguin Books, 1996.

Deng Ruiling 邓锐龄, "Wu Sangui pan Qing qi jian tong diwu bei Dalai lama tongshi shimo," 吴三桂叛清期間同第五輩达赖喇嘛通使始末, *Zhongguo Zanxue* 中國藏學, vol. 57, pp. 16–25, 1998.

Deng Zhongmian 邓中绵, "Lun Wu Sangui 論吳三桂," *Beifang luncong*, vol. 57, pp. 73–79, 1987.

Di Cosmo, Nicola, "Military aspects of the Manchu-Čaqar Wars," in *Warfare in Inner Asian History (500–1800)*, Leiden: E. J. Brill, 2002.

Di Cosmo, Nicola and Dalizhabu Bao, *Manchu-Mongol Relations on the Eve of the Qing Conquest*, Leiden: E. J. Brill, 2003.

d'Orléans, Pierre Joseph, *History of the Two Tartar Conquerors of China*. Rpt. New York: B. Franklyn, 1971.

Duara, Presenjit, "Superscribing Symbols: The Myth of Guandi, Chinese God of War," *Journal of Asian Studies*, vol. 47, no. 4, pp. 778–795, 1988.

Durrant, Stephen, "Sino-Manchu Translations at the Mukden Court," *Journal of the American Oriental Society*, vol. 99, no. 4, pp. 653–661, 1979.

Dzengšeo [Zeng-shou 曾壽], *Beye-i cooha bade yabuha babe ejehe bithe. Sui jun ji xing yizhu* 隨軍紀行譯注. Translated and annotated by Ji Yonghai 季永海, Beijing: Zhongyang minzu xueyuan, 1987.

Elliott, Mark C., *The Manchu Way; the Eight Banners and Ethnic Identity in Late Imperial China*, Stanford, Calif.: Stanford University Press, 2001.

Elvin, Mark, *The Retreat of the Elephants: An Environmental History of China*, New Haven: Yale University Press, 2004.

Fang, Chao-ying, "A Technique for Estimating the Numerical Strength of the Early Manchu Military Forces," *Harvard Journal of Asiatic Studies*, vol. 13, nos 1–2, pp. 192–215, 1950.

Fu, Lo-shu, *A Documentary Chronicle of Sino-Western Relations, 1644–1820*, Tucson: University of Arizona Press, 1966.

Gimm, Martin [Mading Jimu 馬丁·稽穆], "Manzhou wexue shul 芫滿州文學述略," *Manxue yanjiu*, ed. Yan Chongnian 閻崇年, Changchun, vol. 1, pp. 195–208, 1992.

Haenisch, Erich, "Bruchstücke aus der Geschichte Chinas Unter der Mandschu-Dynastie," *T'oung-pao,* Leiden: E. J. Brill, pp. 1–123, 1913.

Han Damei 韩大梅, "Qingdai baqi zidi de xuexiao jiaoyu," 清代八旗子弟的学校 教育, *Liaoning Shifan Daxue Xuebao*, vol. 57, pp. 73–75, 1996.

Hanyu Da Cidian 漢語大詞典, ed. Luo Zhufeng 罗竹风, reduced format edition (*suoyin ben*) in 3 vols., Shanghai: Hanyu da cidian chubanshe, 1997.

Hauer, Eric, "General Wu San-kuei," *Asia Major*, vol. IV, no. 4, pp. 563–611, 1927.

Hosoya, Yoshio "A Document of Shang Ke-xi in the Harvard-Yenching Library," paper presented at the Second North American International Conference on Manchu Studies, Harvard University, pp. 27–29, May 2005.

Hsi, Angela, "Wu San-kuei in 1644: a Reappraisal," *Journal of Asian Studies*, vol. 34, no. 2, pp. 443–453, 1975.

Hu Jianzhong 胡建中, "Qingdai huopao 清代火炮," *Gugong Bowuyuan kan*, vol. 57, pp. 49–57, 87–94, 1986.

Huang, Ray, "The Liao-tung Campaign of 1619," *Oriens Extremus*, vol. 28, no. 1, pp. 30–54, 1981.

Hucker, Charles O., *A Dictionary of Official Titles in Imperial China*, rpt. Taipei: Southern Materials Center, Inc., 1985.

Hummel, Arthur W., *Eminent Chinese of the Ch'ing period (1644–1912)*, rpt Taipei: Ch'eng-Wen, 1975.

Im, Kaye Soon, "The Rise and Decline of the Eight Banner Garrisons in the Ch'ing Period (1644–1911): A Study of the Kuang-chou, Hang-chou, and Ching-chou Garrisons," PhD Dissertation, University of Illinois, 1981.

Jiang Liangqi 蔣良騏, *Donghua lu* 東華錄, rpt Beijing: Zhonghua shuju, 1980.

Jiang Tingyu 蔣廷瑜, "Guangxi suojian 'San Fan' tuguan yin 廣西所見三藩土," *Gugong bowuyuan yuankan,* vol. 57, pp. 71–74, 2003.

Keegan, John, *The Face of Battle*, New York: Penguin Books, 1978.

Kessler, Lawrence, *K'ang-hsi and the Consolidation of Ch'ing Rule, 1661–1684*, Chicago: The University of Chicago Press, 1976.

Kong Deqi 孔德琪, "Lüelun Kangxi di pingding Sanfan zhanzheng zhanlüe zhidao shang de jige wenti 略論康熙帝平定三藩戰爭戰略指導上的幾個問題," *Qingshi yanjiu tongxun*, vol. 57, pp. 14–18, 1986.

Li Yanguang 李燕光, "Qingdai de Baqi Hanjun 清代 的八旗漢軍," *Manxue Yanjiu*, no. 1, pp. 91–103, 1992.

Li Yanguang 李燕光 and Guan Jie 關捷, eds., *Manzu Tongshi* 滿族通史, Shenyang: Liaoning minzu chubanshe, 2003.

Liu, Chia-chü, "The Creation of the Chinese Banners in the Early Ch'ing," *Chinese Studies in History*, vol. XIV, no. 4, pp. 47–75, 1984.

Liu Fengyun 劉風雲, "Shilun Qing chu San Fan fan Qing de shehui jichu 識清初 三藩反清社會基礎," *Beifang luncong*, vol. 57, pp. 62–67, 1986.

Liu Fengyun, *Qingdai Sanfan yanjiu* 清代三藩研究, Beijing: Renmin Daxue chubanshe, 1994.

Luo Ergang 羅爾綱, *Ling bing zhi* 綠營兵志. Beijing: Zhonghua shuju, 1984.

Ma, Chujian, "The introduction of western artillery by the Jesuit missionaries and the consequent changes in the wars between the Ming and the Qing," *Martino Martini: A Humanist and a Scientist in Seventeenth Century China*, ed. Franco Demarchi and Riccardo Scartezzini, Trento: Università di Trento, pp. 307–321, 1994.

Man ming chen zhuan 滿名臣傳, ed. Qing guo shi guan bian 清國史館編, 6 vols, Taipei: Tailian guofeng chubanshe, 1970.

Millward, James , *Beyond the Pass: Economy, Ethnicity, and Empire in Qing Central Asia: 1759–1864*, Stanford: Stanford University Press, 1988.

Morohashi Testuji 諸橋 轍次, *Dai Kan-Wa jiten* 大漢和辭典, 13 vols. Tokyo: Taishūkan Shoten (rpt Taipei, 1992), 1984.

Naquin, Susan, *Peking: Temples and City Life, 1400–1900*, Berkeley and Los Angeles: University of California Press, 2000.

Pant, Gayatri N., *Horse and Elephant Armour*, Delhi: Agam Kala Prakashan, 1997.

Perdue, Peter C., *China Marches West. The Qing Conquest of Central Eurasia*. Cambridge, MA: Harvard University Press, 2005.

Qinzheng pingding shumo fangl 芁親征 平定 朔漠 方署, Chief ed. Wenda 温 達, rpt. Beijing: Zhongguo Zanxue chubanshe, 1994.

Rawski, Evelyn, *The Last Emperors: A Social History of Qing Imperial Institutions*, Berkeley: University of California Press, 1998.

Rhoads, Edward J.M., *Manchus and Han: Ethnic Relations and Political Power in Late Qing and Early Republican China, 1861–192*8, Seattle: University of Washington Press, 2000.

Roth Li, Gertraude, "State Building Before 1644," *The Cambridge History of China, Vol 9, Pt. 1, The Qing Dynasty to 1800*, ed. Willard J. Peterson, Cambridge: Cambridge University Press, pp. 51–72, 2002.

Shang Hongkui 商鴻逵, "Kangxi pingding Sanfan zhongde xibei san Han jiang 康熙平定三蕃中的西北三漢將," *Beijing daxue xuebao* (zhexue shehui kexue), vol. 57, pp. 55–62, 1984.

Shen Lijuan 沈離涓, "Man Han wudao de ronghe," 满汉舞蹈的融合, *Manzu yanjiu*, vol. 57, pp. 82–85, 1998.

Shepherd, John R., "Rethinking Sinicization: Processes of Acculturation and Assimilation," *State, Market and Ethnic Groups Contextualized*, ed. by Bien Chiang and Ho Ts'ui-p'ing. Taipei: Institute of Ethnology, Academia Sinica, pp. 133–150, 2003.

Shi Song 史松, "Ping Wu Sangui cong tou Qing dao fan Qing 評吳三桂從投清到反清," *Qingshi yanjiu tongxun*, vol. 57, pp. 14–19, 1985.

Shiue, Carol H., "Local Granaries and Central Government Disaster Relief: Moral Hazard and Intergovernmental Finance in Eighteenth- and Nineteenth-Century China," *The Journal of Economic History*, vol. 64, 1, pp. 100–124, 2004.

Shore, David H., "Last Court of Ming China: The Reign of the Yung-li Emperor in the South (1647–1662)," PhD Dissertation, Princeton University, 1976.

Shu Liguang, "Ferdinand Verbiest and the Casting of Cannons in the Qing Dynasty," *Ferdinand Verbiest (1623–1688) Jesuit Missionary, Scientist and Diplomat*, ed. John W. Witek, S.J., "Monumenta Serica Monograph Series XXX," Nettetal: Steyler Verlag, pp. 227–244, 1994.

Spence, Jonathan, *Emperor of China: Self-portraif of K'ang-his*, New York: Vintage Books, 1975.

Spence, Jonathan, *The Death of Woman Wang*, New York: Penguin Books, 1979.

Ssu-ma Ch'ien, *The Grand Scribe's Records, vol. 1: The Basic Annals of Pre-Han China*, ed. William H. Nienhauser, Bloomington and Indianapolis: Indiana University Press, 1994.

Struve, Lynn, A., *The Southern Ming, 1644–1662*, New Haven: Yale University Press, 1984.

Struve, Lynn A., *Voices from the Ming-Qing Cataclysm: China in Tiger's Jaws*, New Haven and London: Yale University Press, 1993.

Su Heping 蘇和平, "Shilun Qingchu San Fan de xingzhi ji qi panluan shibai de yuanyin 識論清初三反的性質及其叛亂失敗的原因." *Shehui kexue* (Lanzhou), vol. 57, pp. 107–112, 1984.

The Historical Atlas of China. Zhongguo lishi ditu ji, Chief ed. Tan Qixiang 8 vols., Shanghai: Cartographic Publishing House, 1982.

Ts'ao, Kai-fu, "The Rebellion of the Three Feudatories against the Manchu Throne in China, 1673–1681: Its Setting and Significance," PhD Dissertation, Columbia University, 1965.

Ts'ao, Kai-fu, "K'ang-hsi and the San-fan War," *Monumenta Serica*, vol. 57, pp. 108–130, 1974–1975.

Wade, Thomas F., "The Army of the Chinese Empire: its two great divisions, the Banners or National Guard and the Green Standard or Provincial Troops: their organization, location, pay, condition & c.," *Chinese Repository*, vol. 20, pp. 250–280, 300–340, 363–422, 1851.

Wakeman, Frederic E., *The Great Enterprise: The Manchu Reconstruction of Imperial Order in Seventeenth-Century China*, Berkeley: University of California Press, 1985.

Werner, E.T. Chalmers, *Myths and Legends of China*. London: George Harrap, 1922.

Wittfogel, Karl August, and Chia-shêng Fêng, *History of Chinese Society: Liao, 907–1125*. Philadelphia: American Philosophical Society: distributed by Macmillan Co., New York, 1949.

Wu, Wei-ping, "The Development and Decline of the Eight Banners," PhD Dissertation, University of Pennsylvania, 1969.

Wu Hung, "Photographing deformity: Liu Zheng and His Photo Series 'My Countrymen'," *Public Culture*, vol. 13, no. 3, pp. 399–427, 2001.

Xie Lihong 解立紅, "Hongyi dapao yu Manzhou xingshuai," 紅衣大炮與滿洲興衰. *Manxue Yanjiu*, vol. 2, ed. Yan Chongnian, Beijing: Minzu chubanshe, pp. 102–118, 1994.

Xing Yulin 邢玉林, "Cong pingding `Sanfan' panluan kan Kangxi de junshi sixiang 從平定 '三藩' 叛亂看康熙的軍事思想," *Kang Yong Qian San di pingyi* 康雍乾三帝評議, ed. Zuo Buqing 左步青, pp. 88–106, Beijing, 1986.

Xiu Pengyue 修朋月, "Guanyu Wu Sangui pingjia de jige wenti 關於吳三桂評價的幾個問題," [Some Questions related to Wu Sangyui's appraisal], *Beifang luncong*, vol. 57, pp. 86–91, 1988.

Yang Hongpo 楊洪波, "Lun Wu Sangui pan qing 論吳三桂判清," *Liaoning daxue xuebao* (zhehui shehui kexue), vol. 57, pp. 73–76, 1988.

Zuo Shu'e 左書諤, "Shun Kang zhi ji Wu Sangui pingding Yun Gui tusi shulun 順康之際吳三桂雲貴土司述論," *Guizhou shehui kexue* (wenshizhe), vol. 57, pp. 60–64, 1988.

INDEX TO THE TRANSLATION

This Index includes all names present in the Translation. Together with the maps and the glossary, it is meant to facilitate the identification of people and places mentioned by Dzengšeo.

Breinigsville, PA USA
30 November 2010
250294BV00007B/2/P